Key Concepts in
Community Studies

Recent volumes include:

Key Concepts in Sport and Exercise Studies
David Kirk, Carlton Cooke, Anne Flintoff and Jim McKenna

Key Concepts in Marketing
Jim Blythe

Key Concepts in Radio Studies
Hugh Chignell

Key Concepts in Political Geography
Edited by Carolyn Gallaher

Key Concepts in Sports Studies
Stephen Wagg

Key Concepts in Politics and International Relations
Lisa Harrison

The SAGE Key Concepts series provides students with accessible and authoritative knowledge of the essential topics in a variety of disciplines. Cross-referenced throughout, the format encourages critical evaluation through understanding. Written by experienced and respected academics, the books are indispensable study aids and guides to comprehension.

TONY BLACKSHAW

Key Concepts in
Community Studies

Los Angeles | London | New Delhi
Singapore | Washington DC

First published 2010
Reprinted 2012, 2013

SAGE Publications Ltd
1 Oliver's Yard
55 City Road
London EC1Y 1SP

SAGE Publications Inc.
2455 Teller Road
Thousand Oaks, California 91320

SAGE Publications India Pvt Ltd
B 1/I 1 Mohan Cooperative Industrial Area
Mathura Road, Post Bag 7
New Delhi 110 044

SAGE Publications Asia-Pacific Pte Ltd
3 Church Street
#10-04 Samsung Hub
Singapore 049483

Library of Congress Control Number 2009922162

British Library Cataloguing in Publication data

A catalogue record for this book is available from the
British Library

ISBN 978-1-4129-2843-4
ISBN 978-1-4129-2844-1 (pbk)

Typeset by Cepha Imaging Private Ltd., Bangalore, India
Printed and bound by CPI Group (UK) Ltd, Croydon, CR0 4YY
Printed on paper from sustainable resources

Acknowledgements

I would like to express my sincere thanks to Chris Rojek and Jai Seaman for their support and patience with this project. I would also like to thank Vasu Pillai who is a first class copyeditor. I wish to thank Donna Woodhouse and Beth Fielding-Lloyd for their contributions, and hope that working with me on this book has proved to be a worthwhile learning process for them both. I must also thank the anonymous reviewer who made some perceptive comments, particularly on the structure of the book, which I have duly taken on board.

All of the chapters in this book are written by Tony Blackshaw, with the exception of 'Action Research', 'Community Action', 'Community Development', 'Community Partnerships', 'Community Profiling', 'Community Regeneration' and 'Community Youth Work', which were co-authored with Donna Woodhouse; and 'Community and Identity', 'Locality, Place and Neighbourhood' and 'Virtual Communities', which were co-authored with Beth Fielding-Lloyd.

contents

Community as Policy and Practice

Introduction and User's Guide

The key concepts in this book are arranged into the six themes that comprise the crux of community studies; and within each of these themes, the chapters are arranged in alphabetical order, except the extended essay at the beginning of book 'Setting the Record Straight: What is Community? And What Does it Mean Today?' (*You must read this chapter first.*) As its title suggests, it is an important chapter in this book, as it sets out a way of understanding and appreciating the complexity of a concept that is impossible to escape from these days. However hard you try to avoid it, 'community' seems to spill from nearly every news report, leisure centre, police station, doctor's surgery, university course, government policy, social club and so on and on, filling our world. Its ubiquity might lead us to believe that the idea of community is one of the most distinctive, defining aspects of our times. And it is, but not in the way that most people think it is. The concept of community is a good example of the philosopher Ludwig Wittgenstein's admonition that human thought is often held prisoner by static images. When most people talk about 'community', it conjures up one such image: of a sense of belonging, warmth and companionship. You might say it has a friendly sort of air about it, and like a balmy summer's day it 'feels good: whatever the word … may mean, it is good "to have a community", "to be in a community"' (Bauman, 2001: 1). As Bauman points out, this is because community already has a place in our *doxa* (the knowledge we think with but not about), and it is endowed with an atmosphere all of its own. It transcends its status as a concept – or so it would seem.

The reason for this is that community is *hermeneutical*. It is a concept used to describe things in the world by those who are concerned with social relations connecting people and the problems of understanding and interpreting these. Though there is obviously nothing inherently wrong with this function, the practice of hermeneutics is always potentially problematical because it is burdened by a romantic sensibility, which evokes feelings of *nostalgia* and closeness (Heller, 1999). What this suggests is that hermeneutics and community are two sides of the same coin. One of the major problems with this is that we are always going to have difficulty conceptualizing community without romanticizing it; or in other words, using hermeneutics to interpret the idea of community in new ways that are rich and surprising, while trying to see through our emotional and ideological excesses.

This was certainly one of the major obstacles that faced *community studies* in its formative years, when sociologists such as Stacey (1969) challenged researchers to be more up-front about whether they were actually referring to 'local social systems' rather than communities *per se*. Since this time, most social theorists and researchers have tended to employ community as an *orienting device*, rather than a concept of any refinement or precision, while everyone else seems to use it merely as an *appropriating device* (*see* 'Setting the Record Straight'). The problem with these two trends is that community has become one of the most vague and imprecisely drawn concepts in the social sciences; it seems to mean everything and nothing. This is clearly an unsatisfactory state of affairs, since it invites misunderstanding. It also breaks hermeneutics' promise to the social sciences that they are capable of deepening our understanding of concepts in order to make them more meaningful.

In order to counter this tendency, what I develop in the introductory chapter ('Setting the Record Straight') is my own hermeneutic exercise. The chapter begins by arguing that until the 1980s community was by and large the exclusive property of sociology, or at least that's what sociologists thought. It is subsequently demonstrated that, by the end of the twentieth century, community had been subjected to a conceptualist revolution – or so it seemed. After discussing the implications this has had for community with its new found status as either an *appropriating device* or an *orienting device*, the chapter outlines my own theory of community. This is not a definitive theory as such, but rather a suggested organizing model with a set of four stages of historical consciousness: *community consciousness*, *class consciousness*, *consciousness of classes* and *consciousness of communities*. I present these in order of their chronological emergence, but do not suggest that they constitute a teleological history. What I suggest instead is that these four stages of historical consciousness might constitute a useful way of understanding the shifting configuration of power in the relationship between authenticity and identity and what this implies for community. This model is not my own invention; it is adapted from Agnes Heller's (1999) magisterial thesis in the book *A Theory of Modernity*. What is original about this model, though, is that it is one constructed as a way of understanding community, and more importantly, what it means today.

The rest of the chapters in the book are grouped into six themes, which between them deal with the broad compass of community studies scholarship. Even though these themes have their own specific items of interest, the chapters that make them up are fairly self-contained, which means that it is not necessary to read them by theme, in any particular order, or in fact to read all of them. Readers should select themes and/or chapters according to their own interests. Some readers will want a straightforward 'key concepts' textbook, and for them this book outlines the key themes and the key concepts, theories and ideas in the field, and applies them to community studies. In doing so, it begins each chapter with a thoroughgoing definition of the concept in question and a synopsis of the discussion that follows. The discussion itself provides detailed comment on origins, historical and theoretical developments and thematic connections, as well as an application of the concept to both extant and cutting-edge contemporary developments in community studies. Each key concept is cross-referenced to other concepts included in the book in order to supplement critical assessment. Where it is deemed appropriate, further readings are recommended to facilitate broader in-depth study.

For those readers looking for something more, the format of the book allows them to range beyond a dutiful treatment of community and its many applications – under the theme 'Community as Policy', entries on community care, community health, community policing, etc., have purposely not been included – by challenging them to develop their own critiques of the key concepts in community studies by working out *how* and *in what ways* 'community' has been applied. For example, when these readers have read the chapters on 'Action Research', 'Community Action', 'Community Development', 'Community Partnerships', 'Community Regeneration', 'Political Community' and 'Social Capital', they will know that when politicians talk about developing 'communities', this often means little about community at all, but when community practitioners do, it means something quite the opposite. To take another example, key concepts such as 'Imaginary Communities', 'Imagined Communities', 'Liquid Modern Communities', 'Postmodern Communities' and 'Virtual Communities' can be read separately and then grouped together in order to consider – to paraphrase the philosopher Jacques Derrida – the different ways in which human beings have tried to find new ways of living with community after its 'death' without being haunted by its spectral power.

Used in this way, readers will quickly grasp that the Sage *Key Concepts in Community Studies* is not just a textbook; it is also an attempt to define the current identity of community studies. That as well breaking new conceptual ground by offering its own theories of community, the book is original in at least two other ways. Firstly, in the way it offers a welter of freshly minted concepts and ideas – cleave communities, hermeneutic communities, liquid modern communities, network communities, to name but a few – to community studies. Secondly, in the way it also breaks new conceptual ground by linking together definitional concision and thoroughgoing critique in order to stimulate the sociological imagination. In developing the ability to learn from their sources, pose their own questions, draw their own conclusions and reflect on what they have learned from these original features, it will begin to dawn on readers that the Sage *Key Concepts in Community Studies* is not an impartial book, and that it has been written as an unapologetic, analytically 'engaged' sociology that does not pretend to be 'value-neutral' (Bauman, 2000). An 'engaged' sociology is one that opens a space for the hope that community studies might at last regain some of its critical capacity, that it could even begin to speak in new ways that have not been imagined before.

REFERENCES

Bauman, Z. (2001) *Community: Seeking Safety in an Insecure World*. Cambridge: Polity Press.

Bauman, Z. (2000) '*Afterthought: On Writing; On Writing Sociology*' in Liquid Modernity. Cambridge: Polity Press.

key concepts in community studies

Setting the Record Straight: What Is Community? And What Does it Mean Today?

Over the past 20 years or so, few concepts in the social sciences have undergone such a remarkable transformation than has that of 'community'. When I was a student at the end of the 1980s, we were introduced to the concept by breaking it down into the sum of its parts – namely the three key dimensions of locale, social network and a shared sense of belonging – accompanied with the proviso that community is also more than these individual constituents. We were then challenged with the task of exploring the concept with the range of phenomena encompassed in three key ideas: the rural–urban continuum, community lost and community found (*see* 'Community Studies'). This involved a conversation between the ideas of the founding fathers of sociology – the likes of Durkheim, Weber and Marx, but especially Tönnies (1955), who identified the relentless progression from *Gemeinschaft* (unity based on personal and intimate social relations of family and kinship), roughly translated as 'community', to *Gesellschaft* (impersonal and contractual relations of a more calculating kind) society – and the Chicago School (*see* 'Community Studies'), and how these related to contemporary empirical developments in the field of community studies. And, it was Bell and Newby (1971), in their classic introductory textbook *Community Studies: An Introduction to the Sociology of the Local Community*, who provided the running commentary. There was no doubt about two things: (1) the key theoretical ideas about community could be found in the ideas of the founding fathers, and (2) community belonged to sociology, and broadly speaking, everyone concurred.

Unconcerned that the key ideas about community were supposed to be timeless and universal and the property of just one social science discipline, by the end of the twentieth century, a group of disparate and unconnected scholars had inaugurated what seemed to be a conceptualist revolution. This arguably began with the publication of *Imagined Communities: Reflections on the Origin and Spread of Nationalism* in 1983. In this book, the political scientist Benedict Anderson pointed out that 'all communities larger than primordial villages (and perhaps even these) are imagined' (Anderson, 1991: 6). Drawing on this idea, he also argued that the nation-state has the ability to cultivate an outsize form of belonging as a way of maintaining a coherent sense of national identity, rooted in the consciousness of individuals, who in the same way identify with an imagined national narrative. According to Anderson, the development of new technologies of mass communication, particularly the print media, is the precondition of all modern 'imagined' communities, which as he put it 'are to be distinguished not by their falseness/genuineness, but by the style in which they are imagined' (*ibid*). In the hands of Anderson, community had turned immaterial and phantasmagorical, and it no longer rested solidly upon social foundations – it was now metaphysical.

Two years later, in 1985, the anthropologist Anthony P. Cohen published *The Symbolic Construction of Community*, in which he argued that we must recognize that communities are not only the outcome of the unconditioned agency upon which their existence depends, but also that they do not exist without imagery, boundary marking processes, customs, habits, rituals and the communication of these – in other words, that symbols do not simply describe community; they contribute in some fundamental sense to community being what it is, and in this sense may be said to be a key part of its construction (*see* 'The Symbolic Construction of Community').

The publication of Phillip E. Wegner's *Imaginary Communities* saw a scholar of English attempting to identify, describe and analyse communities that are always a fantastical projection, or in other words, offer lots of alternative ways of conjuring, narrating and making the world. This book served as a reminder to sociology that not only does community have the ability to fire the imagination like no other idea – to pursue an ideal, to embody a dream, to struggle against loss – but also that it is another word for utopia (*see* 'Imaginary Communities'). Although Wenger's book was not published until 2002, it was nonetheless framed with the same basic assumptions as the previous two books; not only is it *connection* where modern community lies, but also that the *feeling of home* (or some other kind of habitat) becomes important when it registers with the imagination. In other words, these authors were unanimous about one important thing: all modern communities are hermeneutic communities. Hermeneutics is the art of dialectical retrieval, in what it sees as changed modern circumstances, and it says community will only be found again by trying to find new ways of meaning for it through interpretation (*see* 'Hermeneutic Communities').

Hermeneutics might have offered the above-named authors some new ways of making meaning for community through interpretation, but conceptually it now hovered somewhere between fantasy and belief – imagination and reality, popping up in publication after publication while often being used with little refinement or concision (Amit, 2002). Community, it seems, had turned out to be an extreme form of dialectics – a concept that is real and imagined. However, what could not be ignored is that these two conceptions – each calling for and implying the other – are antipodal. Indeed, one is the strong refusal of the other. The abomination that the idea of 'imagined' communities represents to those, such as Amit, determined to firmly re-entrench debates about the idea in the real world so that it might regain some of its critical capacity, that it could even begin to describe actually existing social realities again, is, in part, a function of this dialectics.

The upshot of this state of affairs is that community today is by and large used in two ways. In social theory and empirical studies, it is in the main employed as an *orienting device* by thinkers and empirical researchers, who, notwithstanding their belief that we probably have to leave unresolved what terms like 'imagined' communities and 'real' communities might actually mean, demand that we must reinsert the social back into community studies by confronting the concept as an empirical phenomenon. Everybody else – from individuals to nation-states, from football fans to religious groups, from the hoi polloi to politicians – uses it as an *appropriating device*. Let us look at these two uses in turn.

Examples that fit the *appropriating* trend can be found without much difficulty. For example, over the last 20 or so years, 'community' has readily been extended to the public sphere as the new signature truth of policy and practice. In the place of 'health', 'old people's homes and mental institutions', 'tax on the rateable values of people's homes', 'arts', 'sports', 'policing', 'safety', 'town planning', 'fire stations', 'businesses', 'the poor' and the Football Association's Charity Shield match, we now got 'community health', 'community care', 'the community charge', 'community arts', 'community sports', 'community policing', 'community safety', 'community planning', 'community fire stations', 'the business community', 'disadvantaged communities' and the 'FA Community Shield sponsored by MacDonald's'. In most of these cases, the precise details of what a community service might actually involve proper is rarely pursued with care and accuracy (*compare this to* 'Community Development'); if you were to rebuild a community and fill it with people, *appropriating* community was how public policy had to be, even if services and organizations were no more readily open, accessible, reflective of shared interests and responsive to local needs than they had been in the past. It did not very much matter about the detail supporting them either; or that the bulk of these 'community' services were constructed of anodyne doubles that served only as shorthand for real experience and actual emotion, or even that most of the time their content consisted of clichés – 'social capitalism', 'capacity building', 'community empowerment', 'social entrepreneurship' (*see* 'Social Capital') – that held little empirical truth. These were more combinations of gestures and marketing than fully drawn communities, but people seemed nonetheless happy to buy into them because they wanted to believe in the illusions they seem to support: the illusion of security, and of the safety of community.

This branding of community was a consequence of a paradox; it was only when we were no longer sure of community's existence that it became absolutely necessary to believe in it. The other reason community branding has caught hold of the imagination is the emergence of neo-liberalism, the political doctrine that developed in earnest from the close of what Hobsbawm (1995) calls the 'short twentieth century' (1914–1991) onwards, involving the ostensible denial of ideology, the affirmation of entrepreneurship in the light of the opportunities arising from capitalism in the period of intensified globalization, and the substitution of the market state for the sovereign state, which uses the language of community for its own political ends. Spending on the welfare state squeezed by cut backs had to find a new way of delivering its services which not only better included its 'consumers', but was also cheaper.

Dean MacCannell, the most insightful interpreter of the zeitgeist, extends these critical observations to conclude that the community concept in its orthodox sociological understanding has ceased to be of any use in the public sphere, suggesting that the intention of public policy today is nothing less than an ambition:

> to get every thought and action onto a balance sheet, to extend commercial values into every space of human relationship, the central problem … will be to create ersatz 'communities' to manufacture and even sell a 'sense' of community, leaving no free grounds for the formation of

relations outside the corporation. The complexity of this feat of social engineering – that is, the construction of believable sense of community where no community exists – should not be underestimated, nor should the drive to accomplish this feat be underestimated (1992: 89).

For MacCannell, any substance community might once have had has been swept away by its *appropriation*, which has turned it into a spectacle of fictions intent on making the *illusion* of community real to itself and to others. To paraphrase what Terry Eagleton (1990: 209) said of commodities, 'as pure exchange-value, it's as if community has erased from itself every particle of matter; as alluring auratic object, it parades its own unique sensual being in a kind of spurious show of materiality'.

What we can also discern from this discussion is a certain ambivalence about the continuing efficacy of community for sociology; on the one hand, it no longer seems to be an apposite concept for understanding contemporary social phenomena, because it is an insufficiently sophisticated and precise concept to do the sort of critical analysis required of a sociology made to measure of the world today. However, on the other hand, it appears to have been appropriated as a conservative concept tied into the neo-liberal quest for social order based on market principles (*see* 'Political Community'), which suggests that it still deserves the critical attention of sociologists.

As we have already seen, some other social theorists and empirical researchers have taken a different perspective. Concerned that, in the light of the conceptual revolution identified above, hermeneutic community has overtaken the community as social interaction they have set out to revivify *community studies*, which in their view has been sinking into marginality. In so doing, they have also felt obliged to *orient* their definitions of community for their own purposes in order not to invite misunderstanding. The trouble is that this approach has paradoxically served to deepen the problem it set out to overcome. In its ambition to demonstrate that community is still a ubiquitous and powerful feature of everyday life found in lots of different social settings, much empirical work has overstated the significance of social relationships and social solidarity (*see*, for example, Amit, 2002), raising more questions than it has answered. This is also true of those who have attempted to offer definitional reorientations. So, for example, when a highly respected social theorist such as Craig Calhoun tells us that community is best 'understood as the life people live in dense, multiplex, relatively autonomous networks of social relationships. Community, thus, is not a place or simply a small-scale population aggregate but a mode of relating, variable in extent' (1998: 381); what he is offering is little more than the banal observation that on the one hand social relationships are what connect people, and on the other, that any social group is potentially or actually a community. Contrary to the conventional wisdom of the reorientors, it is with the expansiveness of the community concept as an orienting device that we enter the Anderson, Cohen and Wenger territory even more deeply.

This unsatisfactory conceptual state of affairs has led the highly respected historian Eric Hobsbawm to observe that: 'Never was the word "community" used more indiscriminately and emptily than in the decades when communities in the sociological sense became hard to find in real life' (1995: 428). Twenty years after I had been introduced to it as an undergraduate, here community is existing independently of sociology, like a renegade, forever on the run, always one jump ahead of any attempt to identify with it any conceptual precision. By now, it is hard to know whether community has changed, is still the same or was never what we thought it was in the first place. The impossibility of community, the impossibility of there not being such a thing as community, the impossibility of imagining community or, some might say, the impossibility of imagining community differently from the ways in which it has previously been imagined, has resulted in the impossibility of community in all respects – or so it seems.

What the rest of this chapter sets out to do is to offer a critical response to this situation by offering an alternative way of conceptualizing community, so that we might start to get to grips with its meaning today. The best way to do this, I want to suggest, is to offer an *ideal typical* analysis in the Weberian meaning (not be confused with an empirical diagnosis), which attempts to locate the idea of community in the trajectory of the historical consciousness of the human condition. This interpretation relies heavily on Agnes Heller's (1999: 1–4) outline of her theory of modernity. My rationale for developing this kind approach is twofold: first, community as it is used by sociologists is always an *ideal type*, i.e., it is not a description of reality, but an analytical tool which they use to try to understand it; second, there is no such thing as community without human life and there is no human life without historical consciousness.

In offering this alternative way of understanding community, my interpretation takes a number of things for granted. I assume that:

- Pre-modern community is the only community; and that in pre-modern societies it serves as the foundation of human existence. It is in this sense that community should be understood as a *strong ontology* (White, 2005) guided by its own *telos*, which takes it as given that men and women's individual being-in-the-world is absolutely pre-determined (*see* 'A Theory of Community').

- In modern societies, by contrast, community is entirely unfit to serve as such a foundation, since the basis of modern life is freedom (Heller, 1999). Modern men and women are individuals first and foremost. Our lives are governed by our own choices, but also by the contingency of events that are often out of our individual control.

- Communities today are best seen as *weak ontologies* (White, 2005) that have the ability to animate our lives because we have identified something in them to which we attach a fundamental importance, are prepared to deeply commit ourselves to and share what we have with other like-minded individuals, who also have the same shared, deep commitment. *Weak ontologies* have no foundations, and they are always contestable, but we are often deeply committed to them because they have fundamental importance to how we see and reflect on our observations about the world as individuals, our sense of who we are, and how we want to live their lives with other people.

What this last point makes clear is that, in the modern world, human beings can potentially have many identities. However, as Heller points out, in any historical epoch, we are conscious that we are human beings of at least two: we are identical with ourselves, and we are identical with the social group into which we are born. How we understand our individual situation in that social group and the possibilities and responsibilities this affords (i.e., the prospect of becoming an authentic individual *de facto*) comes either *before* or *after* identity. Identity is temporal and spatial, i.e., we are all born into a social group at some time and in some place. The meanings that a social group attributes to its way of life (language, beliefs, ceremonies, etc.) are normalized into a world, and this is the cultural narrative of its people. This narrative raises a number of questions, i.e., 'What are we?', 'Who are we?', 'Who should be included in the social group and who should not?', 'Where did we come from?', 'Where are we going?', and so on. It is the answers to these kinds of questions that Heller calls historical consciousness.

Historical consciousness can be reflected or unreflected, and universal or generalized. As its nomenclature suggests, a historical consciousness that is unreflected is one that is incapable of reflecting. Thus, a body of people with a historical consciousness of unreflected universality is one in which everybody is incapable of reflecting on its existential situation, while a body of people with a historical consciousness of unreflected generality is one in which the incapability of reflecting is widespread. A body of people with a historical consciousness of reflected generality is one in which the capability of reflecting is widespread – but not universal.

I propose that the most illuminating way of understanding community is to summarize its trajectory in the four stages of historical consciousness that broadly reflect the substitution of modernity for pre-modernity and the shift from 'solid' modernity to 'liquid' modernity (Bauman, 2000)[1]:

- *Community consciousness* – Community is the period preceding modernity and is dominated by the consciousness of *unreflected generality*. This is an agrarian subsistence world based on ascribed social stratification and patriarchal social relations. Authenticity comes *before* identity, i.e., one group of people thinks of itself as authentic, and all others are excluded. Social life is built on necessity. The putative harmony and order of community life is an imposed one – a 'mutuality of the oppressed' (Williams, 1973) (*see* 'The "Dark Side" of Community'). Social mobility is not possible. The spiritual class is the church. The figure of time is circular; there is no future, only the repetition of the same.
- *Class consciousness* – Modernity in its formative 'solid' phase begins with a change in consciousness to *unreflected universality*. Society is production-based and capitalist (or quasi-socialist), and made up of social hierarchies built on the work ethic and sustained by economic stratification [upper class, middle class and the working class (Marx)]. The baton of authenticity has been passed on from community to class (classes in themselves and/or classes for themselves). Unlike community relations, class relations are not backed up by any authorized sanctions, but authenticity still comes *before* identity, i.e., freedom is

---

[1] Bauman argues that we have recently seen a shift from a 'heavy' and 'solid', 'hardware-focused' modernity to a 'light' and 'liquid', 'soft-ware-focused' modernity. What sets liquid modernity apart from solid modernity is that it is a social formation the does not, cannot even if it so wanted, resist changes to its shape. And what distinguishes our lives from those of our solid modern counterparts is their utter contingency; no matter what our current circumstances or how certain we individually feel about our lives at the moment, things could always be different.

mitigated by one's place in the social class system. Social mobility is possible, but always circumscribed by class. The spiritual class is the industrialist entrepreneur. The figure of time is linear; the past is the known and the future is presupposed as an element of the unknown.

- *Consciousness of classes* – Modernity Mark Two is dominated by the consciousness of *reflected universality*. Society is production-based, and the work ethic still prevails, but social hierarchies are increasingly defined by consumption and status criteria [leisure classes, housing classes, etc. (Weber)]. The baton of authenticity is still firmly in the orbit of class (classes in themselves and/or classes for themselves). Authenticity still comes *before* identity, but increasing numbers of people are able to imagine themselves in ways outside the class system. Social mobility is widely available. The spiritual class is the legislators (doctors, professors, etc.).The figure of time is linear; the future is modern and it can be known, predicated and conceived.

- *Consciousness of communities* – Modernity in its current 'liquid' phase is dominated by the consciousness to *reflected generality*. This is a consumer-based sociality whose social hierarchies are reflected in culture, judgements of taste and the juxtaposing of different lifestyles. The work ethic exists only for the poor. The baton of authenticity has been passed back from class to communities. Class is still especially important to those in whose interest it is to maintain those paddings of privilege leftover from modernity in its 'solid' phase, but it does not have within its compass an overarching narrative of sufficient power, simplicity and wide appeal to compete with burgeoning *individualization*[2].There is a generalized demand for a better life, but society does not have the economic means for providing all social

---

[2] The casting of society's members as individuals is the trademark of modernity. The major difference between 'solid' modern and 'liquid' modern individualization is that the former is *reflective*, mirroring the underlying tensions between individual agency and the structural determinants of a modern society built on differences such as social class, gender, ethnicity and age (Lash, 2002). With the emergence of liquid modernity, however, individualization has become *reflexive*. As Lash points out, reflexes are indeterminate and immediate and as a consequence of 'liquid' modern change reflexive individuals are those individuals who have to cope with living in an uncertain, speeded-up world, which demands quick decision-making. Bauman argues that with the processes of change associated with 'liquid modernity', individualization ends up transforming human identity from a 'given' into a 'task'.

and cultural groups the means to satisfy it. As a result, extreme social inequalities are palpable. Authenticity now comes *after* identity, i.e., once social stratification based on class stopped being the major determinant of authenticity, communities in the plural are now imaginable. Social mobility is understood as a right. The spiritual class is comprised of the interpreters (the *cultural intermediaries* and the media). The figure of time is pointillist; men and women have no expectations of the future, often look fondly back at the past, but are intent on living life in the here and now.

The fourth stage returns to the first stage (both are stages of consciousnesses of generality and community), except that the fourth stage is a reflected form of the first and community is superseded by communities in the plural. The authenticity baton has now been passed on not only to women, to people of different sexualities (the 'gay', 'lesbian', 'transsexual', 'bi-sexual' communities), to different ethnic groups, but also to those social and cultural groups distinguished by shared leisure lifestyles and leisure tastes: the neo-tribes (Maffesoli, 1996). Even the people from the far-off, the disadvantaged, the poor, the parvenus and the pariahs, can now be 'imagined' as communities.

The modern world in its liquid modern stage creates *open-ended* 'network' communities. Communities now bind the near and the far. They have the ability to forge coherent patterns out of disparate events, create reverberating chains of cause and effect. Just as they can unite individuals across the global, who have never even met one another (*see* 'Virtual Communities'), they can also all of a sudden make some individuals different in the eyes of those who not so long ago shared the same community, were associates, acquaintances and sometimes even friends, transcending what they thought they had in common (*see* 'The "Dark Side" of Community').

If, in a world of *community consciousness*, most men and women are never free; in a world of *the consciousness of communities*, nobody, to paraphrase the existential philosopher Jean-Paul Sartre, is 'free to cease being free'. This means that just as we can choose to be part of a community, we are always free to choose to no longer be part of it. What this suggests is that men and women commit to communities not quite believing in them; that is, we believe in them 'as if' they are 'death do us part' affairs, when in fact they are always 'until further notice'. It seems to me that this is all another way of saying that community today offers us a special kind of freedom.

Indeed, the freedom it affords men and women, who are individuals first and all the rest after, is perhaps the most important aspect of community today. Free individuals like to see themselves as members of various communities. What this suggests to me is that the measure of how we feel about these communities not only has to be understood at the level of the individual (rather than the collective), but also in relation to the ways in which as individuals we are always on the move. After all, modernity is always in motion; it is about perpetual endings and new beginnings. This is often seen as contrary to communities which tend to be imagined as if they might never end, as if Being – what the great existentialist philosopher Martin Heidegger called 'Dasein' – has been detached from the real world and time itself has finished once and for all leaving us forever suspended in a moment of pure possibility. As we will see in the chapter on 'Liquid Modern Communities', however, Zygmunt Bauman argues that, notwithstanding the pulling power of community, time always has the habit of kicking in again and individuals are likely to get quickly bored with community, especially with the wondrous array of other choices on offer in the modern world. It turns out that the real horror of *individualization* is not loneliness *per se*, because this is a horror that all free men and women know that they individually have no choice but to face; it is the horror of community, of too much shared experience, all shared being, all together now.

Bauman (2008: 120, 121) argues that communities today more closely resemble 'social networks'. Unlike communities in the past, 'network' communities are neither sustained by pre-existing structures nor by any pre-defined rules which simultaneously guide their members' conduct and attitudes, and oblige them to follow clearly specified principles of interaction. On the contrary, 'network' communities have no previous history, which means that the past, with its power to guide, monitor and correct, is conspicuous by its absence. In the event, the sense of belonging associated with 'network' communities must be understood as *after* not *before* identity. 'Networks' have their genesis in the imagination and are sustained only through communication, this is because they are – unlike the communities of 'before' identity – forever being born in the course of interaction between men and women who are *individuals* first and all the rest after. As a result, they are always 'individually ascribed and individually focused', which also means that they are only kept alive as long as their individual members deem them important.

What all of this suggests is that it is the individual's experience of departure that is the key to understanding community today. This idea is perfectly illustrated in the work of the novelist Peter Godwin, who argues that community ties are made up of Velcro. As the Collins Dictionary of English informs us, Velcro is the trademark name for a type of 'fastening consisting of two strips of nylon fabric, one having tiny hooked threads and the other a coarse surface, that form a strong bond when pressed together'. Godwin (2007) suggests that we all have ties of Velcro, but these are made up of different strengths. In some situations, Velcro feels very strong, but in others it is much easier for individuals to rip themselves off and attach themselves somewhere else.

The key point emerging from Godwin's analysis is that we do not really know how strong or weak communities are until we leave. As he puts it, it is our experience of departure that is the litmus test, as this tells us how big a part of ourselves we are leaving behind. This is also the key point that underpins Bauman's (2001) theory of community; it was only when we are no longer sure of community's existence that it becomes absolutely necessary to believe in it. In liquid modernity, we are always leaving places we have grown love, and we spend the rest of our lives trying to regain the feeling of them again. This is why communities today are best understood as *cleave communities* – cleave meaning both to slice into episodes and to cling to – which reflect the pointillist and romantic sensibilities that are the basis of contemporary community life. The 'cleaves' of these communities are both noun and verb; we identify with them collectively (especially when we mark their passing), but live them on individual terms. We are thoroughly comfortable with community as somewhere we can visit and then leave after a while. It is a very fine thing, in its place – invariably the *past* – but for it to overrun its bounds of possibility to become something more enduring, or maybe even the *future*, would be conceit.

Even communities of the more enduring kind – those ostensibly self-less creations which, if they become reality, require some degree of self-sacrifice, if not the total abnegation of individual freedom – always have the potential to be forsaken at some point. This is because em-bracing a community life will always be experienced by free men and women as a death of a kind, especially with all the possibilities that the wider world has to offer. What this suggests is that death and community today are inextricably linked – though the death, it should be noted, is always more likely going to be of the community rather than the individual.

We go to these communities for many reasons – Bauman would say to find warmth and security in an insecure world, to feel that we are wanted, to be with people who we perceive are like 'us' and not 'them' (*see* 'Liquid Modern Communities') – but what we are really in search of is not community at all, but life itself. And therein rests the paradox of community today; we are attracted to it first and foremost to be entertained, instructed, diverted, surprised, enlightened and entranced to enjoy epiphanic and cathartic experiences (*see* 'Liminality, Communitas and Anti-Structure'). Men and women today use community as Foucault (1984) suggested we should use art – in order to fashion an authentic existence. Like art, community offers us new ideas about how to live, as well as inspiration, moral lessons, comfort and tales of the lives of others and how these might inform how we might live ourselves. It is through this 'care of the self' that community becomes manifest, where we perceive we can become somebody, can find an authentic existence through self-discovery and self-fashioning.

All of this would seem to confirm Bauman's argument that community is intractably an individual concern and that our obsession with it merely reflects the cult of consumerism that prevails in contemporary society (*see* 'Liquid Modern Communities'). However, once individuals recognize the fact that today it is possible for them to live an authentic life, they are also likely to recognize that, as individuals, they themselves are the foundation of all values – as Agnes Heller points out, freedom itself is entirely unfit to serve this function because it is a foundation that cannot found – which also means that they are inseparable from all others, because their free choice of values determines the conditions under which others themselves choose. It is on this basis of interdependent responsibility for the self and the Other that the art of living prospers as a universalizable ethical mode of existence. Implicit in this idea of the 'care of the self' is also 'care of the Other', since according to Foucault those who progress to authenticity, and realize their own personal autonomy, also develop an original voice through their art, and it is this that is likely to encourage others to undertake such an enterprise for themselves.

This is the possibility that community offers us today: the possibility of *personal* transcendence, to become an authentic self, which is nothing less than an individual world – each individual separate and unique but still bound to one another through the felt presence of their shared humanity. This is why community, like all other *personal* things – homes, bodies, relationships, friendships – is so relentlessly aestheticized; it is in the process of making life a work of art that its importance is signified, and its depth.

This is a different view of community, and surely not the only possible or valid one, but it is one that compels us to look at the concept in a way that is both analytical and conceptually precise.

REFERENCES

Amit, V. (2002) 'Reconceptualising Community' in V. Amit (ed.) *Realising Community: Concepts, Social Relationships and Sentiments*. London: Routledge.

Anderson, B. (1991) (2nd ed.) *Imagined Communities: Reflections on the Origin and Spread of Nationalism*. London: Verso.

Bauman, Z. (2000) *Liquid Modernity*. Cambridge: Polity Press.

Bauman, Z. (2001) *Community: Seeking Safety in an Insecure World*. Cambridge: Polity Press.

Bauman, Z. (2008) *Does Ethics Have a Chance in a World of Consumers?* London: Harvard University Press.

Bell, C. and Newby, H. (1971) *Community Studies: An Introduction to the Sociology of the Local Community*. London: George Allen and Unwin.

Calhoun, C. (1998) 'Community without Propinquity Revisited: Communications Technology and the Transformation of the Urban Public Sphere', *Sociological Inquiry*, 68 (3): 373–397.

Cohen, A. P. (1985) *The Symbolic Construction of Community*. London: Tavistock.

Eagleton, T. (1990) *The Ideology of the Aesthetic*. Oxford: Blackwell.

Foucault, M. (1984) 'On Genealogy of Ethics: An Overview of Work in Progress', in P. Rabinow (ed.) *The Foucault Reader: An Introduction to Foucault's Thought*. Harmondsworth: Penguin.

Godwin, P. (2007) 'Truth in Black and White', in P. Stanford (ed.) *The Independent Arts and Books Review*, 9th March.

Heller, A. (1999) *A Theory of Modernity*. Oxford: Blackwell.

Hobsbawm, E. (1995) *Age of Extremes: The Short Twentieth Century 1914–1991*. London: Abacus.

Lash, S. (2002) 'Foreword: Individualization in No-Linear Mode' in U. Beck and E. Beck-Gernsheim (ed.). *Individualization*. London: Sage.

MacCannell, D. (1992) *Empty Meeting Grounds: The Tourist Papers*. London: Routledge.

Maffesoli, M. (1996) *The Time of the Tribes: The Decline of Individualism in a Mass Society*. London: Sage.

Tönnies, F. (1955, 1887) *Gemeinschaft und Gesellschaft* (trans. *Community and Society*). London: Routledge.

Wegner, P. E. (2002) *Imaginary Communities*. London: University of California Press.

White, S. K. (2005) 'Weak Ontology: Genealogy and Critical Issues', *Hedgehog Review*, Summer: 11–25.

Williams, R. (1973) *The Country and the City*. London: Chatto Windus.

Community as Theory

A THEORY OF COMMUNITY

This chapter draws its inspiration from the philosopher Agnes Heller (1999) in order to present *a* theory of community. In other words, it offers *one* theory of community among any number of possible theories.

Section Outline: After problematizing the idea of community in the socio-logical tradition of thought, the chapter traces its historical career progress in the light of the substitution of modernity for feudalism. It is suggested that community went from being a way of life that was total, transcendent, universal, unified and all-seeing to a dead thing, whose prospects of being made real are only possible through the human imagination.

The word 'community' is encountered everywhere these days, notably not only in the writings of communitarian philosophers, sociologists and political scientists, but also in the talk of movers and shakers as diverse as politicians, police commissioners and university vice-chancellors. As one would expect of a word that has acquired such universal affection, community has also become the idiom of the street, the sports arena and the playground. It even appears in the most unlikely places, such as the market (the business community) and that once-upon-a-time monolith of Fordist brutality – the welfare state. 'Community' is a word most agreeable to modern ears, or so it would seem. Not only does it come ready-made with its own inner glow, but it also has a hand-made, home-made quality about it. You might say that community is one of the front-line feelings of our age. People feel happy when they hear and see the word. This is why marketing experts trade on the idea and have become so astute at design that traps its warm textures and homely, feel-good features in the themed package-holiday brightness of their glossy bro-chures: pop-up 'communities' in rainbow colours – black and white and yellow and brown – helping the local community 'bobby' solve crimes in 'their' neighbourhood, popping into 'their' community centres to cast their votes at election time or descending on the local sports stadium to watch 'their' teams, and so on. However, though the concept of community is so ubiquitous, few people today seem to much consider what conception ought to be framed of the word, which everybody ostensibly admires, and is very often keen to celebrate, but hardly ever calls into question, or seems capable of discussing in any critical way.

Perhaps this is why George A. Hillery in the article 'Definitions of Community, Areas of Agreement' (1955) identified 94 meanings for the word, and as good as suggested we ditch the lot after reaching the conclusion that if there is one thing that could be found in all of them, it was that they each dealt with social relations connecting people, but beyond this common base there could be no accord about the precise meaning of the word. No one paid any notice to him, of course. Not least Robert A. Nisbet, that most passionate advocate of the sociological tradition of thought, who suggested that although the word evokes the feeling of something 'once upon a time', of the ways and means of a world that is no longer ours, it nonetheless has deep roots in much nineteenth- and twentieth-century thought, and remains a way of knowing one another and living together that 'encompasses all forms of relationship which are characterized by a high degree of personal intimacy, emotional depth, moral commitment, social cohesion, and continuity in time' (1967: 47). According to Nisbet, in keeping with the simultaneously collective and universal context of human being-in-the-world, community is:

> founded on [humankind] conceived in [its] wholeness rather than in one or another of the roles, taken separately, that [men and women] may hold in a social order. It draws its psychological strength from levels of motivation deeper than those of mere volition or interest, and it achieves its fulfillment in a submergence of individual will that is not possible in unions of mere convenience or rational assent. Community is a fusion of feeling and thought, of tradition and commitment, of membership and volition. It may be found in, or be given symbolic expression by, locality, religion, nation, race, occupation or crusade. Its archetype is the family, and in almost every type of genuine community, the nomenclature of family is prominent. Fundamental to the strength of the bond of community is the real or imagined antithesis formed in the same social setting by the non-communal relations of competition or conflict, utility or contractual assent. These, by their relative impersonality and anonymity, highlight the close personal ties of community (*ibid*: 47, 48).

In Nisbet's view, community is deeply entrenched in our awareness of the world; whether we know it or not; this is because it summarily signifies a special way of being together, which seems as if it already has a room in our *doxa* (the knowledge we think with but not about), and not only that, but it is also endowed with an atmosphere all of its own: it stands out among other words (Bauman, 2003).

Notwithstanding this vital observation, there is another important reading of the word emanating from Nisbet's painstaking definition: community is a positive concept that represents the converse of all the things that are negative about the brutalism of modernity (especially the modern state), otherwise known as the social formation that most astute philosopher–guide Agnes Heller calls the 'modern social arrangement', which made its spectacular appearance on the world stage over three centuries ago. In direct opposition to the modern social arrangement, community is remarkable. Community is transcendent. Community is founded on humankind conceived in its totality. Community is wholesome. Community is a warm summer's day. Community is gentle tranquillity itself. Community is morally improving. Community is the family. Community is home. Community is domesticated. It feels good to be in a community. Community, above all, is bigger than individuals – we are something much more than individuals when we are part of community. And this is how things ought to be.

In the midst of this rush of enthusiasm for the word, however, Nisbet fails to acknowledge any downbeat versions of community that lay bare the fragile divide between its majesty and its misery. That is, those ways of being together, which if they conjure the undeniable 'solidity' of community relations, built on mutual identification and reciprocity, also express their solidarity in opposition to a supposedly threatening Other, and unite themselves by vilifying and constantly mocking that Other. In other words, what Nisbet ignores are community's ready-made outlets for prejudice and excessive emotionalism, which are often located in vicious rivalries that define themselves largely as and by resistance to their bitterest of opponents, blossoming whenever 'we' expunge 'them', achieving their sensual union through the depredations of their necessary Others – a sense of community that is essentially based on and stands for one-way or mutual hatred.

This is community that is exclusive. This is the imposed community (Williams, 1973), featuring the 'mutuality of the oppressed', whereby the 'peasantry' is forced to live in abject poverty exploited by the 'lords of the manor' and subject to their every whim. This is community that is a home that is far from homely. This is community that is cold: the summer of communality is an illusion, and so is warmth between people; the reality is that – like winter – community attempts to freeze-frame everything; in a world in which our being together is the prevailing way of life, there will never be a thaw. Community is terrifying. Community is even crueller than individuals, so that historically, since time immemorial, men and women, both together and apart, have had to shield themselves from its most repellent forces.

But the real scandal of Nisbet's definition lays not so much in the way that it ignores the *dark side of community*, but in its failure to acknowledge that any claim that community's existence can be inferred from the order and intricacy of the world is pre-modern. That is, the mind-set of a *telos* that was rendered unfeasible with the substitution of modernity for the pre-modern social arrangement that had hitherto prevented, or at the very least limited, the scope and the form of human curiosity and soul searching, that would eventually shape the twin driving forces of democracy and revolution, which together would form the basis of what Agnes Heller calls the dynamic of modernity – 'the constant and ongoing querying and testing of the dominating concepts of true, the good, and the just' (2005: 64) – that was, and to this day remains, the midwife of the modern social arrangement. Put another way, the tacit assumption that such as thing as a community in the originary sense of the word could exist once that seismic shift in the processes of history occurred, when the swinging pendulum of human expression and behaviour shifted decisively in favour of freedom over constraint to found a new world without the foundations of locality, feudalism (with its closed system of social stratification), religion and tradition, is untenable.

It is, of course, impossible to be precise about the why, the when, the where and the how of the substitution of modernity for community: at what point did the dynamic of modernity usurp the *telos* of the pre-modern social arrangement of community locked into a timeless present, a totality marked by subsistence, casual brutality and ignorance of the world beyond its bounds? Who knows? Still, it would not be too far wrong to suggest that at some point in the seventeenth century, community was broken by a combination of factors that accompanied the progress of freedom from its roots in the Reformation, the Age of Reason and the Enlightenment; these were on the one hand the large technological transformations that had their basis in the Industrial Revolution and which formed the platform for the modern hegemony of science, and on the other, the end of absolute monarchy that accompanied the democratic revolutions at the end of the eighteenth century, most notably in France.

Before we go on to look at the consequences of these seismic shifts in the processes of history for the fate of community, however, let us first of all consider the precise meaning of community life in the eyes and minds of the men and women who inhabited the pre-modern social arrangement.

To begin, what the reader needs to grasp first and foremost is that the *varieties* of 'community' we encounter in modern societies are quite a different proposition from the *singularity* of community in the pre-modern social arrangement. The community of the pre-modern social arrangement is irreducible to modern definitions. Its existence is inferred from the order and intricacy of the world. Community has its own *telos*; that is, it dwells in the comfort of its own clarity, and it exists entirely for its own sake. Community is absolutist; it makes a total claim on the individual; to the men and women of the pre-modern social arrangement, it would have seemed a universe, while being *the* world in miniature. What is most striking about community is its completeness, the integration of subject and object, individual and society. To this extent, community does not have to justify its existence. It is simply *there* – it is an achievement of social unchange. As Raymond Williams once observed, it is in this way that community 'always has been'. To reiterate, it exists – like God – independent of any other ground because its presence is sufficient explanation for its existence. A world that is as full of certainty as a community can have no place in it for self-reflection. As such, pre-modern men and women (without reflexive consciousness) can dwell in the world as it is, and be content (as we will see, this is an indulgence that is not open to modern men and women). In all of these senses, pre-modern community is the only true community, unreflectively steadfast to itself and to its time.

In this sense, the pre-modern social arrangement is reminiscent of what the philosopher Martin Heidegger called *zuhanden gelassenheit*. It has the capacity to simply let things be what they are, to leave them in order that they may sediment and acquire their own intractable existence, as if they came into being of their own volition, or by divine ruling. The *zuhanden* kind of world is 'at once unchanging and arbitrary. Life must follow the ways of the past; and at the same time life cannot be planned … patterns of life are fixed in ways that cannot, must not, be broken just because they are traditional; at the same time unpredictable, unreliable, miraculous' (Abrams, 1982: 93). In such a world, men and women are *embedded* in the dense folds of community. The place that they occupy in the social hierarchy is determined by their individual function in life. So, for example, in the same way that aristocrats and the landed gentry ruled the roost in the feudal estates found in pre-modern Europe, clergymen were charged with the holy orders, and the serfs were tied to the land where they lived and worked – there would have been almost no possibility of them escaping their shared fate, because it was God's will that they stay put. As Heller points out, what this tells us is that freedom, as modern men and women know it, is not an option in this community world, except for the minority who are born free and for some unlikely reason lose that freedom.

To draw on Heidegger's terminology once again, it was those seismic shifts in the processes of history that swung the pendulum of human fate from constraint to freedom – the discovery of culture, the substitution of rationality and reason for irrationality, the shift from stasis to progress, the dethroning of God and the discovery of the individual, to name just the four most striking new 'facts of life' emanating as a result of dynamic of modernity – that, to paraphrase Zygmunt Bauman (2004: 8), pulled the world out of 'the dark expanse of *zuhanden* (that is, 'given to hand' and given to hand matter-of-factly, routinely and therefore 'unproblematically'), and transplanted it on to the brightly lit stage of *vorhanden* (that is, the realm of things that, in order to fit the hand, need to be watched, handled, tackled, kneaded, moulded, made different than they are). As Anderson (1991) has convincingly argued, these altered conditions of existence led to the collapse of three key conceptions of the world: the idea that religion offered privileged access to truth; the belief that monarchs were persons apart from the rest of humankind and were some how pre-ordained to preside over them; and an understanding of the past and the present in terms of some creation myth – three conceptions, we might add, that rooted human lives firmly in community.

With the onset of the modern social arrangement, a new era of self-determination had arrived, and no longer could men and women sleep-walk through their lives; from now on, they had to learn how to wake themselves up and make their own destinies. This substitution of the penumbra of *zuhanden* and its stultifying confines for the searchlight and spotlights of *vorhanden* meant that there could no longer be any escape from the consequences of contingency, no return to whatever world there was before the dynamic of modernity took over. In other words, modernity had succeeded in displacing the pre-modern social arrangement, and community could never be community again. It was caput.

This is why Zygmunt Bauman argues that community in the modern social arrangement:

> can only be numb – or dead. Once it starts to praise its unique valour, wax lyrical about its pristine beauty and stick on nearby fences wordy manifestos calling its members to appreciate its wonders and telling all the others to admire them or shut up – one can be sure that the community is no more .... 'Spoken of' community (more exactly: a community speaking of itself) is a contradiction in terms (Bauman, 2001: 11, 12).

What Bauman is suggesting here *vis-à-vis* Agnes Heller is that 'it is "the end" that renders meaning in a contingent world' (Heller, 1993: 70). Indeed, it is only from its very demise that we can begin to understand the idea of community. In other words, community's voice was only found in the shock of its bereavement. 'The owl Minerva', the great philosopher Hegel wrote, 'begins its flight only with the onset of dusk'; as the sun set for community, dawn broke for its afterlife. In our time, men and women embrace community with such fever precisely because in reality there is no longer any such thing. There is no such thing as community in modernity because there exists no solid ground under which the conditions of a community could ever be realized. We can only 'imagine' the grey and grey of community today because it 'always has been'.

See also: *'Setting the Record Straight'; 'Hermeneutic Communities'; 'Imaginary Communities'; 'Imagined Communities'; 'Liquid Modern Communities'; 'Nostalgia'; 'Postmodern Communities'.*

FURTHER READING

Read 'Hermeneutic Communities' after this chapter. The arguments put forward here should also be compared with the more conservative Durkheimian approach of Nisbet (1967).

REFERENCES

Abrams, P. (1982) *Historical Sociology*. Shepton Mallet: Open Books.

Anderson, B. (1991) (2nd ed.) *Imagined Communities: Reflections on the Origin and Spread of Nationalism*. London: Verso.

Bauman, Z. (2001) *Community: Seeking Safety in an Insecure World*. Cambridge: Polity Press.

Bauman, Z. (2003) 'Plenary Lecture: Community' presented at the *Communities Conference*, Trinity and All Saints College, Leeds, 18th September.

Bauman, Z. (2004) *Europe: An Unfinished Adventure*. Cambridge: Polity Press.

Heller, A. (1993) *A Philosophy of History in Fragments*. Oxford: Blackwell.

Heller, A. (1999) *A Theory of Modernity*. Oxford: Blackwell.

Heller, A. (2005) 'The Three Logics of Modernity and the Double Bind of the Modern Imagination', *Thesis Eleven*, 81 (1): 63–79.

Hillery, G. A. (1955) 'Definitions of Community, Areas of Agreement', *Rural Sociology*, 20 (2): 111–123.

Nisbet, R. A. (1967) *The Sociological Tradition*. London: Heinemann.

Williams, R. (1973) *The Country and the City*. London: Chatto Windus.

HERMENEUTIC COMMUNITIES

Originating from the Greek words *hermēneuein* and *hermēneutikos*, meaning 'to interpret' and 'expert in interpretation', respectively, the term 'hermeneutics' is derived from the herald of the gods, Hermes, whose role it was to make intelligible to humankind that which could not otherwise be grasped. In the modern meaning, the term is generally used to refer to the theory or the art of the interpretation of texts. The ways in which hermeneutics and communities are connected have their basis in the idea that the pre-modern world was founded on the basis of a singular community; that is, community was once upon a time the *archē*, or the underlying source of the being of all things human. As hermeneuticians point out, the modern world, in marked contrast, is founded on the basis of freedom, which means not only that it is destined to be a world without an *archē* (in other words, community), but also one which is always in the process of reinventing itself (Heller, 2005). This societal rupture not only left men and women with a lasting *nostalgia* for community, but also with the resolve to expound its sense for them as moderns. In other words, it was the substitution of modernity for community that made the very idea of hermeneutic communities possible.

Section Outline: *After outlining the theoretical basis of the theory of hermeneutic communities, this chapter argues that John Milton's masterpiece Paradise Lost is the founding cornerstone of the philosophy of community as it took root in the modern imagination in the seventeeth century.*

Thereafter, the chapter discusses the impoverishment of the ways and means of the theory of hermeneutic communities in the light of the emergence of postmodernity. The chapter concludes by suggesting that by engaging in a reinvigorated hermeneutics, we can not only overcome the limits placed on community by both postmodernism and fundamentalism, but also in the process transform individual contingency into collective destiny, and in so doing, we might even make a better world possible.

In the broadest sense, the use of the term 'hermeneutic communities' refers to any philosophy whose starting point is that the birth of modernity ushered in a new phase for community, which if restricted in its hegemony and rather dimmed in personality, nonetheless saw it ingeniously empowered by the human imagination. To paraphrase what Agnes Heller (1999: 125) said about culture more generally, with the onset of modernity, community was transformed from a way of life to a narrative, a task of interpretation; or in other words, it was to become a hermeneutical exercise. That is, once community ceased to be a thing in itself, it instead became more and more meaning, something like what Martin Amis (2006) recently called the ridiculous category of the *unknown known* – the kind of 'paradise, scriptural inerrancy' usually associated with God. In modernity, then, it is hermeneutics that deepens community, rather than a specific set of social and cultural relations and their associated bonds and ties. It is hermeneutics that makes community more meaningful to modern men and women. This interpretation of the word strengthens community's aura, for it evokes the feeling of nostalgia and recognition. Modern men and women say: 'Here is a work of culture which is either different from ours or close to ours'. And, in this regard, community is special because, through interpretation, both difference and closeness are made to look attractive.

To continue with Heller's summary, it is meaning, the appeal to the *unknown known*, to the nostalgia and/or the appeal to closeness, that has placed community 'over time' at the top of the modern hierarchy of culture. It is placed high because it has the potential to serve for infinite interpretability, and it has already been interpreted from various academic and lay perspectives again and again (*see* 'Imaginary Communities'). In the modern world, community performs a function, then – the function of rendering meaning and evoking the feelings of nostalgia and closeness. This conception presupposes that there is *something* in the originary concept of community (its *unknown known*) that cannot be disciplined – its *secret*. The secret of community is beyond interpretation, and we do not know, cannot know, about its secret; rather, we *feel* its warm glow, we *sense* it.

The key peculiarity about the shift from the community of the pre-modern world to this modern yearning for community is the one that Raymond Williams would have called *unaware* alignment turned into *active* commitment, or in other words, the moving of social relationships to human consciousness. Unaware alignment is pre-modern, in the sense that it is what you are stuck with, while active commitment is something that is modern and is *felt* as a duty, an obligation, a responsibility and especially a desire. Indeed, it is not so much the perfection of realizing something as authentic as being part of a community that is the goal of active commitment, but the desire that accompanies it. This is what Zygmunt Bauman would call the ambivalence of modern community.

This reassessment of community as hermeneutics is perhaps best expressed in Benedict Anderson's (1991: 6) famous assertion that all modern communities 'are to be distinguished not by their falseness/genuineness, but by the style in which they are imagined' (*see* 'Imagined Communities'). However, arguably its origins lie in John Milton's masterpiece *Paradise Lost*, which can be considered the founding cornerstone of hermeneutic community as it took root in the modern imagination in the seventeenth century. Put another way, the modern obsession with community is Miltonic.

Published in 1667, *Paradise Lost* is an epic poem concerned with the expulsion of Adam and Eve from the Garden of Eden, which can be seen as a metaphor for the substitution of the hermeneutic community for the originary community way of life. In other words, humankind's love affair with community begins with Adam and Eve, who, having eaten the forbidden fruit, are driven out of the door of Paradise into the new empty world before them. If physical self-consciousness is the first symptom of their exit, this is quickly followed by the recognition that some mistakes are irredeemable and that Paradise will always be lost – and regretted – that the present cannot be escaped, and that from this point onwards Adam and Eve will have to make their own lonely way through life, either together or apart – the choice is individually their own.

As Milton (1968: 292) puts it in the closing lines of *Paradise Lost*:

> The world was all before them, where to choose
> Their place of rest, and Providence their guide.
> They, hand in hand with wand'ring steps and slow,
> Through Eden took their solitary way.

Adam and Eve have two options: they can either look back nostalgically at Paradise in the hope that if they look hard enough they will find all the fragments of its broken totality, and that if they can put these back together without any cracks, that what has vanished might reappear, that the scattered shards and dust of Paradise might be reunited by a word, that something consumed by the fire of human curiosity might be made to bloom once again from a pile of ash. Milton, the champion of Cromwell's republican movement, knows that this is an illusion. The true magic of *Paradise Lost* lies in the ability of the world it contained to vanish, to become so thoroughly lost, that it might never have existed in the first place. The enduring message of Milton's poem is that if men and women are prepared to support one another beyond Paradise (read: after community) from which they have been forever exiled, they will begin to recognize that they have the world 'all before them'.

In other words, humankind might have been exiled from the old world of community, but it has the opportunity to make a new kind of community in the modern world. The archangel Michael tells Adam and Eve as they leave the Garden of Eden that if they practise Christian virtues, they will find Paradise *within* themselves. Christianity's teleological foundation has metamorphosed into a never-ending homelessness, a fate at once both acknowledged and resisted by a modern imagination nourished on faith. As Claire Tomalin (2008) has suggested, however, Milton has to be read as a 'man full of ideas that are sometimes in conflict with each other'. Indeed, Milton's ideas emerge from a Christian foundation but will not be bound by it; he is too greatly attached to Christianity's hermeneutical tendencies to purge himself of its diction. In the event, the central message emerging from *Paradise Lost* can also be read as republican and secular in spirit: community emerges from a Christian base but is no longer bound by it. Men and women need not feel nostalgic about *Paradise Lost* because they have the gift to find Paradise *between* themselves, and with it the potential to be 'happier far' than they ever were in Eden.

Milton's poem indicates that hermeneutics is much more than a compliment we pay to sentences; not only is it a useful art for dealing with human solidarity in the modern world, but when practiced effectively it has something useful to say about how modern men and women might live authentic, good and just lives together – that might be something like a community but without a foundation, without an *archē*. To paraphrase the great Mexican novelist Carlos Fuentes (2005), what this suggests is that hermeneutics has the ability to restore the life in humankind that was disregarded by the haste of history. In other words, hermeneutics makes real what history forgot (this means that it also has the capacity to reveal community's negative as well as positive attributes). And because the history of community has been what it was, hermeneutics will offer us what has not always been; or in other words, an alternative modern version of community that does not consign itself to the past and limit the possibilities of what it might be in the future.

Since the publication of *Paradise Lost*, humankind has conjured a seemingly inexhaustible number of community narratives (*see* 'Imaginary Communities'). However, whereas Milton blends the past and the future, turning the hermeneutics of community into a critical, reflective and reflexive process which proposes that if humankind wants to make a better world it needs to practice Christian values which chime with human endeavour, creativity and solidarity, most other approaches do not perform hermeneutics very well. The problem is that most interpretations merely try to present community as a luxury biscuit collection fresh out of the box, when the truth is that what you are actually getting is a bag of broken digestives, quite a few of which have bits of ideological fluff sticking to them, while most of them taste just the same. What this suggests is that hermeneutic communities have hitherto not performed their function very well.

The reasons for this are threefold. The first can be identified in Heller's (1999) analysis of modernity. The function of hermeneutics is to render meaning, but as she suggests, it is burdened by a romantic sensibility which evokes feelings of nostalgia and closeness (*see* 'Nostalgia'). Second, historical evidence suggests that hermeneutic communities inevitably seem to be accompanied by ideology and dreams of utopia. Most worrying amongst these are the fundamentalisms, such as religious fundamentalism, which have hardly anything to do with religion or community and everything to do with gaining ideological power and influence. Third, there has, over recent years, been another profound shift in how community is interpreted, in most uses, it has become just a word.

As Zygmunt Bauman would say with regard to this third shift, the idea of community has by now become only a postmodern surface ideal which merely *stands for* deep mutuality and long-standing reciprocal relationships, and it is saved from commitments and lifetime guarantees by the shadow of kitsch, which ensures that it *seems* to be an admirable way of living, while – like all good consumer durables – redeeming its ostensibly functional qualities. What this suggests is that hermeneutics as a higher art form has been superseded by something of lower standing; to use an art analogy, liquid modern hermeneutics is to hermeneutics what muzak (the trademarked and thoroughly domesticated 'light music' played in shopping malls and restaurants) is to music: hermeneutics-as-muzak.

What this suggests is that it is still the elusiveness of community, the 'thing itself', the Kantian *Ding an sich*, that is today the pressing concern. Indeed, the question 'what is the meaning of the word "community" in the modern world?' could be an emblem for liquid modern life itself, constantly in flux, evolving, changing its meaning. Yet, the concept has become increasingly vulnerable, as no other has, to this question. For as we have seen, unlike most other words, 'community' cannot contain in its own self the reason why it came into being, what it is now and what it will be in the future. The fate of community is in the hands of men and women. It has been since the birth of the modern world, but we simply have not yet fully grasped the implications of what this means.

What Wittgenstein once said, about philosophers specifically, is true of modern men and women more generally, especially in our dealings with community. We strived to find this liberating word 'community', that is, that word that finally permitted us to grasp what, up until the point we found it, had been intangibly weighing down our consciousness. However, when we found 'community', we wallowed in its nostalgia and its feelings of closeness, and after that, effectively 'discontinued the divine vocation of Hermes' (Heller, 1999: 150), when what we should have been doing instead, was trying to find new ways of meaning for community through interpretation.

In other words, using hermeneutics to interpret community in new ways that are rich and surprising, all the time trying to see through our own ideological and emotional excesses, engaged in making meaning that is forever unfinished, perhaps unfinishable. As Heller points out, good interpretation deepens words and makes them more meaningful, creating its own democratic operating principles as it proceeds, while convincing the rest of us that it is an actual world we have stumbled on, rather than remaining something utopian or ideological. Hermeneutics is the opposite of postmodernism and of fundamentalism. It is not an ism; it is cultural discourse. To this extent, hermeneutics makes something like a community possible; if we engage in hermeneutics, we can transform *individual* contingency into *collective* destiny, and we might even make a better world possible. The challenge hermeneutics presents to modern men and women, we can conclude, is with making a world which is universal, but never universalizing, and where all humanity can be at home both together and apart. This is the same world in which there will perhaps be many communities, none of which will come with any lifetime guarantees, but each will be continually re-imagined on the basis of collective commitment to the virtues of human kindness, tolerance, justice and solidarity and, most of all, freedom.

See also: *'Setting the Record Straight'; 'A Theory of Community'; 'Imaginary Communities'; 'Imagined Communities'; 'Liquid Modern Communities'; 'Nostalgia'; 'Postmodern Communities'.*

REFERENCES

Amis, M. (2006) 'The Age of Horrorism: Faith and the Dependent Mind', *Observer Review*, 10th September.

Anderson, B. (1991) (2nd ed.) *Imagined Communities: Reflections on the Origin and Spread of Nationalism*. London: Verso.

Fuentes, C. (2005) 'Time Will Tell, Maybe Time Will Sell: The Privileged Space of Incertitude', *Le Monde Diplomatique*, December.

Heller, A. (1999) *A Theory of Modernity*. Oxford: Blackwell.

Heller, A. (2005) 'The Three Logics of Modernity and the Double Bind of the Modern Imagination', *Thesis Eleven*, 81 (1): 63–79.

Milton, J. (1968) *Paradise Lost and Paradise Regained*. New York: Airmont.

Tomalin, C. (2008) 'The Devils Advocate', the *Guardian Review*, 1st March.

LIQUID MODERN COMMUNITIES

This concept is predicated on the idea that the more our lives have become separated from community, the more we long to experience it. It might be said that liquid modern communities came of age once people began to recognize that the safe, familiar world of modernity in its formative era was vanishing forever, and when they found consolation for this in their passion for a community life that could not help but be missing.

Section Outline: The starting point of this chapter is Zygmunt Bauman's assertion that community must be understood in the context of the shift from a solid modern society to a liquid modern sociality. After outlining what Bauman means by the term 'liquid modernity' and discussing what implications the emergence such a sociality has for the ways in which men and women imagine themselves and the ways they relate to one another, the chapter explores what this tells us about the ontological, ethical and aesthetical status of community. The chapter closes with a critique of Bauman's theory and a counter response.

Why community? And why now? The starting point of Zygmunt Bauman's theory of liquid modern community is the paradox that it was only when we were no longer sure of community's existence that it became absolutely necessary to believe in it. For Bauman, community is the great desiderata of contemporary social existence. He argues that men and women living today know deep down that they have to live without the glowing warmth that people born of a community are able give out to one another, but also the largely 'predictable and therefore manageable' habitus of the 'heavy' and 'solid' hardware-focused modernity, which replaced the pre-modern social arrangement (Bauman, 2000). This is because modernity has, in the last 30 years or so, been transformed by a combination of economic, political, social and cultural factors that have resulted in the emergence of a more 'light' and 'liquid' software-focused world. In marked contrast to the *producer* society of solid modernity, liquid modernity is a *consumer* sociality in which *individuals* have become simultaneously the promoters of commodities and the commodities they endorse (Bauman, 2007). This should not surprise us since industrial production has by and large been superseded by consumerism as the mainstay of global capitalism and, at the same time, the task of the art of living has become increasingly about *individualization*, which Bauman argues is liquid modernity's own indelible force.

The foremost difference between 'solid' and 'liquids' is that the latter do not tolerate the pressure differences between any two points; in adopting this law of physics as an analogy, what Bauman is suggesting is that the world we inhabit today is underpatterned and underdetermined, rhizomatic rather than rooted, its trains of experience busy with unremitting new arrivals and speedy departures, as well as unexpected diversions, derailments and cancellations. In other words, the modern world has developed into a particular form of modernization, the most striking feature of which is its lability, its undecidability.

Liquid modernity is characterized by *Unsicherheit* (the German term that Bauman uses to describe the complex combination of uncertainty, insecurity, precariousness) which is reflected in the makeup of economic inequality, social upheaval, collisions of culture, political instability, existential insecurity, environmental risks, the daily dread of dangers of terrorism, etc., all of which have come to the forefront in liquid modernity. It is these too that are a sign of the relentless change, uncertainty, fragmentation and the concomitant absences which mirror the dislocated lives that men and women lead today, which involve them wandering in-between worlds, shuttling between identities. Left alone, rootless and worn out by *Unsicherheit*, liquid modern men and women look for some semblance of belonging, rootedness and respite in community.

In marked contrast to men and women who inhabited the more secure and relatively stable worlds of pre-modernity and solid modernity, liquid modernity's inhabitants are both forced and choose to live their lives on the hoof, with social relations experienced as speedy, fleeting and transitory, and in effect governed by 'the continuation of disembedding coupled with dis-continuation of re-embedding' (Bauman, 2002: 2). The upshot is that modern men and women today live their lives in *pointillist* time which means they experience it in episodes (Bauman, 2007), and community, when it does live, lives similarly, devoid of any kind of extended unity save for that contingently imposed on immediate events – a victory for their team in an important football match or good holiday. What Bauman is also suggesting is that modern men and women today have become shape-shifters whose identities lie not within them, so much as in the current form they assume at any particular moment and in their ability to metamorphose, while defying any tacit expectations about gender, age, ethnicity and social class, never mind expectations about community values such as mutual obligation and reciprocity.

With liquid modernity, a postulated unity of interests gives way to more specialized *habitats* and associated lifestyles and individuality, and men and women become '*operators* who are willing to forego a secure source of fruit for a chance to connect more of the world' (Wellman et al., 1988: 134). Men and women invest their hopes in 'networks' rather than 'communities', 'hoping that that in a network there will always be some mobile phone numbers available for sending and receiving messages of loyalty' (Bauman, 2006: 70). Consequently, individuals going their own way in a world tend to hook up with other individuals with whom they share common interests to form what Maffesoli (1996) calls neo-tribes. In this sense, communities today are nothing more than self-defined communities, conceptually formed 'by a multitude of individual acts of *self-identification*' (Bauman, 1992: 136). Sucked as it has been into the soft melt of liquid modern identity making, community is but an individualized expression, painted only for individuals, which is also part of its liquid modernity. The truth is that liquid modern community does not deliver any universal cheer; it is imagined only for individual consumption not to alleviate collective shiver. This is community updated for twenty-first century consumer loneliness and ennui.

'Each person is truly alone', somewhat ironically wrote Ferdinand Tönnies (1955, 1887), the author of that classic account of community *Gemeinschaft und Gesellschaft* (translated Community and Society). What Tönnies could never have anticipated, however, is the irrefutability of Bauman's argument that community is by now merely a nourishing antidote to what has become an unquestionably *individualized* life. It is individualization rather than community which sets the template for men and women's lives and lifestyles. As Bauman (2006: 114) points out, 'none of us, or almost none, believes (let alone declares) that they are pursuing their own interests', but that is exactly what a life governed by individualization demands of each and every one of us. Community is merely a conduit for our individualized hopes and fears, and it is the fact that men and women know that they are today truly alone that is what makes it so absorbing. Indeed, if community cannot help but be absent, modern men and women nonetheless miss it in their individuality, in the privatized style of independence which they value even more, and which they consider to be the supreme source of their happiness. It is this observation that holds the most important clue to the central meaning of community in liquid modernity.

Liquid moderns only want community the way *they* want community: individually wrapped for individual consumption. Individualized men and women live their lives as if they do not need the support and backing of the world, with its ready-made fixtures and fittings, its conventional points of orientation. They are so individualized and independent that they can live their lives anywhere, and wherever they are is potentially home – for the time being at least. Liquid modern men and women are the point of their own orientation, their own landmarks. They merely need an old-fashioned solution to deal with the intermittent loneliness which comes with being an individual *de facto*, and they find the answer in community.

Community is imagined (*see* 'Imaginary Communities'; 'Imagined Communities') to be something that will transport liquid modern men and women into a place where they believe that they will not mind that many of their other future options have been closed off with the fateful 'I commit myself to this group of people'. The trouble is that liquid modernity is a world 'marked by the dissipation of social bonds, that foundation of solidary action. It is also notable for its resistance to a solidarity that could make social bonds durable – and reliable' (Bauman, 2006: 21). When they have been transported to that place, they invariably find that they really do mind, very much; and they cannot wait to leave. Indeed, instead of being drawn into the community and embracing the responsibility that living one's life in a community brings, the individual is inevitably going to distance him- or herself from it. You might say that liquid modern men and women hanker for the certitudes of community, but they know deep down that they need most of all the latest aids to liquid modern living – both the equipment (most of all their precious mobile phones) and attitude (individualistic and about me, me, me) – in reserve to face the present and the future.

In the event, the idea of community is a gloss which merely *stands for* deep mutuality and long-standing reciprocal relationships. It is saved from commitments and lifetime guarantees by the shadow its own impermanence, which ensures that it remains an admirable way of living, while – like all good consumer durables – redeeming its ostensibly functional qualities. Community has been stripped of its original identity and turned into a commodity for private consumption which makes it a concept made to the measure of the current liquid modern for shaping and training its inhabitants 'as consumers first, and all the rest after' (Bauman, 2004: 66). The upshot of this is that community, in common with other goods on offer in liquid modernity, is likely to self-destruct once it has been consumed, leaving no trace behind it. It is the very definition of depthless, disposable consumer culture. If it came in a packet, it would have to feature the following consumer warning: 'as you might expect, just one discernable flavour, but no detectable staying power' (although quite useful for making its purchasers feel momentarily fulfilled).

Bauman's theorization of community brings our attention to the throwaway nature of the contemporary consumer world, which is best understood through his idea of 'cloakroom communities'. This is the kind of community that boils over rather than one that simmers – that is its brilliance and its difficulty. According to Bauman, these magnesium-flare-like ways of relating – usually nothing more than the 90 minutes or so that constitute a cup final win or the 2 weeks that sustain a good holiday – beg a certain intimacy, but they are not likely to be reciprocated or sustained only because they are too self-contained. A good example of this kind of community is that which became known as the 'Summer of Love' of rave culture that hit Britain in 1988. This was associated with illegal dances held in the open air, the use of the drug 'Ecstasy' (MDMA) and new music that encouraged participants to lose themselves in each other. In other words, a narcotically charged sort of community which was eagerly swallowed by those who wanted to swoon in its excesses and experience a weird and wonderful high – a sense of community which is more real than the real thing. The thing was as the last vestiges of its tranquilizing power hit the wall, they came down and wondered who the hell they had been hugging.

The postulated contract according to which men and women indenture themselves when entering these cloakroom communities requires them to accept that the strength of the bond that they will find there plays itself out in an autonomous ontological realm. However, the reality is that, more often than not, it is only half-heartedly that men and women accept the truths that hold good within these ontological realms. Indeed, if they do accept one of these postulated contracts, it is usually *without* the proviso that they must put aside for the duration any belief they might have entered a community presided over by an ultimate authority, which anchors all feeling and thought, commitment and volition.

On the contrary, liquid modern community tends to come with hollow seal of holiday promises or is swathed in the light of post-football-match-victory positivity, whose 'predigested forms and programmed effects', which Hal Foster calls, after Adorno, 'fictional feelings' that anybody can experience, but no individual can quite possess (Foster, 2005). So arbitrary is liquid modern community in its genesis, so swift is its evolution, so ephemeral is its crescendo and so quickly is it cut off, that it hardly has the substance to support any weight loaded onto it.

In Bauman's schema, such experiences are evidence of the false front of what Guy Debord (1995) might have called the spectacle of community, whose adherents are quick to shed their carnival masks once the partying is over. Bauman (2006: 68) suggests that these brief carnivals of 'targeted solidarity' and 'targeted patriotism' disguise the fact that by and large we treat the 'others' who we encounter on a daily basis as rather 'a vague, diffuse threat', instead of a stream of opportunities for coming together. These communities operate with the kind of image that you leave looking forward to a second viewing, but few encounters are likely to invite continued experience as the vitality of the spectacle tends to die in its performance. Indeed, these are not communities which are intended to outlast the celebrations for which they have been manufactured. Their adherents may treasure the community's collective imagination for its reciprocation of their individual passion to it, and this is why they return time and again, but the spectacle's potency is likely to fade with too much exposure and its seemingly extraordinary closeness may well crumble at the first sign of ennui, and what was once tacit can quickly seem tepid. In liquid modernity, nowhere stays wondrous for very long once you are there, and community is no different.

The big question surrounding Bauman's theory of liquid modern community and one that hardly registers in his analysis is the difference between *consumers* of community and those *producers* of community committed to enduring reciprocal relationships and group solidarity. As Adam Brown (2008) demonstrates in his research on community in football, we can discern major variations in degrees of faith and dedication between two ideal types of football supporter communities – those lightly committed in their performativity and those who are heavily committed. There is no doubting that for those inclined to light commitment, 'community' has a job on its hands trying to compete with other creedal currency on the market – the shelves are simply overstocked with alternative identities begging for their attention – while in those inclined towards heavy commitment, there is one cultural identity that is important in their lives, and they are not only fully committed to it but also insistent on politicizing it, as was the case with the emergence of FC United of Manchester, a community-based club set up by a collective group of fans who withdrew their support from Manchester United as a result of a corporate takeover.

However, what Bauman's critics fail to recognize is that he does not refer to this type of collective activity in his discussions of community because, following the logic of his critique, these do not carry the stamp of a liquid modern community. They should instead be discussed on the basis of what they actually are: *collectivities* – the kinds of institutions that form 'a bounded area of social order reproduced and recreated by actors who have a sense of membership of that social order' (Malešević and Haugaard, 2002: 2), which are constituted by like-minded individuals, generous reciprocation and the necessary ups and downs that accompany them.

As that most astute chronicler of the zeitgeist Adam Phillips (2006: 31) recently put it in another context, 'there is something about modern life that generates fantasies of closeness, of intimacy, that are way in excess of human possibility'. We can wrap up this discussion of liquid modern communities by reiterating Bauman's central message: community today might come with its own uplifting messages, but the shame is that it is hardly ever convincing. And, following Malešević and Haugaard, we can conclude that the movers and shakers behind groups like FC United of Manchester constitute not communities at all, but collectivities *with their own* consciousness (as opposed to imaginary or imagined communities *without their own* consciousnesses). In addition, we can conclude that, in this regard, Bauman's central message is this: if we are going to use the conception of community, we not only need to use it *critically*, but also *appropriately*, and certainly not in contexts where there are available alternatives (such as the concept of collectivity) better made to the task in hand.

See also: *'A Theory of Community'; 'Imaginary Communities'; 'Imagined Communities'; 'Liminality, Communitas and Anti-Structure'; 'Postmodern Communities'; 'The Symbolic Construction of Community'.*

FURTHER READING

The idea of community is a recurring theme in Bauman's work. *Community: Seeking Safety in an Insecure World* (2001) is the best starting point, but there is also a good introductory chapter in *Liquid Modernity* (2000).

REFERENCES

Bauman, Z. (2000) *Liquid Modernity*. Cambridge: Polity Press.
Bauman, Z. (2001) *Community: Seeking Safety in an Insecure World*. Cambridge: Polity Press.
Bauman, Z. (1992) *Intimations of Postmodernity*. London: Routledge.
Bauman, Z. (2002) 'Cultural Variety or Variety of Cultures?', in S. Malešević and M. Haugaard (eds) *Making Sense of Collectivity*. London: Pluto Press.
Bauman, Z. (2004) *Identity: Conversations with Bendetto Vecchi*. Cambridge: Polity Press.
Bauman, Z. (2006) *Liquid Fear*. Cambridge: Polity Press.
Bauman, Z. (2007) *Consuming Life*. Cambridge: Polity Press.
Brown, A. (2008) '"Our Club, Our Rules": Fan Communities at FC United of Manchester', *Soccer and Society: Special Issue: Football in the Global Context*, 9 (3): 346–358.
Debord. G. (1995, 1967) *The Society of the Spectacle*. New York: Zone Books.
Foster, H. (2005) 'Yellow Ribbons', *London Review of Books*, 27 (13): July.
Maffesoli, M. (1996) *The Time of the Tribes: The Decline of Individualism in Mass Society*. London: Sage.
Malešević, S. and Haugaard, M. (2002) 'Introduction: the Idea of Collectivity', in S. Malešević and M. Haugaard (eds) *Making Sense of Collectivity*. London: Pluto Press.

community as theory

Phillips, A. (2006) 'Thwarted Closeness', *London Review of Books*, 28 (2): January.

Tönnies, F. (1955, 1887) *Gemeinschaft und Gesellschaft* (trans. *Community and Society*). London: Routledge and Kegan Paul.

Wellman, B., Carrington, P. and Hall, A. (1988) 'Networks as Personal Communities', in B. Wellman and S. Berkowitz (eds) *Social Structures: A Network Approach*. Cambridge: Cambridge University Press.

POSTMODERN COMMUNITIES

On the face of it, the idea of a 'postmodern community' is an oxymoron, a conceptual contradiction in terms, when judged by what are taken to be the basic premises of postmodernism and community. On the community side, there is belief that 'community' summarily signifies a special way of being together, founded on an ideal of transparency and propinquity, where a group of people share a set of understandings held common, as well as strong and deep. In stark contrast is the postmodern premise that there is no one special way of being together. Community is merely another modern grand narrative, which more often than not fails to come up to scratch under its own limited terms of reference; this is reflected precisely in the way its adherents try to claim special privilege for the world it creates. The reality is that living in the contemporary modern world means living without foundations; it also means living with difference. According to the postmodern perspective, community's adherents not only choose to ignore both of these 'truths', but they also evince a tendency to ignore the *dark side of community*. In marked contrast, the postmodern outlook is more interested in the ways that community always seems to let us down.

Section Outline: For conceptual expediency, this chapter distinguishes between 'positive' postmodern community and 'negative' postmodern community. After identifying the postmodern attitude to life, it begins by arguing that if there is such a thing as community today, it is always being denied any fixed vantage. It is also demonstrated that, from the perspective of postmodernism, the status of knowledge has today been radically altered and with this performativity and the language of the market have now become the language of community, and the world as a whole. In discussing 'negative' postmodern community, it is argued, using a number of pertinent examples, that as a result of this change in status, the idea of community has simply become an empty signifier, a rallying point appropriated by all manner of individuals, public organizations and institutions in the hope that technology might restore to it an immediacy that always seems missing. Thereafter, it is demonstrated that no perspective understands the possibilities and perils of community more acutely than 'positive' postmodernism, and that the never-ending conversation between 'us' and 'them', 'same' and 'other', is its biography, its obsession and its destiny.

Whatever 'postmodern community' means, it is contrary to community in the orthodox sociological sense (*see* 'Setting the Record Straight'), and we can assume from this fact alone that it should be examined seriously. However, having said that, it is almost impossible to do justice to such an intriguing idea within the necessary limits placed on this overview. For this reason, the present chapter will demonstrate how the term can be understood in two basic ways, which for reasons of expediency we will call 'negative' postmodern community and 'positive' postmodern community. As the reader will see, in common with 'negative' postmodern communities, 'positive' postmodern communities are fragmentary and vulnerable to discontinuity, appear in weird and wonderful shapes, accord to no standard and conform to no certain rules, but what marks them out as different is the manner of their ethics and the ways in which they take political responsibility.

Before we look at the idea of 'negative' postmodern community, we first of all need very briefly to consider the ways in which postmodern existences are lived, as well as put some more flesh on the basic premise of postmodernism that community is a grand narrative. According to Deleuze and Guattari (1987) the 'natural' habitat of postmodern life lies neither in the dense folds of community nor in rootedness; it is a 'just-below-the-surface', 'borderline' kind of existence. In other words, to live a postmodern life is choose to live it rhizomatically, a way of life altogether less entrenched than the obstinacy of a conventional community life, full of twists and branchings that are always liable to alter life's course. To this extent, a postmodern existence is an altogether transplantable and transferable way of life, leading in several directions at once: backwards, forwards, sideways (*see the entry of* 'Liquid Modern Communities' for a comparison) – without ever rooting or getting entrenched in one place.

As result, as Lyotard (1984) famously pointed out, it should not surprise us that the postmodern attitude to life is marked by an 'incredulity towards metanarratives', or in other words, the collapse in our time of the illusions that gave energy to the modern imagination. In keeping with the social, cultural, political and economic changes that are consistent with the large-scale socio-historical transformations associated with the emergence of postmodernity, there has been a conspicuous shift in the way in which knowledge claims come to be legitimated. Lyotard's basic premise is that modern knowledge attempted to establish its monopoly of 'Truth' through the use of grand narratives, or big stories (in this instance community), which not only promised justice at the end of inquiry, but were also able to legitimate themselves in such compelling ways that they were hardly ever questioned. Lyotard argues that, with the emergence of a critical postmodern sensibility, this is no longer possible.

However, this has not stopped those who adhere to particular grand narratives from trying to concoct stories that are made to the measure of their own preferred understandings of the world. In a postmodern world governed by what Lyotard calls the 'performativity criterion', rather than the absolutist grand narratives of the past, states, governments and other organizations, just like individuals do, recognize that like businesses they need to get noticed, and this means that they must assert their identities in the most efficient ways they have at their disposal. In other words, it seems that today we all need narratives which, if they are never going to be universal, are going to be convincing. Community is one such story that is governed by this 'performativity criterion'. Its adherents attempt to claim for it such status because they see it as *the* stalwart safeguard against contemporary modern uncertainties. In this sense, 'negative' postmodern community can be understood as a sustained attempt to assert the identity of community in order to make the world think and speak under the ways and means of the discourse of community. And, in order to establish the possibility and validity of the communication of this discourse, the ideal of a communication community beyond all other 'language games' must to be established.

The paradox of 'negative' postmodern community is its belief that the language game of community can offer us that most valuable gift: the pragmatics of a singularity of one vision (Readings, 1989). Not only is it the case that, in direct opposition to the *uncertainty* of modern life, the discourse of community is *certain*, but to this extent, it is also a discourse that is capable of both captivating and capturing of the postmodern imagination. Pragmatically, who would not want to resurrect community? After all, it signifies the idea of a wonderful world: 'its siren-song … is all about the warmth of togetherness, mutual understanding and love; such a relief from the cold, harsh and lonely life of competition and continuous uncertainty!' (Bauman, 1995: 277). Since community itself cannot be brought back (*see* 'A Theory of Modernity'), the next best thing is to get a convincing alternative to perform its songs and go through its routines.

The upshot is that the language game of community might sometimes appear to be suffering a kind of personality disorder, unsure whether it has been resurrected to celebrate art or commerce, to empower local communities, or simply to assuage the limitations of market forces, but these issues do not really matter that much, because it exists only in its performativity. What is really required of it is merely a *presence*: on the one hand, the aesthetic appearance to look the part of a community, and on the other, the technological ability to carry off community's ostensible authenticity.

Whatever it is, postmodern community is in no way anything like its adherents claim. It is simply the case that modern life is a technological problem that needs to be solved (Heller, 2005). The pragmatic solution to this is to appropriate the idea of community, and transform it through technology by altering its intensity and scope so that it is not averse to surface relations and short-life encounters; and this is done by assigning to it some wholly different and incongruous functions, and in the event ends up, not so much redefining it, as turning it into something ready-made. Just like its pre-modern predecessor, postmodern community is still in the main a flesh and blood encounter, experienced with indubitable human spirit, but it is not by knowing and committing themselves to one another that men and women in postmodernity find community. On the contrary, it is by knowing and committing themselves to the idea of *kitsch* – 'that beautiful lie, which hides all the negative aspects of life' (Čulík, 2000). In the event, this 'negative' postmodern version is used to 'stand for' (rather than is) the warmth and the weight of community; it might appear to be inseparable from its 'legend', but when you scratch beneath the surface, you find that there is little that the two have in common. The unifying thing about postmodern community is surface; there is no sub-surface unity in postmodern community. For example, individuals, who claim that they are committed to one another and that their lives are guided by *deep* and *ethical* concerns for their fellow human beings, are more often than not creatures of *surfaces*, more concerned with their own *individual* welfare and given to *excluding* rather than *including* others in their 'communities'.

To take another concrete example, it could be argued that during the late 1980s, 1990s and the early 2000s, the language game of 'negative' postmodern community became so-pervasive, so driven by the events that had smashed the originary concept, that it could no longer lie down, bewitching public policy discourse in the United Kingdom (*see* 'Setting the Record Straight'). As their critics were to argue, these community labels were rarely designating anything, precisely or otherwise – neither offering any new horizons for renewed political thought, nor suggesting a truly shared categorization of the world (*see*, for example, Butcher, 1993). On the contrary, in this 'negative' usage, the idea of community became simply an empty signifier, a rallying point appropriated by all manner of public organizations and institutions in the hope that technology could restore to community a lost immediacy (Deutscher, 2005: 63); lost because modernity is a cold, harsh and uncertain world where community cannot help but be missing.

What public policy was experiencing here is what Baudrillard (2005: 18) has described as the substitution of 'Integral Reality' for 'Objective Reality', or in other words, the substitution of a language game 'without limits in which everything is realized and technically materialized without reference to any principle or final purpose [*destination*] whatsoever' for a reality related to *real* meanings and representation. For some critics, what this process of change in public policy was in fact signalling was nothing less (and ironically) than the technological appropriation of community to facilitate 'the realization of the capitalist fantasy of the socialist goal of a classless society' (MacCannell, 1992: 100).

What MacCannell's observation suggests is that the capitalist desire for the security of community is made neither in any deep sense nor even as a yearning for something lost, but on the basis of a prize to be bagged. This makes postmodern community's adherents what Deleuze and Guattari would call 'desiring machines', who desire community only capitalistically (and inevitably in privatized and individual ways), simply in order to exploit, consume or perform it. In other words, community is the fuel which enables capitalism to continue running – without which it is likely to break down, or so it seems. This leads Jean-Luc Nancy to conclude that 'if we do not face up to the challenge of the homogeneity … [of such] … actions, the likelihood is that our political aspirations will desert us, abandoning us to … technological communities, if it has not already done so. And this will be the end of our communities, if this has not yet come about' (Nancy, 1991: xli).

Like 'negative' postmodern community, 'positive' postmodern community is not an attempt to revivify the grand narrative of community, but it is a mode of existence which, if it recognizes both the needs of the individual and the collective, is also a process (rather than an unchanging fixity) and is always in the plural. That said, 'community' from this perspective, as it is for 'negative' postmodern community, is located not in the actually existing reality, but in discourses of power–knowledge through which our understandings of the world are inscribed. Indeed, because adherents of 'positive' postmodern community have no desire to turn the concept into a grand narrative, its meaning must always be denied a presence; that is, the ideal of community must always be at best provisional or 'until further notice'. According to thinkers such as Jacques Derrida, this is because the discourse of community is constituting of and constituted by the inequity of binary oppositions, which we use to classify and organize everyday life. Ultimately what constitutes community is always dependent on what Derrida (1973) calls the 'play of difference' between community and its associated meanings – 'us', 'same', the 'established' – which are mobilized to render their 'inferior' oppositions – 'them', 'other', the 'outsiders' – by definition, absent (see 'The "Dark Side" of Community').

The other problem with community from Derrida's perspective is that its name is so powerful and pervasive that it has become its own signature word. And, like all other signature words, it comes with the promise to consign the present to the future, and with it limit the possibilities of what the future might hold. Community's signature says: 'I was produced in a present that is now former and I will remain what I am in every present to come, as will the truth of everything I have been used to validate' (Lucy, 2004: 165). This is the promise that community keeps on repeating again and again in the way that it is forever invoking and putting its own validating stamp on its own ready-made central organizing principles and mythologies, for example, national *identity* and its destiny, cultural similarity and its vitality, *communitarian* political expediency and its validation, and so on and so forth.

If the signature of community is a defining problem, then so is the potential for its misrepresentation. As we have seen with the examples of public policy discussed above, like all other signatures, community is all too easy to forge. Following Derrida, at least two levels of misrepresentation can be identified with the signature word 'community'. First, misrepresentation occurs, not in the conventional way in which forgeries are carried out, but when community, in attempting to perform its own performativity tries to pass itself off in an 'authentic' or 'genuine' way, which is in line with traditional community's 'once only-ness'. Moreover, here is the paradox of community. In putting new stamps on its own signature, it makes the false promise of trying to pass itself as the original. More obvious, though, is the second level of misrepresentation. As we have seen, Derrida argues that every signature comes with a promise, but how do we know that community in its reiteration will honour that promise? The signature of community can never be a promise of anything in itself, because it comes without any certainties or guarantees about what might happen in the future.

To paraphrase Lucy, it is in these two duplicitous forms of misrepresentation that community presents its own paradox; on the one hand, its signature aspires to be seen as a sign of its own presence, to be untranslatable, while on the other, it always reaches out for confirmation, for the Other's counter-signature. That it is stuck with this undecidability means that not only is community destined to be a death-in-life zombie category[3] – caught somewhere between a 'genuine' and a 'false' promise – but what this reveals is that it has been 'haunted by its own mechanical ghost, from the beginning' (Derrida, quoted in Lucy, 2004: 166). What this tells us, Derrida suggests, is that it is *not* community that we should be putting our faith into, but taking responsibility for our own world, the world of the present. Indeed, we must not be afraid of writing our own signatures (read: imagining new communities), but we must write them not to bring some *presence* to what is *absent*, but in order to 'bring about new events with untranslatable marks – and this is the frantic call, the distress of a signature that is asking for a *yes* from the other, the pleading injunction for a counter-signature (*ibid*)'.

In other words, we should be looking to replace community with alternative cultural practices which we might put in its place

---

[3] In both ordinary language and in sociology, the term 'zombie' refers to the idea of the 'living dead'. The concept zombie category was developed by Ulrich Beck (2002) from Derrida's philosophy as a response to the major epochal changes that have transformed the relationship between sociology, individuals and existing social formations and institutions. For Beck, zombie categories are essentially stock sociological concepts which, if they seem self-apparent, have in fact lost their conceptual and explanatory powers.

(Rorty, 2007), that operate on the basis of 'a sort of groundless ground of community', and which are founded on the straightforward promise that they will be open and will seek at all times to maintain their relation to others, and importantly, other ways of being-in-the-world. When I say 'yes' to my community, I am saying '"yes" to another, that is, I inaugurate a promise to remain open to whatever might come, to others who may come unexpectedly or in forms I may not have been able to predict. It is this, and not my nation's laws or my culture's traditions, that puts me in touch ... with a sense of community – one which is not organized around differences' (Lucy, 2004: 163). The issue for 'positive' postmodernism is how we are to live together, and accept our differences.

Like Salman Rushdie (2005) in his novel *Shalimar the Clown*, adherents of 'positive' postmodern community look forward to a time when cultural differences are more like 'descriptions' rather than 'divisions'. With this in mind, we can conclude that 'positive' postmodern community is a community that is yet to come. Not only does it offer an alternative way of thinking about community that gives our minds a new world to travel in, but it is also suggestive of an alternative language game of cultural politics, which revels in the art of the possible (Rorty, 2007).

See also: *'Setting the Record Straight'; 'A Theory of Community'; 'Cosmopolitanism, Worldliness and the Cultural Intermediaries'; 'Imaginary Communities'; 'Imagined Communities'; 'Liquid Modern Communities'; 'Political Community'.*

REFERENCES

Baudrillard, J. (2005) *The Intelligence of Evil or the Lucidity Pact*. Oxford: Berg.

Bauman, Z. (1995) *Life in Fragments: Essays in Postmodern Morality*. Oxford: Blackwell.

Beck, U. (2002) 'Zombie Categories: Interview with Ulrich Beck', in U. Beck and E. Beck-Gernsheim (eds) *Individualization*. London: Sage.

Butcher, H. (1993) 'Introduction: Some Examples and Definitions', in H. Butcher, A. Glen, P. Henderson and J. Smith (eds) *Community and Public Policy*. London: Pluto Press.

Čulík, J. (2000) *Milan Kundera*. http://www.arts.gla.ac.uk/slavonic/kundera.htm.

Deleuze, G. and Guattari, F. (1987) 'Introduction: Rhizome', in G. Deleuze and F. Guattari (eds) *A Thousand Plateaus*. Minneapolis: University of Minnesota Press.

Derrida, J. (1973) *Speech and Phenomena, and Other Essays on Husserl's Theory of Signs*. Evanston: North Western University Press.

Deutscher, P. (2005) *Derrida*. London: Granta.

Heller, A. (2005) 'The Three Logics of Modernity and the Double Bind of the Modern Imagination', *Thesis Eleven*, 81 (1): 63–79.

community as theory

Lucy, N. (2004) *A Derrida Dictionary*. Oxford: Blackwell.

Lyotard, J-F. (1984, 1979) *The Postmodern Condition: A Report on Knowledge*. Minneapolis: University of Minnesota Press.

MacCannell, D. (1992) *Empty Meeting Grounds: The Tourist Papers*. London: Routledge.

Nancy, J-L (1991) *The Inoperative Community*. Minneapolis: University of Minnesota Press.

Rorty, R. (2007) *Philosophy and Cultural Politics: Philosophical Papers*. Cambridge: Cambridge University Press.

Rushdie, S. (2005) *Shalimar the Clown*. London: Jonathan Cape.

Community as Method

ACTION RESEARCH

Action research is a form of social inquiry which seeks to bring together action and reflection and theory and practice. In so doing, it deconstructs the relationship between researchers and those conventionally seen as their 'subjects' by empowering the latter as participants through joint working and the cogeneration of knowledge, with the view to effecting social change. As such, action research is particularly pertinent to research with communities of disadvantage.

Section Outline: This chapter begins by outlining the central tenets of action research. After a brief discussion of the origins of this approach to social inquiry, it goes on to discuss the key relationships of power in the research process, and in the light of identifying these, the specific political orientation of action research. Thereafter, the chapter discusses what action research means in practice. The final part of the discussion considers the ostensible weaknesses of action research, claiming that these largely depend on the epistemological position of the critic.

According to its adherents, action research is not simply another methodology in the narrow and broad meaning of 'research methods', but is better understood as an *orientation* to social inquiry, which 'has different purposes, is based in different relationships, and has different ways of conceiving knowledge and its relation to practice' (Reason, 2003: 106). If action research has one specific goal, it is to bring about social change. This observation notwithstanding, it might be said that the emphasis of action research is not merely social change (e.g., increased participation in active sport and leisure activities that lead to better health and well-being), but it is also with articulating the world through new ways, rather than being caught in the entrenched vocabularies of either social science or politics. Reason suggests that, to this end, action research 'is an approach to human inquiry concerned with developing practical knowing through participatory, democratic processes in the pursuit of worthwhile human purposes, drawing on many ways of knowing in an emergent, developmental fashion' (p. 108).

The origins of action research are contested. However, its antecedents can be traced back to the mid-1940s, when Kurt Lewin constructed the first theory of action research, arguing that in order to 'understand and change certain social practices, social scientists have to include practitioners from the real social world in all phases of inquiry' (McKernan 1991: 10). Uses of the term 'action research' are also contested. Gornahug and Olson (1999) identify three variants: co-operative inquiry, action research and participative action research. In so doing, they demonstrate that while born of the same orientation to inquiry, each differs on a number of counts: in terms of the methods employed to collect information; the importance placed on reflection; the degree of involvement of participants; and in terms of underlying theories.

No matter what disagreements may exist about its origins or the finer points of its application, action research may usefully be thought of as a method of social inquiry whose key aim is not merely to attempt to achieve social change but also develop new ways articulating the world – ways which might not yet exist in the traditional vocabularies of social science. What this suggests is that action researchers are very much aware that, just as society has different *bases* of power (e.g., status, knowledge, authority), different *forms* of power (e.g., influence, manipulation, control) and different *ends* (e.g., academic ends, political ends, community ends) of power, so too does the research process. What most commentators agree on is that it is an approach to social inquiry that is rooted in a social democratic desire for social justice, progress and change. Action research is *democratic*, in the sense that it has as its primary goal the participation of all people; it is *equitable*, in the sense that it acknowledges people's equality of worth; and it is *liberating*, in the sense that its primary aim is to provide communities with freedom from oppressive, debilitating conditions (Stringer, 1999). This desire to effect social change suggests that action research is concerned to move the objectives of research far beyond mere description, understanding and explanation.

Engaged as it is in self-reflective inquiry undertaken to improve social justice, action research seeks to shape what happens around it; its *modus operandi* being oriented towards *positive action*. Action research, in this sense, may be viewed as a vital tool of *community development* which can assist people in extending their understanding of the social situations in which they find themselves and resolving problems that confront them. The approach's epistemological attraction for some researchers is illustrated by Hooley (2005: 68), who claims that the notion of truth that action research operates with 'is more transient and localised than permanent and generalised', which makes it much more alert than orthodox social science research approaches to the complexity of the lives of individuals and local communities. As a result, action research is invariably locally based, and it often has a community as well as organizational orientation. Either way, one of its primary purposes is to produce practical knowledge that is useful to people in the everyday conduct of their own lives. As has already been suggested, on a wider societal level, action research can also been seen as an approach to inquiry that seeks to bring about the increased social, psychological and economic well-being of individuals and communities.

Central to the idea of action research is the idea of cogeneration of knowledge. It is a mode of research which aims to build democratic, participative, pluralist communities of social inquiry by 'conscientizing' individuals and community groups whose lives are circumscribed by social, cultural, economic and political inequalities (e.g., Friere, 1970). Herein, action research points to a kind of *praxis* where theory and practice meet in purposive action to interpret 'practice', to make sense of it, and find as yet 'hidden' possibilities for change. In this way, action research also points to the *possible*, in the sense that it signifies something that has not yet happened. The idea of *possibility* also signifies a refusal to be constrained within the limits of 'how things seem to be' (*see* Bauman, 1976), which means that action research is also suggestive of socialist politics (rather than Marxist politics) that seeks to alter the world in ways that cannot be achieved at the level of the individual. That said, practitioners are also alert to the tension that may exist between praxis and necessity, i.e., there is not going to be a revolution so we need to get on with changing *our* world for the better. In this second sense, action research has close affinities with pragmatism.

Action research is, in this sense, an efficacious way to research community issues, usefully providing in complex contexts what Selby and Bradley (2003: 123) refer to as 'space in which uncertainties can find articulation and differing realities can be negotiated in public'. In terms of its specificity, it is concerned with observing, reacting to and making sense of events *in situ*, rather than mechanically following a pre-determined research programme, which is not appreciative of the idiosyncrasies of contingency, time and place.

The literature shows that action research has historically been carried out in a number of different settings, but especially in education, health and *community development*, and that it can be initiated and developed by academics, practitioners, individuals or community groups. It is much more likely to be initiated by agencies or practitioners in community development contexts. However, when this occurs, there is usually a commitment to community participation which seeks to shift control of the planning and management of research process away from outside 'experts' to local 'stakeholders', leading to the development of flexible, locally appropriate methods of inquiry rather than externally defined, fixed methods of assessment. By immersing themselves in the sites of study, researchers can develop better understandings of those sites and can then convey this to a wider audience.

Action research in this sense can be seen as a useful counter to the statistics-obsessed quantitative research which tends to dominate current public policy and is often not capable of capturing the complex and evolutionary nature of how communities function, helping to communicate the social structures, processes and contexts in which people dwell (Crabbe et al., 2005). Indeed, the approach produces information which has much more 'richness' than that associated with much quantitative research, and which can generate at times intense investment by stakeholders, meaning that the findings are more likely to be respected than findings provided by more distant, non-negotiated research. Action research is a collaborative process underpinned by the ethos to 'give back' what the researcher 'takes out', and the hands-on nature of the methodology allows the researcher to take on (to some extent) the role of a worker/activist. Although the interests of the researcher may be foregrounded, the action research approach facilitates a consistent exchange of skills and establishes a context in which mutually respectful relationships may be built. This 'give and take' has obvious benefits in a community setting, where resources can often be absent or stretched.

For those engaged in action research, the importance of language in the dissemination of research findings is pivotal because it can help to refocus what are often subjective judgements which often offer unrepresentative calculations about poverty, where communities of disadvantage are portrayed as 'deficient', not just in material terms, but also with regard to their social attitudes and culture. Just as the focus is turned from external 'experts' to those with local know-how, so the language of research findings should be such that findings are capable of reaching as wide an audience as possible, using evocative communication which attempts to avoid muffling the voices of those involved in the research. Rather than delivering 'findings' at the end of the research process, in keeping with the reflective, learning ethos of action research, work to effect change, including the sharing of findings, should take place as the research is happening, which lends weight to Chandler and Torbert's (2003) observation that research is about timely action *in the present*, seeking to transform historical patterns into future possibilities.

For all these strengths, there are, according to its critics, two undeniable weaknesses with action research. The first problem lies with its unpredictability. Hammersley (2004), for one, suggests that action research is inherently unpredictable and unstable, arguing in the process that most attempts at linking practice and theory are routinely contradictory. However, this viewpoint is based on the belief in a false immersion/detachment binary, and it evidences a tendency to privilege theory over practice. As Chandler and Torbert (2003: 134) usefully remind us: 'action and research are inherently intertwined in real life, not polar opposites of one another, as they appear to be under the assumptions of empirical positivism'. The second objection to action research is that it is an approach to social inquiry that lacks rigour and replicability, and objectivity and reliability. In addition to constructing action research as something of a straw target, this critique assumes that the research methods favoured by those who adhere to a more positivistic research approaches possess some universal, or at least, consistent qualities, a claim that is not only contestable but which also presupposes that objectivity is always beneficial to the research process.

What these counter critiques suggest is that what critics of action research see as weaknesses can be viewed as strengths. As Williamson and Prosser (2002: 588) point out, 'the formal documentary life of mission statements, policies and procedures may contrast sharply with the informal private life of organisations'. What action research is good at is revealing the 'unofficial' lives of community interventions. The advantages of using action research in this way can be illustrated by looking at the evaluation of programmes which aim to address the 'problematic' behaviours of young people using sport as a diversionary tool. Conventional approaches to research in *community development* work have traditionally struggled to provide 'hard' evidence that interventions have a significant impact on patterns of crime (Coalter, 1989). What evidence is available tends to come from internal assessment or quantitative evaluations which often provide no more than a snapshot and failing in the process to untangle the impacts of the project being examined from other potential causes of measured reductions in offending behaviour. As Selby and Bradley (2003) point out, this is precisely what action research is good at: documenting idiosyncratic situated local knowledge (Selby and Bradley, 2003). It is through this kind of commitment to the cogeneration of knowledge that action research acts to counter the impulse to provide instant answers, which often lead, at best, to only partial solutions. As Ellis and Kiely (2000) conclude, the value of action research lies in the way it is embedded in the everyday lives of those who, under auspices of other research approaches, would be considered 'subjects' for analysis. In so doing, it places those who traditionally have research done 'to' them democratically at the centre of the research process. It is this as much as any social, economic or political gains that makes this approach ideal for carrying out research in communities of disadvantage.

Co-authored with Donna Woodhouse.

FURTHER READING

The *Handbook of Action Research* (Reason and Bradbury, 2001) is packed with examples of different approaches to action research.

REFERENCES

Bauman, Z. (1976) *Socialism: The Active Utopia*. London: Allen and Unwyn.

Chandler, D. and Torbert, B. (2003) 'Transforming Inquiry and Action. Interweaving 27 Flavors of Action Research', *Action Research*, 1 (2): 133–152.

Coalter, F. (1989) *Sport and Anti-Social Behaviour: A Literature Review*. Edinburgh: Scottish Sports Council.

Crabbe, T., Blackshaw, T., Brown, A., Choak, C., Crabbe, T., Gidley, B., Mellor, G., O' Connor, K., Slater, I. and Woodhouse, D. (2005) *'Getting to Know You': Engagement and Relationship Building. First Interim National Positive Futures Case Study Research Report*. London: Home Office.

Ellis, J. and Kiely, J. (2000) 'The Promise of Action Inquiry in Tackling Organisational Problems in Real Time', *Action Research International Paper 5*. http://www.scu.edu.au/schools/gcm/ar/ari/p-jellis00.html

Friere, P. (1970) *Pedagogy of the Oppressed*. New York: Seabury.

Gornahug, K. and Olson, O. (1999) 'Action Research and Knowledge Creation: Merits and Challenges', *Qualitative Market Research*, 2 (1): 6–14

Grundy, S. (1982) 'Three Modes Of Action Research', in S. Kemmis and R. McTaggert (eds) (1988) *The Action Research Reader*. Geelong: Deakin University Press.

Hammersley, M. (2004) 'Action Research: A Contradiction in Terms?', *Oxford Review of Education*, 30 (2): 166–180.

Hooley, N. (2005) 'Participatory Action Research and the Struggle for Legitimation', *The Australian Educational Researcher*, 32 (1): 67–82.

McKernan, J. (1991). *Curriculum Action Research. A Handbook of Methods and Resources for the Reflective Practitioner*. London: Kogan Page.

Reason, P. and Bradbury, H. (eds) (2001) *Handbook of Action Research. Participative Inquiry and Practice*. London: Sage.

Reason, P. (2003) 'Pragmatist Philosophy and Action Research: Readings and Conversation with Richard Rorty', *Action Research*, 1 (1): 103–123.

Selby, J. and Bradley, B. (2003) 'Action Research Intervention With Young People: A City Council's Response', *Australian Psychiatry*, 11 (Supplement): 122–126.

Stringer, E. (1999) *Action Research: A Handbook for Practitioners*. Newbury Park: Sage.

Williamson, G. and Prosser, S. (2002) 'Action Research: Politics, Ethics and Participation', *Journal of Advanced Nursing*, 40 (5): 587–593.

COMMUNITY PROFILING

Community profiling is a social research method which involves building up a picture of the nature, needs and resources of a locality or community, with the active participation of its members, the aim being to create and implement an action plan to address the issues unearthed.

Section Outline: This chapter starts by outlining the different ways in which community profiling has been identified in the literature. Thereafter, it offers a critical discussion of these approaches, demonstrating that this research method has hitherto not been used to its fullest potential with local communities.

In the words of Hawtin et al. (1994: 5), a community profile is 'a comprehensive description of the needs of a population that is defined, or defines itself, as a community, and the resources that exist within that community, carried out with the active involvement of the community itself, for the purpose of developing an action plan or other means of improving the quality of life in the community'. Twelvetrees (in Hawtin et al., 1994: 161) argues that the 'purpose of a community profile is first, to gather information about the needs of a locality and the potential for action and second, to provide the basis for an analysis of possible alternative courses of action from which to chose priorities'. A profile then is not a document that merely reports on the conditions of existence of a community, it is also part of a process which aims to move beyond the identification of needs and assets to the formulation and implementation of an action plan to improve those conditions.

Payne and Payne (2004) outline three types of profiling. The first approach, rapid appraisal, draws on extant data and uses a mixture of social research methods, including observation and discussions with key informants in the community. This is a popular method which can be carried out relatively quickly and cheaply, compared to commissioned research. However, this approach has a tendency to rely on 'common sense' understandings of community needs, and is also often carried out by untrained staff. The idea that profiling is 'common sense', that it can be carried out cheaply and quickly, and by anyone, is an underestimation of both the composite difficulties associated with working in communities and the skills required by profilers. In terms of literature produced around community studies, the popularity of this approach is reflective of what Payne and Payne (2004: 42) call the 'intellectual and political bankruptcy' of the British community work movement, which they suggest operates with an ideological indifference towards good research.

The second type of profiling identified by Payne and Payne is priority searching, which is a research package developed by Sheffield City Council in the late 1980s. This approach identifies a focus group in the community, which is asked a general question. The responses emanating from the focus group are then used to form the basis of the survey, usually in the form of a data set posed in a questionnaire, with the aim being to unearth underlying consistencies in opinion. A similar approach is also used in the third type of profiling – the patented package called 'Compass', developed by the Policy Research Institute in Leeds and the Countryside Community Research Unit, which is a 400-item questionnaire that allows respondents to add their own questions. This approach is not widely used by community groups as it still requires sampling and report-writing expertise.

Whilst there are limits with the first of these three approaches to community profiling, it is the latter two approaches which cause the most consternation. To reduce what should be a shared project between practitioners and communities to a computerized process is anathema to community development. It is an illustration of how, when faced with the 'threat' of having to work with communities, many organizations incorporate and mutate 'community work/development' to fit their own structures, rather than adapting those structures to usefully incorporate ways of working that are conducive to the needs of local communities.

Community profiling is a much broader approach to social inquiry than any of the three types discussed above suggest. As the term suggests, community profiling is essential to identifying community need and is used to inform planning, delivery, target setting and monitoring and evaluation. Although profiling can be initiated by an individual or group, it is a tool often employed by local authorities and their partners to identify and address need, which is seen as a legitimate basis on which to deploy statutory sector resources. Community groups and third-sector organizations also use profiling to demonstrate *unmet* need and campaign against developments, in order to hold policy makers accountable.

A clear advantage of profiling is that, in addition to using community knowledge, it has the ability to flag up community assets, as opposed to portraying communities as places of deficit. The ideal profile would be carried out with the highest resource level that a statutory agency can make available and with a high level of participation – from conception to dissemination – of people located in the community being profiled. The community, possessing local knowledge, is capable of producing a fuller profile than that which would be generated solely by practitioners, one which is more likely to aid good decision-making.

Participation in profiling also has the ability to empower communities. However, in order to satisfy the ethos of *community development*, it is argued that profiles should fulfil a number of criteria. Firstly, the community or communities in question must be involved at all stages of the research process to allow for ownership and meaningful contribution from local people. The work should be sensibly timetabled, so that the profile is generated at the community's pace. The profile must also seek to generate ideas and discussion which leads to action. Accordingly, profiling requires good communication mechanisms. To this end, it should draw on a range of research methods which encompass group and individual working in the collection and presentation of information. These methods, if they are going to be effective, should also be appropriate to the community, in order to generate interest and accessibility. The results of the work should be made publicly available, and need not be in traditional report form. Instead, they can take the form of stories, events, pictures, blogs and so on, in order to communicate findings. Finally, community profiling should always try to take on board a variety of views across a wide range of subjects, making connections between issues and acknowledging differences within communities.

There are always likely to be varying levels of involvement amongst community participants in profiling. The wider community may have been informed of the research and be a source of information, there may be members of the community who volunteer to help in a more practical way and, perhaps, a core group that helps to plan and manage the work. Ideally, and responding to community development's call for self-determination and democracy, the community should be empowered to carry out the profile, with support and advice from practitioners who work in a non-directive ways. A positive of using profiling in this way is that it can identify skills and knowledge which already exists within communities, making for a much more comprehensive profile than would have been generated solely by practitioners. Profiling can also act as a prompt or focus for learning if there is a skills deficit identified in the process.

Profiles, if they are to be influential, should be seen to be 'professional' in their methods. However, this should not be allowed to suffocate experimentation and dictate if what is produced is dry or formulaic. Profiling should never be imagined as a one-off event, but rather as part of a continuing exercise in participation; it is at its best when not seen as a technical exercise but rather as something which is integrated into local policy making and political processes. The argument goes that, in situating the 'codified knowledge' of researchers alongside the 'experientially grounded' (Percy-Smith and Sanderson, 1992: 13) knowledge of people from communities, the technique has the potential to 'challenge bureaucratic departmentalism as well as more accurately reflecting the reality of people's lives' (Hawtin et al., 1994: 5), helping agencies to recognize the weaknesses of their own structures and practices.

However, despite a growth in recent years of community consultation and user involvement by statutory and third-sector agencies, it is still the case that the shapers and deliverers of services are compelled by funders to take on board, and attempt to respond to the opinions of 'client' communities. One of the upshots of this is that consultation often only takes place in relation to a research proposal, is perfunctory and can engender cynicism. The rhetoric of genuine community involvement is seldom matched by a wholesale, committed and quality reality. As we examine various approaches to community profiling, below, this disturbing gap between the rhetoric and the reality of working with communities becomes apparent.

Although the use of community profiling has enormous potential as part of a broader community development approach, there are further issues with how the process is often operationalized on the ground. One of the realities which local authorities must acknowledge when using profiling is the problematic issue of territoriality and ways of defining community, with administrative boundaries often not corresponding to how local people view 'their' community. This can both reduce participation and skew results. Coupled to this is the use of extant data, which are often partial, not least because it has not been collected with the help of local people, limiting its validity both technically and in the eyes of local communities.

Another issue is that much community profiling is still very much 'top down', with resources, timetabling, the production of reports and the ability and willingness to act on them still owned by commissioning agencies. Haggstrom (in Hawtin et al., 1994) speaks of community as *object* as opposed to the *acting* community which identifies its own needs and participates in collective action. Many professionals 'act on' communities as objects, believing that this is in the community's best interests; however, such approaches can create apathy and dependency. In the event, practitioners and policy makers may well see the use of community profiling as empowering, but communities still lack power *vis-à-vis* policy *making*. Ultimately, profiles may raise hopes, but, without a commitment to community development, the necessary policy responses to the findings of profiles may not be implemented, engendering cynicism.

In what can be disparate communities, generating a consensus on needs and priorities may also be problematic; so here, power relations *within* the community, rather than between community and agency, can cause difficulty. Additionally, if profiles are being carried out by various communities, it is possible that these communities will end up vying for a share of scarce resources, generating hostility, rather than cohesion. Some workers choose not to use profiling as it tends not to attract additional resourcing and in the event can be demanding, not only in terms of time taken to carry out profiles but also to train community participants.

For those workers and community representatives who have lived through several cycles of initiatives, especially if they have not borne much fruit, profiling might be seen as a way of delaying 'doing something' or as something which should be done by academics or 'experts'.

Community profiling also has several *technical* aspects that can prove problematic. Methodologically and epistemologically, community profiles are often too close to the still dominant 'scientific' paradigm, and local authority culture increasingly being driven by measurement, profiles tend to generate quantitative, rather than qualitative, data. In this atmosphere, inputs are often misleadingly seen as outputs and outcomes, e.g., the number of GPs in an area may be taken as a substitute for the level and quality of primary health care available. Agencies often only collect information that they are compelled to collect and in a format which suits managerial rather than community needs. These two issues mean that both the validity and comprehensiveness of data gathered through community profiles can often be called into question. However, profiling can provide information that is reliable, valid and relevant, and if a model is used consistently, comparisons about equity of resourcing can be made. In response to this habit of favouring quantitative data, some people carrying out research in communities may choose the explicitly qualitative *action research* approach, as opposed to community profiling.

Community profiling, if executed well, is not merely an end in itself. Indeed, the skills community members and practitioners gain during profiling can be as important as the 'data' generated by them. Like other approaches to community development, profiling can be used disingenuously, as a mere sop, or as something that, in reality, is not community driven, but driven by the needs of those who do commissioning. At their best, however, community profiles can both 'up skill' those involved in carrying them out, and identify community needs and resources, putting in place effective mechanisms and policies, at the same time engendering a culture of participation in local politics. However, the evidence would seem to suggest that such a positive scenario seems unlikely, currently, when much that is potentially radical about work with communities has become stultified by agencies keen to control ways of working that run contrary to their own putative assumptions about how best to operate.

See also: *'Action Research'; 'Community Development'; 'Locality, Place and Neighbourhood'.*

Co-authored with Donna Woodhouse.

community as method

59

REFERENCES

Hawtin, M., Hughes, G. and Percy-Smith, J. (1994) *Community Profiling. Auditing Social Needs.* Buckingham: OUP.

Payne, G. and Payne, J. (2004) *Key Concepts in Social Research.* London: Sage.

Percy-Smith, J. and Sanderson, I. (1992) *Understanding Local Needs.* London: IPPR.

COMMUNITY STUDIES

'Community studies' is the term used to describe a particular variety of empirical research (usually ethnographic and often carried out by researchers in communities of which they are a member) which traditionally has been concerned with the study of the social networks, kinship ties and face-to-face social relations that constitute the social structure of a clearly defined geographical locality, place or neighbourhood.

> *Section Outline: This chapter begins by explaining the ways and means of community studies. Thereafter, it discusses the historical development of community studies as they emerged in the United Kingdom during the twentieth century, in the process identifying some of the metaphysical and theoretical problems suggested by this research tradition. After briefly discussing the theoretical implications for developing community studies in the light of recent societal changes, the chapter closes with a discussion of some of the practical and ethical implications of developing community studies and a brief comment on their usefulness in a world that is modern in different ways than it was in the past.*

The starting point of community studies is that, notwithstanding the processes of change by which traditional societies achieved modernity, localism is still a significant principle of social organization. In other words, it works with the assumption that community, with its emphasis on social networks, kinship ties, face-to-face social relations, shared identity, values and spirit of belonging, not only serves certain societal functions, but also continues to be a meaningful social formation for individuals. Community studies are thus concerned with the study of 'local social systems', to use

Margaret Stacey's (1969) apt expression, invariably using approaches which involve researchers living, or spending significant amounts of their time, in communities identified for investigation (*see* 'Ethnography'). Because the practice of community studies has traditionally been dominated by the idea that community is a delimited space, most communities that have come under its purview have tended to be compact. Historically, these studies have been carried out in both rural and urban areas. Having said that, community studies have in the main evinced a tendency to focus their attention on community life in the city, which is reflected in their obsession with finding evidence of life based on mutuality, belonging and intimate social relations in the very place considered to be the most impersonal, artificial, lonely and where it is assumed that social relations are of a more calculating kind.

Crow and Allan (1994) identify three phases in the evolution of British community studies. The first phase, which began at the end of World War II until the late 1960s, can be seen, with the benefit of hindsight, as a critical response to two key ideas that had hitherto predominated in sociology: the loss of community thesis and the rural–urban continuum (*see* 'Community: An Interim Career Report'). Although both of these ideas can be traced back to the founding fathers – especially the work of Durkheim and Tönnies – they emerged most powerfully in the work of the Chicago School in the United States in early twentieth century.

This work was characterized by a rather pessimistic view of community life which suggested that urbanism had become the basis of modern life because the city is so dominant. As a result, the city served as the primary research site for these scholars who introduced and developed a specifically urban sociology concerned with what Robert Park (1916) famously called 'the investigation of human behavior in the urban environment'. In his formative work in urban sociology, Park identified an urban world featuring the breakdown of local attachments where people 'touch but do not interpenetrate'. However, the more influential work on what was to become essentially a treatise of urban isolation was developed by Louis Wirth (1938), who in his famous essay, *Urbanism as a Way of Life*, argued that the size, density, diversity and heterogeneity of modern city life weakens social bonds and produces social relations that are 'impersonal, superficial, transitory and segmental', concluding that, in the city, communal relations, such as kinship and neighbourliness, and the sentiments arising out of these, are likely to be absent or, at the best, weak. Turning his critical eye away from city to the countryside, another Chicago scholar Robert Redfield (1947) took up the idea of 'folk society' to focus his attention instead on the ways of rural life. However, by and large, he reached the same conclusions as his colleagues: community can be equated with 'ruralism as a way of life', while 'urbanism as a way of life' is suggestive of the anonymity and impersonal rules of city living.

As suggested above, the impetus behind the challenge to the loss of community thesis and the rural–urban continuum model, which together had summarily failed to consider how modernization processes outside the city and the countryside contributed to societal change and impacted on social roles, groups and social networks, came from nascent community studies in post-war United Kingdom. Influential work in this formative work can be broken down into two distinct focal points: the discovery of urban communities and the discovery of urbanism in the village. These researchers, all working at the sharp end of empirical community studies, were by and large persuaded of community's existence as a material and observable reality. What their studies were telling them was that community had merely been changed by modern forces rather than was lost, and it was these researchers who summarily signalled the rediscovery of community in the first half of the twentieth century.

Urban studies research revealed the existence of relatively stable, closely knit communities in urban areas. Good examples of these are Richard Hoggart's (1957) personal rendition about his formative experiences in Hunslet, Leeds, in *The Uses of Literacy* and the classic empirical study of 'Ashton', a West Yorkshire mining community in *Coal is Our Life* (Dennis et al., 1956), which focused its attention on the important communal influences of work, leisure and family. However, this type of study is perhaps best exemplified in the longitudinal work of Peter Willmott and Michael Young in the United Kingdom (Dench, Gavron and Young, 2006; Willmott, 1963; Willmott, 1986; Willmott and Young, 1960) which began with Willmott and Young's (1960) classic study *Family and Class in a London Suburb*. This first phase of studies showed that, in urban settings, social networks and mutual support were strong, particularly in working-class localities and industrial areas. While rural studies, such as *Life in the Welsh Countryside* by Rees (1950), Williams' (1956) work in Gosforth *The Sociology of an English Village* and Littlejohn's (1963) study *Westrigg: the Sociology of a Cheviot Parish*, revealed forms of sociality and sociability more readily associated with the city – impersonality, loneliness, social class divisions and contractual social relations.

However, despite the rich literature it produced, this phase of community studies was marked by a sense of unease about the way that the majority of these research projects were using the idea of community. According to their critics, these community studies had a tendency to highlight community solidarity rather than discord, with some accusing their adherents of producing 'very sympathetic ... over sympathetic – portraits of a locality' (Bell and Newby, 1971: 55) (*see* 'Nostalgia'). This problem led Stacey (1969) to challenge researchers to be more up-front about whether they were referring to a 'local social system' or not; this would make sure they avoided the nostalgic and ideological associations with 'community'. Bell and Newby (1971) were less reproachful, but agreed that 'community studies' should only refer to a *method*, not an object.

According to Crow and Allan (1994), however, Elias (1974) was hinting at the real problem when he observed that 'the theoretical aspects of community studies are less advanced than the empirical work in the field'. What these critics also failed to consider enough was the fact that it is the very peculiarity of community studies that they perhaps must leave unresolved what terms like 'real' communities and 'imagined' communities might actually mean. What could not be doubted was that at the very heart of the majority of these studies was the desire to confront an empirical phenomenon; that is, to try to understand why people are so attached to their localities by trying to capture a sense of their shared experiences and the collective meanings they attach to these.

Stacey's (1960) Banbury study analysed the changing nature of community as established social formations and culture were confronted with incomer populations and the effects this had on local social relations and institutions. Importantly, this research also discussed concerns about the operational use of the term 'community'. In so doing, Stacey's work signalled the emergence of a more reflective second phase of community studies in which theoretical concerns were addressed more squarely. The housing estates that had emerged from the slum clearance programmes carried out in the post-war period also provided a focus for many other studies, which explored 'new' communities marked by a wide variety of social groupings, including those more conscious of their careers and conspicuous consumption than class and continuity. Willmott's (1963) *The Evolution of a Community: A study of Dagenham after Forty Years* is a good example of this kind of work.

The third phase of community studies, from the 1980s onwards, saw researchers moving back into the field with a methodologist's keen eye for research-related issues and a politician's concern about the decline of the manufacturing industries. Stacey et al. (1975) produced follow-up work to the Banbury study, and Parker's (1986) work in the northeast of England examined communal changes and tensions in the midst of industrial decline. The Isle of Sheppey study (Pahl, 1984) and its associated work (Wallace, 1985) also made an important contribution to this third phase, putting the emphasis on the household division of labour and the impact of wider social and structural forces on community. What all of this work served to confirm was Pahl's (1966: 322) earlier assertion that 'any attempt to tie particular patterns of social relationships to specific geographical milieux is a singularly fruitless exercise'. In this third phase of studies, Wellman and his colleagues (1979; 1988) also argued that personal communities were now much more significant than local ones. These observations notwithstanding, it was difficult to argue with the fact that locality was still a significant reference point for many people in their everyday lives. Even today, many people still have a sense of belonging to a particular area and think of the kinship and friendship ties that they have there as their 'community'.

As community has become less place-dependent (*see* 'Virtual Communities'), however, it has become increasingly clear that community studies which focus on locality provide only a partial portrait of a world in which all-embracing solidarity has given way to more specialized forms of community and associated lifestyles characterized by individuality, and more reliance on formal organizations for those needs which used to be fulfilled informally (Wellman, 1979; Wellman et al., 1988). While not underplaying the centrality of place to many people's lives, what this shift suggests is that researchers must now embrace yet another phase of community studies, acknowledging the complexity of how many people today experience community, incorporating an understanding of Giddens's (1987; 1990) theorization of 'late' modernity where time and space are re-organized such that the texture of day-to-day life is bound up with more contingent and ephemeral kinds of belonging and associated social networks and identities (*see* 'Liquid Modern Communities'; 'Postmodern Communities'). Blackshaw's (2003) study in Leeds is an example of such work, which focuses its attention on the social networks and leisure lifestyles of an imagined community of working-class men, arguing that leisure, with its intermittent and contingent life-worlds, much more than work, is now the central arena in which some individuals define their shared identities and sense of belonging.

Whilst early studies tended to focus on community as a physical place, this more sophisticated work helps us to consider community as something symbolic, imagined and imaginary (*see* 'The Symbolic Construction of Community'; 'Imaginary Communities'; 'Imagined Communities'). To reiterate, this is not to say that place is no longer important in community studies, but rather to argue that its centrality to people's experience of community should not be taken as a simplistic given. The value of approaches that are not dependent on spatially delimited definitions of community is that they help to foreground the importance of the social relationships that are often at the heart of both solidarity and conflict.

Glass once called community studies 'the poor sociologist's substitute for the novel' (cited in Bell and Newby, 1971: 13). This criticism reflects the descriptive nature of much early work in community studies, which meant that it could be easily dismissed as social history offering little contribution to our knowledge of historical continuity and modern change. However, as we have seen, more contemporary work has addressed this issue and attempts not just to describe and analyse the site of research, but to link that site to a wider social context, and in doing so, is more theoretically robust. The eschewing or only negligible use of quantitative research approaches may mean that few community studies can be compared in order to measure their reliability and validity, which in some people's eyes is cause for concern. However, the search for typicality or difference has never been the aim of community studies, which do not claim to be cumulative in the orthodox social scientific sense. Community studies do not produce a once-and-for-all understanding of the world, and the 'realities' that their adherents articulate in their published output are clearly at odds with positivist approaches that seek to do this. Carrying out a community study is not a form of abstracted empiricism, and the 'facts' of the field cannot speak for themselves – they have no intrinsic meaning or value and take their meaning from the ways in which they are interpreted by researchers and bound together with theory. Ultimately, then, we base our judgements of the validity of such studies not on their ontological status, but on their ability to compel, as well as the respect we have for the author and our confidence in their individual integrity and that of their informants.

With regard to the field difficulties associated with community studies, it is more likely today than in the past that researchers are going to be relative strangers in the sites where they choose to carry out their studies. Researchers are also more likely these days to have to build relationships with key informants who become 'sponsors' helping them to access communities and key informants. This 'getting to know' the field is indicative of community studies as a process, with the three broad phases of: entry, maintaining a position and exit. Fieldwork is taxing, with the dialectic between researcher as stranger and friend, capable of causing personal uneasiness, if not distress. The idea of detachment is also problematic. If researchers appear too aloof, they may not be able to access the rich insights they seek, but equally if they are perceived by peers as too immersed, they risk accusations of 'going native', of losing their objectivity.

Ethically, researchers have a duty of care towards their respondents. Convention has it that individuals, and even the communities themselves, should remain anonymous in the writing up of research findings. However, it is difficult to disguise people and settings in community studies without losing the 'feel' of them. In terms of conduct, researchers should not make it impossible, through their behaviour during and after the research, for another researcher to follow their initial forays into communities, which Frankenberg (1966) once called the 'cardinal principle'. In terms of learning from the findings of such studies, Coleman (cited in Bell and Newby, 1971) argues that community studies tend to be written in such ways that render them limited, or at least uninteresting, and the upshot is that actual community members have little to gain from taking part. This is because it seems that the findings of community studies invariably end up being presented in ways suited to the academy rather than the worlds from which they ostensibly emerge, making it difficult for those unfamiliar with academic language to glean much useful information from research.

For all the limits of community studies, however, and not least the parochial concerns that make them both 'appealing and infuriating' (Bell and Newby, 1971: 250), there are few other approaches to the study of social life that are capable of matching their ability to elucidate the complexity of the huge and opaque tissue of inter-human connections. Indeed, community studies continue to act as an important barometer of key changes in the ways modern life is experienced, telling us a great deal about how social networks operate in a modern setting and the ways in which these are underpinned by values that are both shared and often come into conflict, maintaining their tradition of informing us about the richness and complexity of humanity in the process.

See also: *'Setting the Record Straight'; 'Action Research'; 'Community Development'; 'Community Policy'; 'Ethnography'; 'Liquid Modern Communities'; 'Locality, Place and Neighbourhood'; 'Nostalgia'; 'Postmodern Communities'; 'The Symbolic Construction of Community'; 'Virtual Communities'.*

Tony Blackshaw and Donna Woodhouse.

FURTHER READING

Bell and Newby (1971) is the classic introduction to community studies. Crow and Allan (1995) and Day (2006) are also worth following up for discussion of more recent studies.

REFERENCES

Bell, C. and Newby, H. (1971) *Community Studies: An Introduction to the Sociology of the Local Community*. London: George Allen and Unwin.

Blackshaw, T. (2003) Leisure Life: *Myth, Modernity and Masculinity*. London: Routledge.

Crow, G. and Allan, G. (1994) *Community Life: An Introduction to Local Social Relations*. London: Harvester Wheatsheaf.

Day, G. (2006) *Community and Everyday Life*. London: Routledge.

Dench, G., Gavron, K. and and Young, M. (2006) *The New East End: Kinship, Race and Conflict*. London: Profile Books Ltd.

Dennis, N., Henriques, F. and Slaughter, C. (1956) *Coal is our Life: An Analysis of a Yorkshire Mining Community*. London: Tavistock.

Elias, N. (1974) 'Foreword – Towards as Theory of Communities', in C. Bell and H. Newby (eds) *The Sociology of Community: A Selection of Readings*. London: Frank Cass.

Frankenberg, R. (1966) *Communities in Britain. Social Life in Town and Country*. Harmondsworth: Penguin.

Giddens, A. (1987) *Social Theory and Modern Sociology*. Cambridge: Polity Press.

Giddens, A. (1990) *The Consequences of Modernity*. Cambridge: Polity Press.

Hoggart, R. (1957) *The Uses of Literacy*. London: Chatto and Windus.

Littlejohn, J. (1963) *Westrigg: the Sociology of a Cheviot Parish*. London: Routledge.

Pahl, R. (1966) 'The Rural–Urban Continuum', *Sociologia Ruralis*, 6 (3–4): 299–329.

Pahl, R. (1984) *Division of Labour*. Oxford: Basil Blackwell.

Park, R. (1916) 'The City: Suggestions for the Investigation of Human Behavior in the Urban Environment', in R. Sennett (1969) (ed.) *Classic Essays on the Culture of Cities*. Englewood Cliffs: Prentice-Hall.

Parker, T. (1986) *Red Hill: A Mining Community*. Sevenoaks: Coronet.

Redfield, R. (1947) 'The Folk Society', *The American Journal of Sociology*, 52 (3): 293–308.

Rees, A. (1950) *Life in a Welsh Countryside*. Cardiff: University of Wales Press.

Stacey, M. (1960) *Tradition and Change. A Study of Banbury*. Oxford: Oxford University Press.

Stacey, M. (1969) 'The Myth of Community Studies', *British Journal of Sociology*, 20 (2): 134–47.

Stacey, M., Batstone, E., Bell, C. and Murcott, A. (1975) *Power, Persistence and Change. A Second Study of Banbury*. London: Routledge & Kegan Paul.

Wallace, C. (1985) 'Forms of Work and Privatisation on the Isle of Sheppey', in B. Roberts, R. Finnegan, and D. Gallie (eds) *New Approaches to Economic Life: Economic Restructuring, Unemployment and the Social Division of Labour*. Manchester: Manchester University Press.

Wellman, B. (1979) 'The Community Question: The Intimate Networks of East Yorkers', *American Journal of Sociology*, 84 (5): 1201–1231.

Wellman, B., Carrington, P. and Hall, A. (1988) 'Networks as Personal Communities', in B. Wellman and S. Berkowitz (eds) *Social Structures: A Network Approach*. Cambridge: Cambridge University Press.

Williams, W. (1956) *The Sociology of an English Village: Gosforth*. London: Routledge & Kegan Paul.

community as method

Willmott, P. (1963) *The Evolution of a Community: A Study of Dagenham after Forty Years*. London: Routledge & Kegan Paul.

Willmott, P. and Young, M. (1960) *Family and Class in a London Suburb*. London: Routledge & Kegan Paul.

Willmott, P. (1986) *Social Networks, Informal Care and Public Policy*. London: Policy Studies Institute.

Wirth, L. (1938) 'Urbanism as a Way of Life', *The American Journal of Sociology*, 44 (1): 1–24.

ETHNOGRAPHY

In community studies, 'ethnography' is the term generally used to refer to a specific study of the collective interest or way of life that a particular group of people share. It is also used to describe a particular research method which at its most basic level can be defined as one culture studying another culture. This usually refers to a researcher who participates in a community over some length of time, either overtly or covertly in some masquerading role, watching things that happen, listening to what is said, smelling, touching and tasting, taking note of things that are tacit, such as the non-spoken interaction that goes deeper than verbal communication, and in the light of these observations asking the members of that community pertinent questions, while linking all of this with what he or she knows already and has imagined as a consequence.

Section Outline: After outlining the historical development of ethnography in social anthropology and sociology, this chapter discusses the role of this research method in community studies by focusing on William Foote Whyte's (1943) classic ethnography of 'Cornerville' in Street Corner Society. Thereafter, it is demonstrated that there has, over the years, been a slow but profound shift in the ways in which ethnography is both practiced and written – one which has also altered, deeply, our entire view about the ability of this research method to capture the everyday lived experiences of communities.

According to its adherents, ethnography is the social research method best equipped for investigating, capturing and providing detailed accounts of the meanings and attachments associated with the everyday lived experiences of community life. Its origins as an academic research method can be traced back to the book *Primitive Culture* written by Edward B. Tyler, published in 1871, which 'laid out the rudiments of a new approach to the study of human life' (Colls, 2001: 245). As Colls goes on to point out, by 1896, when Tylor became Professor of Anthropology at Oxford, the idea of 'primitive culture' was ubiquitous in anthropology, and it was to have a massive impact on the subsequent development of ethnography as it was established in functionalist social anthropology in British and American universities in the early part of the twentieth century.

As Kuper (1988) demonstrates, the idea of 'primitive culture' was used by these anthropologists as the inverse of 'modern culture'. The upshot of this was that most early ethnographic research began in places such as Africa, South America and Australasia with the study of non-literate tribal communities. However, once it was adopted by the Chicago School in American urban sociology, ethnography moved closer to home, in the city: sociologists as ethnographers exploring the social structure of community as something preserved in local neighbourhoods, while being under threat in the wider urban context, just as their anthropological predecessors saw village life in Africa, South America and Australasia being preserved in spite of an increasingly encroaching modernity.

William Foote Whyte's classic study of 'Cornverville' in *Street Corner Society: The Social Structure of an Italian Slum* (1943) raised three central themes pertinent to the emergence of ethnography in social anthropology and sociology, but in a new context: it established living among a community and participating in the daily life of its inhabitants over a period as an accepted research method; it analysed one community as a social structure made up of various small groups, leading to the development of the popularity of sub-cultural analysis; and it dispelled the tacit assumption that slum areas were by definition disordered and disorganized, bringing to light evidence that suggested such 'communities' should be understood as ordered and organized, even if only on the basis of crime, racketeering and local politics (Boelen, 1992).

Whyte's thinking on this last theme indicates something about the one-dimensional way in which he viewed life in 'Cornerville'. That is, if it was a community, it was one that exhibited the typical pathological

community as method

69

features of the persistent social problems associated with other immigrant areas in large cities, such as run-down housing amenities and high rates of poverty and crime. As Boelen (1992: 27) points out: 'What Whyte considered an organized "slum" ridden with gangs, racketeers, and corrupt politicians was in [his] opinion an "urban village", whose patterns of association and communal activity make more sociological sense when interpreted in the appropriate context of Italian village life rather than in a foreign context of a city slum'.

This self-confessed inability 'to take a self-critical view of the values of his own social world' (1943: 164) to 'defamiliarize the familiar' by asking questions about 'Cornerville' no one had even remembered asking, let alone had answered before (Bauman, 1990), highlights a general problem associated with outsiders carrying out ethnography in local communities, and this is that their research is going to be limited if they do not recognize that empathy is a key cultural practice. As Boelen (1992) concludes, Whyte was insufficiently concerned with the distance that separated him from the community that he was researching, and his ethnography was always going to be inadequate because not only did he not speak Italian, but he was also unfamiliar with the Italian culture, which would have undoubtedly distanced him from this community. These specific criticisms aside, what Whyte's study lacked was the recognition that ethnography comes with a universal promise to commit itself to the infinite subtlety and suggestibility of community life, especially the non-spoken interaction that goes deeper than verbal communication.

What should be clear by now is that ethnography is a research method that demands a high level of skill and competence from its practitioners. Even when these are in place, however, it can still present several problems. Gaining access to communities is not always easy, and even when it is made possible through key informers, too much reliance on these individuals can skew the research in particular ways. For example, according to Boelen, Whyte over-relied on his main informant 'Doc' to the extent that he ended up putting too much emphasis on 'gang' structure in 'Cornerville' than it actually merited. There is another problem with relying too much on key informers in ethnography. With acceptance, there is the possibility that researchers will become too confident about their newfound status, imagining they are more accepted than they actually are, or in some extreme cases, become so compulsively gripped by the community under scrutiny that they become oblivious to its invisible tensions and connections. Notwithstanding these general methodological problems associated with ethnography, there is the more specific problem that faces all ethnographers carrying out research in community contexts, and that is the difficulty that, even if they can observe community life in ways that are unmediated by their presence, they can never be sure that they are observing it in a way that unmediated by their own expectations of what a community is, should look or feel like.

This last point leads us on to a counter critique of Boelen's denigration of Whyte's study, and this is that it works with the assumption that if ethnographers are highly skilled and ethnography is resolutely and systematically executed, it is possible to capture the essence of any community under scrutiny. However, the critique of this ethnography as 'realism', or what has been described as a kind of *correspondence theory of truth,* has been overwhelming in recent years. There are few if any ethnographers around today who believe that what they practice in their work is an approach to qualitative research which has as its central aim the 'discovery' of an accurate representation of some objective reality, in order to produce a 'true' or accurate picture of a community or any other form of social and cultural life.

In the light of this critique, ethnographers have become less ambitious in their endeavours and ethnography today stands for the belief that community exists, and it does so in the knowledge that our ability to know that reality is fated to remain incomplete, because every ethnography, no matter how assiduously researched, is bound to be irredeemably ignorant of some matters. Correspondingly ethnographers today have replaced the quest for epistemological and ontological certainty and methodological rigour with culturally grounded interpretations of truth that prove themselves to be, as Richard Rorty would say, 'good in the way of belief, *and good, too, for definite, assignable reasons',* and which ultimately help us see that community life is much more complex than we once imagined. Not only that – as Barker (2004) has suggested, ethnography today tends to have personal, poetical and political rather than metaphysical justifications, and as a result ethnographers have focused their attention more closely on developing innovative political ways of writing about community and culture in all their diversity.

While most enlightened ethnographers have come to recognize that their research findings will always remain partial, they have also become more aware of the limitations of traditional ethnographic forms of writing, which suggest that the meticulous and gradual observation of social phenomena provides a grounding for theory *vis-à-vis* Glaser and

Strauss (1968) – an approach which assumes that theory emerges from research 'data', which is typically illustrated with characteristic examples of 'data' from field notes, such as interview quotations. Instead, they have increasingly looked to develop ethnographic writing techniques which attempt to reflect the worlds of the communities under scrutiny. This new kind of ethnography revels in accretions of detail and theory, speaking of the important things that govern men and women's lives: their loves, their memories, their families and the many other beauties and truths and quiddities and epiphanies that give meaning to their individual and shared existence. It also works on the basis that the best ethnography works its magic through the ability of its author(s) to *convince* its readers about the reality under scrutiny, rather than through any direct correspondence with that reality. This approach to ethnography works with the assumption that, like all good novels, ethnography must be well written, but its real strength and power lies in the researcher's ethnographic imagination. That is, its thick descriptions, as Geertz (1973) called them, should be free of sociological jargon and editorializing, and capable of engaging the reader with what makes community intimate and real, by evoking the actual feeling of day-to-day, week-to-week, year-to-year of community life.

In this view, ethnography is a creative way of telling a factual story. This suggests a shift in ethnographic writing which means that if ethnography is as compelled as it ever was in its ambition to capture everyday life, it also now has an ambition to create atmosphere, whether it is a single consciousness or the atmosphere of a shared consciousness – even the consciousnesses of communities that are contingent, shape-shifting rather than enduring. Blackshaw (2003) argues that it is only by such staging that ethnographers can reach a more profound level of truth that cannot otherwise be found. What some commentators now call ethnographic fiction relishes the task of transporting its readers by telling them how people who share a particular fate think, speculate, desire, understand, live their lives but in a way which makes every gesture, every attitude, every word spoken by its respondents, part of its imaginative and deliberate study.

Blackshaw's *Leisure Life*, which is a study of an *imagined community* based on working-class men's leisure, is a good example of this kind of ethnography. By alternating perspectives, seeing events unfold through 'the lads' eyes and then from the view of the ethnographer, Blackshaw manages to do more than simply analyse this leisure lifeworld. He attempts to coax the reader into walking in the shoes of 'the lads' to 'lad-like' experience their worldview. This is nothing less than about reinventing the ethnographers writing craft by making fact read like fiction, using language charged and poetic which takes its readers on a cultural ride in order to find the truth – physically transporting them. In this way, this alterative way of writing ethnography permits and requires greater descriptive detail than was previously the case.

There are critics who will no doubt argue that the borrowed prestige of fiction can limit as well as liberate ethnography. That is, to liken ethnography to fiction may suggest that ethnography verges on fiction. But, such a reaction fails to recognize that even the most empirical of accounts are prey to cosmetic enhancement. The real world is contingent, chaotic and crowded with inessentials, while sociology requires order, themes and structure, so researchers can transform the accumulation of their experiences into an object of analysis. One of the upshots of this is that the temptation to sharpen an observation here or make better a quote there can be tempting to any researcher. At what point does fact pass into the fiction?

Blackshaw and Crabbe (2004) sidestep this question by stressing that this alternative way of writing ethnography should not be understood as in any way deceitful on the part of ethnographers, but more precisely ethnography looking at itself in the mirror and recognizing that it can still do everything it used to be able to do *and* much more. The trick of ethnographic fiction is that it is able to tell the 'truth' about the social world while not being exactly deceitful, but embellishing that 'truth'. In this sense, rather than trying to make the reader believe in the 'facts' of the reality that it deals with in its pages, ethnographic fiction simply conjures the 'real' instead. As Blackshaw and Crabbe demonstrate through their own work, this changed economy of narration typically leads ethnographers to write in self-consciously cinematic ways, which tend to draw on rhetorical devices, such as metaphors, metonymies and synecdoches, which they use *not* to replace the real, but to clarify, reinforce and enhance our understanding of community and other socio-cultural formations. What this suggests, to paraphrase what Malcolm Bradbury once said of Salman Rushdie's historical novels, is that it is the tricks of literature that show us with what fantasy the real world must now be written – if, that is, we are to penetrate it, and in the process save ethnography.

See also: *'Community Crime Control'; 'Community Studies'; 'Imagined Communities'; 'Imaginary Communities'; 'Locality, Place and Neighbourhood'; 'The "Dark Side" of Community'; 'The Symbolic Construction of Community'.*

FURTHER READING

The reader should explore the two ethnographic community studies discussed in this chapter as well as the references in the chapter 'Community Studies'.

REFERENCES

Barker, C. (2004) *The Sage Dictionary of Cultural Studies*. London: Sage.

Bauman, Z. (1990) *Thinking Sociologically*. Oxford: Blackwell.

Blackshaw, T. (2003) *Leisure Life: Myth Masculinity and Modernity*. London: Routledge.

Blackshaw, T. and Crabbe, T. (2004) *New Perspectives on Sport and 'Deviance': Consumption, Performativity and Social Control*. Abingdon: Routledge.

Boelen, W. A. M. (1992) 'Street Corner Society: Cornerville Revisited', *Journal of Contemporary Ethnography*, 21 (1): 11–51.

Colls, R. (2001) *Identity of England*. Oxford: Oxford University Press.

Geertz, C. (1973) 'Thick Description: Towards an Interpretive Theory of Culture', in *The Interpretation of Cultures*. London: Hutchinson.

Glaser, B. and Strauss, A. (1968) *The Discovery of Grounded Theory*. London: Weidenfield and Nicholson.

Kuper, A. (1988) *The Invention of Primitive Society: Transformations of an Illusion*. London: Routledge.

Tyler, E. B. (1871, 1903) *Primitive Culture*. London: John Murray.

Whyte, W. F. (1943) *Street Corner Society: The Social Structure of an Italian Slum*. Chicago: University of Chicago Press.

SOCIAL NETWORK ANALYSIS

Social network analysis is concerned with the chains of relations and ties that lie at a community's core. It is both a specific paradigm of social research and a powerful analytical tool which draws on a range of strategies, or what social network analysts call units of analysis, in order to plot, clarify and understand patterns of human affiliation and social solidarity.

Section Outline: After outlining the central tenets of social network analysis as it relates to community studies, this chapter outlines the different approaches and the main tools used by social network analysts and what these tell us about the ways in which communities are formed and operate. It concludes by discussing the limits of this approach as both a tool of social analysis and a paradigm of social inquiry.

It might be assumed then that from the perspective of social network analysis, community is generally understood as a very particular kind of social network that is made up of tightly bound solidarities and densely knit ties of reciprocity, and that as a result of this assumption, social network analysis itself is concerned with trying to identify how these work as well as with understanding the effects they have on different individuals and social groups. This is not the case. On the contrary, its adherents stress that the utility of social network analysis for the study of community is that 'it does not take as its starting point putative solidarities – local or kin – nor does it seek primarily to find and explain the persistence of solidarity sentiments' (Wellman, 1979: 1203); instead, its analytical strength lies in the way it is able to identify patterns of *social structure* in communities.

To this extent, social network analysts take relations and ties as the key focus of their attention (rather than making any putative assumptions about community in order to examine how these can help explain different kinds of behaviours and attitudes). They are interested in answering questions such as: 'Who talks to whom in a community?' (the composition of relations and ties); 'About what?' (the content of relations and ties); 'How are relations and ties maintained over time?'; 'How do interpersonal relations and status relations affect communities?'; 'Who are the key movers and shakers in a particular community?'; 'How do the links between the most strongly connected individuals and groups in a community operate?'; 'Who is included in a community, who is not, and why?'; 'How do support networks work in communities?'; and 'How do social networks operate in communities that are neither bound by locality nor by tightly bound solidarities?'. In other words, the social network approach allows researchers to get away from the metaphysical problem of community. That is, in emphasizing the study of primary social relations, social network analysis does not make the mistake of identifying community as a reified structural entity (Bulmer, 1985).

Most commentators trace the origins of the social network perspective back to Bott's (1957, 1971) classic studies of family and marriage, or Barnes's (1954) research on the social networks of a Norwegian island community (Knox, 1987; Scott, 1991; Crow and Allan, 1994; Stokowski, 1994). When compared to more recent social networks research, these early studies can appear overly simple; however, all social network analysis has the basic aim of illustrating the structure of social interaction in communities by representing individuals as 'points' and treating their social relationships as connecting 'lines' (Granovetter, 1976; Knox, 1987; Scott, 1991).

Information about social networks is gathered through a number of research methods, including questionnaires, interviews, focus groups, diaries, observations and participant observations and ethnography. Within all these approaches, attention is given to relations and ties. As adherents of social network analysis point out: 'To discover how A, who is in touch with B and C, is affected by the relation between B and C … demands the use of the network concept' (Barnes, 1972: 3). How some of the more recent analyses tend to differ most from earlier studies is either in their use of graph theory and increasingly computer-generated mathematical models for analysing and representing empirical evidence (e.g., Scott, 1991), or on the basis of their adherence to a particular theoretical paradigm (e.g., the structural analysis of Wellman et al., 1988).

The graph theory model melds mathematics with theory as a way of measuring the structural components of social networks. Its basic approach is to use sociograms in order to map the social networks of relations within a community, with the aim of revealing patterns of communication, which can help researchers identify where power relationships lie between individuals and within social groups, in order to explain social structure. This model is venerated by John Scott, who argues that social network researchers should make best use of mathematics, while arguing that it is imperative that they, rather than the models they have utilized, should determine the shape and presentation of their work. As Scott points out, for all its ability to enable researchers to identify different concentrations of social networks and their structural characteristics, graphs alone cannot account for notions of distance and the organization of space in the 'real' world, because they are limited to presenting multidimensional social agency in a two-dimensional format. For Scott, it is imperative that researchers determine the shape and presentation of their work, and not the mathematical models they have utilized. This is where graph theory comes into its own, because it 'consists of a body of mathematical axioms and formulae which describe the properties of the patterns formed by the lines' (Scott, 1991: 13).

In his various studies of personal communities, Barry Wellman (1979; 1988) also offers an approach to social network analysis whose overriding concern is to theorize social structures. To this extent, Wellman argues that his approach reflects a shift from methodological individualism common in sociology today towards a structural analysis proper. Moving beyond the rather sterile 'community lost' versus 'community saved' debate that tends to accompany many understandings of modern community, Wellman (1979) argues that by the second part of the twentieth century community had been transformed and, as a result, we now see the co-existence of communities which represent, to different degrees, close-knit preindustrial, or traditional, communities *and* more personalized forms of community that can be described as post-industrial. In the latter type of community, all-embracing solidarity gives way to more specialized forms of community and associated lifestyles characterized by individuality, and more reliance on formal organizations for those needs which used to be fulfilled informally (Wellman, 1979; Wellman et al., 1988). From this viewpoint, community can be seen to have been 'liberated', in the sense that modern, cosmopolitan urban areas with their highly developed communication and transport networks facilitate multiple-interest-based communities. The rationale underpinning this argument suggests that 'people are not so much antisocial or gregarious beings as they are *operators* who are willing to forgo a secure source of fruit for a chance to connect more of the world' (Wellman et al., 1988: 134).

Working with these assumptions, Wellman and his colleagues made use of the social networks of people's *personal communities* to explore the *diversity* of the various communities within the locality of East York in Toronto (*see* Wellman, 1979; Wellman et al., 1988). In doing this, they used various data pertaining to social relations, such as friendships, kinship ties, leisure networks, interpersonal support and informal social control. Crucially, as they point out, this use of the social network approach ensures that the research is not constrained to investigating a community which is restricted to one locale; communities may span the city and beyond.

As has already been suggested, the two main tools used by social network analysts to analyse communities are relations and ties, but within these two categories are included some more sophisticated units of analysis, including the following:

- Bonding and bridging ties
- Strong and weak ties
- Network density
- Multiplexity
- Partitioning networks

A brief sketch of each of these provides an illustration of how social network analysts have or might use them in community research.

As social network theorists might argue, most people in a community belong to some kind of social network or other and can be involved in any number of relations, which may be reciprocated by others to a greater or lesser extent. It is these ties that connect social actors. Putnam (2000) argues that two basic features are characteristic of the ties that constitute communities: *bonding ties*, which signify interaction between 'like people' whose social networks are inward looking and exclusive; and *bridging ties*, or inter-group links, which are more outward looking and inclusive (*see* 'Social Capital; 'Communitarianism').

As Stokowski (1994) demonstrates in her discussion of community networks in leisure, however, some networks will be equally reciprocated, but not all community ties are necessarily symmetrical, and people are most likely to experience nonreciprocal relations with those of a higher social status (Johnson, 1971). In other words, who interacts with whom in a community is also likely to be dependent on a number of other factors, including social class, ethnicity, religion, gender and age. This last observation notwithstanding, its foremost adherents are keen to stress that social network analysis is an attempt to look beyond the specific attributes of individuals in order to understand the nature of interaction among social actors (Wellman et al., 1988).

One way they do this is by distinguishing between *strong* and *weak ties*. What are considered to be either *strong* or *weak ties* may differ from context to context, but as their nomenclature suggests the former are more likely to include intimate and enduring relations between close friends and families, which tend to be guided by familiarity, high levels of reciprocity and self-disclosure, while weak ties are generally more infrequently maintained, detached and non-intimate.

At first glance, it would appear that *strong ties* provide the more useful units of analysis of the two for understanding how communities operate, particularly given that much community-based research seems to suggest that social actors who have strong ties are more likely to share resources (*see*, for example, Wellman and Wortley, 1990). However, contrary to this assumption, the important research of Granovetter (1973, 1974) on how people get jobs through informal contacts suggests that weak ties are perhaps more useful units of analysis for understanding how communities work. This is not only because community ties typically tend to be weak, but also because they are indispensable to individuals' opportunities and to their integration into communities. This leads Blackshaw and Long (1998) to hypothesize that strong ties are more likely to breed local cohesion, but in the process lead to overall fragmentation in local communities; and that weak ties are not generative of alienation.

Network density can be defined as 'the ratio of actual ties existing in the network to the potential number which would exist if all those involved knew one another (Crowe and Allan, 1994: 180). This unit of analysis is concerned with the kinds of multiple connectednesses found in communities and what this tells us about durability and intimacy and the levels of support found in dense social networks. In more recent studies, this unit of analysis has been replaced by *multiplexity*, which is also used to explore what happens when social networks become more dense. Research in the field of virtual communities made via the Internet and e-mail, for example, which has drawn on this approach, asserts that, contrary to what conventional wisdom would seem to suggest, people are able to make and maintain online community relations that are multiplex, or in other words, voluntary, intimate, supportive and durable (*see* Wellman and Gulia, 1999).

Identifying the composition and pattern of social networks is crucial to understanding the different ways by which relations and ties are made and maintained in communities. Garton, Haythornthwaite and Wellman (1997) identify three units of analysis for understanding these, which they summarize under the label 'Partitioning Networks' – groups; positional analysis; and network of networks.

According to the social network analysts, *groups* are not merely collective units that are bound by common interests; they are empirically discovered structures that are often formed and maintained on the basis of cliques or exclusivity. Social network analysts want to know the sort of things that people look for in groups, e.g., the basis of their personal 'community' relationships and the kinds of mutual support they receive from others in a community group. They are also concerned with the ways in which community groups define and sustain themselves and express their sense of collective identity.

Positional analysis is concerned with the ways groups situate themselves in relation to other groups in communities. Although it does emanate from social network analysis, Elias and Scotson's (1994) classic study of *The Established and Outsiders* is a good example of how members of a community, who hold a similar position in a community, divide themselves from those with less power to both limit their opportunities and maintain extant social boundaries (*see* 'The "Dark Side" of Community').

The idea of *networks of networks* is derived from Georg Simmel's observation that 'webs of group affiliations' both facilitate and constrain social networks and is concerned with the way in which groups and other forms of identification combine (Garton, Haythornthwaite and Wellman, 1997). With their structured global networks and cohesiveness, international terrorist organizations are a good example of 'communities' that can be studied through this unit of analysis. Take, for example, *al-Qaeda*, which according to one commentator (Burke, 2003) is a group consisting of a *network of networks* made up of four elements: the 'al-Qaeda hard core', Osama bin Laden's inner circle; the scores of militant Islamic groups in over 50 different countries which have, or had, some kind of relationship with bin Laden or his inner circle; and the apparent scores of young Muslims around the world who have no formal connection at all with bin Laden and his followers, but whose attitudes, behaviours and actions demonstrate that they are keen to link themselves with *al-Qaeda*.

Notwithstanding the obvious attractions of social network analysis for researching community by making explicit the structure of relations and ties and their cross-cutting networks (Knox, 1987), its critics argue that it can only ever aspire to expose to view a portion of social reality, and an overly structured one at that (Blackshaw and Long, 1998). For, without doubt, social network analysis, particularly Wellman's structural approach, makes no attempt to overcome the 'duality' of structure and agency, but only a vague attempt to understand and explain social action in terms of structural constraints on activity. Stokowski (1994) has attempted to overcome the deterministic nature of this structuralism and its marginalization of social action by combining it with grounded theorizing, statistical testing and phenomenology by using Giddens' theory of structuration. Unfortunately, this approach remains unconvincing as the central tenets underpinning the structural approach are too much at variance with the axioms of phenomenology – it is not easy to accommodate autonomous decision-making and personal feelings within mathematical models. Indeed, implicit to Giddens' sociology is the view that agents actively create their own meanings and reciprocally based sociality in their everyday encounters with each other. Perhaps this is why 'the merging of phenomenology with structuralism is not common in sociology' (Stokowski, 1994: 97).

Abrams (1982) also felt that, in the social network perspective, there was real potential for investigating critical aspects of community life, particularly neighbouring. As Bulmer (1986: 91) points out, though, he ended up rejecting it for more historically grounded approaches to social analysis underpinned by qualitative methods. This was because he thought that social network perspective tends to emphasize form at the expense of content (Bulmer, 1985: 437). To be sure, for all their apparent use value, intricate maps and graphs may evince little of the real substance of relationships found in contemporary community life. As Abrams explains, commenting on network density as a unit of analysis for understanding *neighbouring*:

> One of the main reasons why so many of the proposed relationships between density and other factors cannot be found effectively in the real world is … precisely because density, insofar as it is taken seriously as a formal property of interaction, has to be measured in terms of all links in a network. The varying content of actual links is deliberately ignored; equal weight has to be given to all links, regardless of the varying significance they might have for those concerned. If one recognizes that different links can have widely different values for individuals within a network, one may get much closer to an explanation of the relationship in which one is interested but the explanation is no longer grounded in the notion of density as a formal property of interaction; it is an explanation in terms of the significant content of relationships, not the structure of networks (Abrams in Bulmer, 1986: 89).

This led Abrams to the conclusion that social network perspective had failed to build on its earlier potential because it was held back by its positivism; and this is probably why his use of the term always remained a metaphorical one (Bulmer, 1986: 90).

See also: *'Community Profiling'; 'Social Capital'; 'Locality, Place and Neighbourhood'; 'The "Dark Side" of Community'; 'Virtual Communities'.*

REFERENCES

Abrams, P. (1982) *Historical Sociology*. Shepton Mallet: Open Books.

Abrams, P. (1986) in M. Bulmer (ed.) *Neighbours: The Work of Philip Abrams*. Cambridge: Cambridge University Press.

Barnes, J. A. (1954) 'Class and Community in a Norwegian Parish', *Human Relations*, 7 (1): 39–58.

Barnes, J. A. (1972) *Social Networks*. Reading: Addison-Wesley.

Blackshaw, T. and Long, J. (1998) 'A Critical Examination of the Advantages of Investigating Community and Leisure from a Social Network Perspective', *Leisure Studies*, 17 (4): 233–248.

Bott, E. (1957, 1971) (2nd ed.) *Family and Social Network*. London: Tavistock.

Bulmer, M. (1985) 'The Rejuvenation of Community Studies? Neighbours, Networks and Policy', *Sociological Review*, 33 (3): 430–448.

Bulmer, M. (ed.) (1986) *Neighbours: The Work of Philip Abrams*. Cambridge: Cambridge University Press.

Burke, J. (2003) 'What is Al-Qaeda?', *The Observer*, 13th July.

Crow, G. and Allan, G. (1994) *Community Life: An Introduction to Local Social Relations*. London: Harvester Wheatsheaf.

Elias, N. and Scotson, J. L. (1994) (2nd ed.) *The Established and the Outsiders*. London: Sage.

Garton, L., Haythornthwaite, C. and Wellman, B. (1997) Studying online social networks. *Journal of Computer-Mediated Communication*, 3 (1). http://jcmc. indiana.edu/vol3/issue1/garton.html [*Reprinted* in S. Jones (ed.) (1999), *Doing Internet Research* (pp.75–105). Thousand Oaks, CA: Sage.]

Granovetter, M. (1973) 'The Strength of Weak Ties', *American Journal of Sociology*, 78 (6): 1360–1380.

Granovetter, M. (1974) *Getting a Job*. Cambridge: Harvard University Press.

Granovetter, M. (1976) 'Network Sampling: Some First Steps', *American Journal of Sociology*, 81: 1287–1303.

Johnson, S. K. (1971) 'Sociology of Christmas Cards', *Society*, 8: 27–29.

Knox, P. (1987) (2nd ed.) *Urban Social Geography: An Introduction*. New York: Longman.

Scott, J. (1991) *Social Network Analysis: A Handbook*. London: Sage.

Stokowski, P. A. (1994) *Leisure in Society: A Network Structural Perspective*. London: Mansel.

Wellman, B. (1979) 'The Community Question: The Intimate Networks of East Yorkers', *American Journal of Sociology*, 84 (5): 1201–1231.

Wellman, B. (1988) 'Structural Analysis: From Method and Metaphor to Theory and Substance', in B. Wellman and S. Berkowitz (eds) *Social Structures: A Network Approach*. Cambridge: Cambridge University Press.

Wellman, B. and Berkowitz, S. (eds) (1988) *Social Structures: A Network Approach*. Cambridge: Cambridge University Press.

Wellman, B., Carrington, P. and Hall, A. (1988) 'Networks as Personal Communities', in B. Wellman and S. Berkowitz (eds) *Social Structures: A Network Approach.* Cambridge: Cambridge University Press.

Wellman, B. and Gulia, M. (1999) 'Virtual Communities as Communities', in M. A. Smith and P. Kollock (eds) *Communities in Cyberspace.* London: Routledge.

Wellman, B. and Wortley, S. (1990) 'Different Strokes from Different Folks: Community Ties and Social Support', *American Journal of Sociology*, 96: 558–588.

Community as Place

COSMOPOLITANISM, WORLDLINESS AND THE CULTURAL INTERMEDIARIES

From the Greek word *kosmos* meaning 'world' and *polis* meaning the place 'where we can meet each other as *equals*, while recognizing our diversity, and caring for the preservation of that diversity as the very purpose of our meeting …'(Bauman, 1994: 33), the sense of the term 'cosmopolitanism', as it is used by proponents of critical cosmopolitanism, does not merely invoke the idea of having a familiarity with or even empathetic interest in the many different parts of the world, neither does it merely reflect a political philosophy which is concerned with humankind as a single global community. To be critically cosmopolitan is to recognize Bauman's (2004: 4) pivotal observation that the planet we inhabit today is 'full', and what this means is that if there are no places left to colonize or to dump the products of human waste, there are also no longer any places left to hide from our mutual responsibilities and obligations to each other.

Section Outline: This chapter starts by outlining the rudiments of a critical cosmopolitan sociology which has recently emerged as a response to intensified processes of globalization that have quickened in the last 20 years with the fall of communism and the concomitant rise of free markets and

> *goods produced and marketed on a global scale, the continued strengthening of Western cultural hegemony, the spread of information networks due to technological advances, and a surge in the worldwide movements of population. It is subsequently argued that the critical cosmopolitan revels in otherness – it is the Other that fires the cosmopolitan imagination – and in this regard, comparisons are drawn between Beck's sociology and Edward Said's idea of worldliness. In the light of these comparisons, the chapter concludes by identifying a number of problems confronting critical cosmopolitans, especially the challenge of breathing life into the cross-fertilization of communities of different cultures and the pivotal role of cultural intermediaries in this process who stress the need to pay people from different cultural groups the compliment of taking them seriously as individuals and communities with moral intelligence.*

As the above definition suggests, to be critically cosmopolitan is to be blessed with the cosmopolitan imagination, the unshakable prescience which is on the one hand to know the futility of trying to escape the weight of the world and on the other to care about the intractable fate of the global community. You might say, then, that if the cosmopolitan turn is a new phenomenon that has recently emerged in the light of intensified processes of globalization, its *raison d'être* was already inscribed in Karl Marx's (1888: xi) abiding observation that: 'The philosophers so far have only interpreted the world in various ways; the point is to change it'. This dedication to changing the world for the better leads Delanty (2006: 35) to suggest that critical cosmopolitanism is reflexive in the sense that it operates on the basis of self-problematization in its commitment to world openness and transformation.

In developing a distinctive cosmopolitan approach to sociology which deconstructs the usual territorial boundaries, Beck and Sznaider (2006) suggest that the cosmopolitan imagination has three interrelated commitments. The first is the widespread recognition that the new century is not only global but it marks a re-enlightened *age of cosmopolitanism*. Secondly, those who share the cosmopolitan imagination also share a critique of *methodological nationalism* or a commitment to the idea that research practice cannot be reduced to nationalist preoccupations. As Beck (2002) has observed, the writing of sociology has been marked and limited by national perspectives. However, this is not simply a problem of which countries and whose ideas loom largest in sociological accounts, but it also affects the kinds of research agendas pursued and the sorts of questions asked by researchers. As Beck points out, *national sociology* tends to be governed by a 'monological imagination' which when it is confronted with 'others" alternative cognitive frames, rather than changing its grammar, has a propensity to merely *translate* their contents into its own nationalistic language rather than trying to imagine what those cognitive frames might mean if they remained as *untranslatable* languages (Blackshaw, 2005).

In the third instance, Beck and Sznaider point out that there is a collective recognition with cosmopolitan sociology that shorthand dichotomies like global versus local, the national and the international, East versus West, and so on, have dissolved and therefore no longer hold good, which implicitly begs the question of the continuing relevance of the cognitive frames underpinning extant social science conceptual and empirical approaches. What Beck and Sznaider are explicitly suggesting through this third commitment is that as sure as concepts like class, state and community are only marginally useful for understanding the globality of our present predicament – as useful as sociology's other key meta-concepts – so are the tried and tested methodologies and ways of narration associated with all conventional social sciences. What is elemental to this third critique, then, is a shared commitment to developing a new research agenda built on some kind of multi-perspective *methodological cosmopolitanism*.

Implicit to Beck's (2002) work is the argument that the idea of sociology as a discipline whose practitioners operate under the auspices of nation states has had its day and that both the present and the future predicament of the human condition needs to be understood globally. To this extent, what Beck calls *cosmopolitan sociology* is better placed than *national sociology* to interpret and endeavour to change for the better the lives of people in the global community because, not only is it characterized by a 'dialogic imagination', but it is also able to deal locally – or as Beck might say, glocally – with the day-to-day experiences of '*internal* globalization, globalization *from within* national societies' (p. 17). What this suggests is that critical cosmopolitanism is fundamental to telling us something about the lived conditions of globalization processes from *within* local communities rather than merely describing them from *without*.

We can see that what Beck is most interested in is developing a kind of sociology which shifts its focus from the domestic canvas of nationality to the wider issues and problems of globalization but which is still locally rooted and reflects a world where most if not all people have become 'visitors' – anything from economic migrants, refugees, asylum seekers and exiles to terrorists and tourists – as well as remaining in some sense 'locals' or 'natives'. What Beck is trying to map through his work is a sociology fit for a speeded-up world in which social, cultural, economic and political conditions mean that by way of either choice or necessity potentially everybody is on the move and in the event might be looking to make a 'home' anywhere, even if when they arrive they might be unwelcome there and everywhere else, too. In other words, he wants to develop a critical cosmopolitanism whose purpose is to try to get to grips with 'every act of production and consumption and every act of everyday life [which] links actors to millions of unseen others' (Beck and Sznaider, 2006: 22); and, we might add, is capable of capturing something about the millions of tiny fragments of public and private history, ranging from what individuals and groups watch on the television to what they think about their new overseas neighbours across the street.

Beck is also at pains to stress that this methodological approach is against the idea of cosmopolitanism as merely the privileged activity of the affluent members of the globality, who safe in the knowledge that their passports allow them to pass through any port of call, can roam the world, seemingly at will, seeking out cultural otherness. However, perhaps what he does not register enough is Tom Nairn's (2006: 12–13) caustic observation that if globalization is us, it 'means many different things, but among them is the conversion of the world into an unavoidable, forced terrain of confluence, a cross-fertilisation from which escape is impossible: the global village, in other words – not self-conscious cosmopolitans playing at being villagers, or scheming to become shamans of the largest imaginable community'. This criticism not withstanding, Beck's (2002: 19) cosmopolitan sociology is attentive to the point that the contemporary global world is part of lots of places and lots of people who have '"roots" and "wings" at the same time. So it rejects the dominant opposition between cosmopolitans and locals as well: there is no cosmopolitanism without localism'.

As it has been suggested already, with its dialogical imagination cosmopolitan sociology is able to challenge other binary oppositions, such as the one between East and West, subject and object, insider and outsider, in order to move beyond their ethnocentric foundational inequities and the tacit propensity to homogenize everyday community life that accompanies them. Of course, Beck is not the first intellectual to turn this dichotomous corner. As Edward Said (1978) famously showed, the *Orientalist* mindset was one which constructed the East as an exotic mystery which assumed that it took Western rationality to know about.

Drawing on Foucault's (1972) idea of discursive formations, Said forcefully argued that the Orient was (and perhaps still is) the West's mysterious and exotic Other. In Said's account, this Orientalist discourse did more than render the Other mysterious and exotic, though, because it also left who or what the Other 'really' was out in its version of events. As Said made clear, the procedures which constituted Orientalist discourse were authoritative and tacit and they also had an 'official' feel about them despite achieving their existence and power in day-to-day language and cultural practices. In the event Orientalism could do nothing other than give the wrong impression about the 'Orient' and its subjects, through an anaesthetizing discourse which set the parameters for 'dealing with it by making statements about it, by authorizing views of it, describing it, by teaching it, settling it, ruling over it: in short, Orientalism as a Western style for dominating, restructuring, and having authority over the Orient' (Said, 1978: 3). As Homi Bhabha (1994) was to subsequently point out, there was an added irony with colonial Orientalist discourse, which meant that its success was dependent on its own failure: the colonized Other was obliged to mimic the language and the culture of colonialism but this mimicry merely revealed it to be neither at home with the colonizers nor at home with itself. In the event, the colonized was never, could not be authentic, and was destined to remain 'almost the same, *but not quite*'.

As is well known, in response to this state of affairs, Said set about constructing his own 'critical elaboration' of the world which was wrapped up in the consciousness of who he himself was as a contingent product of the historical process to date, which in the words of Antonio Gramsci had sedimented in him, as a Christian Palestinian, 'an infinity of traces, without leaving an inventory' – and it was in *Orientalism* that Said took up the challenge of compiling such an inventory. However, the concept which Said came to use in the context of responding to the stocktaking and the filling out of his historical record of being an *Oriental* in the eyes of the West (Viswanathan, 2004: xv) was that of *worldliness* (Said, 1978), which clearly resonates with Beck's idea of cosmopolitan sociology, because on the one hand it too is not limited by disciplinary constraints, and on the other, it has an in-built mechanism for resisting the propensity for intellectual tourism.

Worldliness is not merely contrary to the 'monological imagination of the national perspective, which excludes the otherness of the other'

(Beck, 2002: 18); then, it is also defined by what Said (2004: 140) calls an 'omnicompetent interest' in the Other and is anchored in the quotidian of real struggles and real social movements. Like critical cosmopolitanism, *worldliness* is also inspired by an outlook that imposes a responsibility on researchers which compels them to continually question their ways of working, as well as the inevitability of their own ethnocentricity, and the idea that what they might just be developing through their analyses is another form of cultural imperialism. In other words, *worldliness* challenges the idea of *all* hegemonic institutions, be they *Orientalist* fantasies, national identities and communities, or academic disciplines with their ready-made methodologies.

These linkages notwithstanding, what the concept of *worldliness* also suggests is that Beck's cosmopolitan sociology can be criticized for failing to acknowledge and reflexively contemplate the truth that cosmopolitanism shares in common with *Orientalism* some key intuitive and practical contingencies, which in turn raise some key ethical questions for cosmopolitan researchers. For example, Beck never considers the crucial truth that the two intrinsic pleasures of *Orientalism* – on the one hand, the freedom and ability to move across geographical boundaries and, on the other, the power to imagine the Other – are both also crucial aspects of the cosmopolitan imagination. In the light of this observation, we should add that what should be made implicit to the perspective of critical cosmopolitanism is the self-reflexive questioning of the freedoms and pleasures that *worldliness* brings, which means being, at all times, critically aware of the values, moral and political imperatives involved in making cosmopolitan judgements.

Beck also fails to consider the fact that just as colonialism relied to a greater or lesser extent on cultural intermediaries to do its work, so ultimately does methodological cosmopolitanism. This raises key questions, not only about the power relationships between 'cosmopolitans', their 'go-betweens' and their respondents, but also about the value of the 'stories' they develop through these encounters. Notwithstanding the need to be critically aware of the potential limitations and ethical dilemmas posed by making such cosmopolitanism associations, the role of the cultural intermediary is crucial to developing cosmopolitan community because, not only does it provide a political strategy to help dissolve the binary systems of 'subject' and 'object', 'same' and 'other', 'us' and 'them', 'global' and 'local' and so on, but it is also, in the words of Walter Benjamin (1996), a very effective way of translating the 'way of meaning' of one community to another. To this extent, Appiah (2006) argues that if people from vastly different cultural and religious communities are going to live together without ignorance, intolerance, distrust and violence, they must master these arts of conversation, and with these the ability to know that that to appear to communicate without a message is a more powerful way of conveying one.

The final problem with Beck's perspective is that although it makes a powerful ontological case for cosmopolitan sociology on the basis of the changing social structure accompanying processes of globalization, it is limited by its quietism on issues of epistemology and methodology. In other words, Beck's *methodological cosmopolitanism* – despite its claims about overcoming *methodological nationalism* – is unfortunately lacking because, on the one hand, it fails to adequately consider what happens when cosmopolitans enter imaginatively into realities that would otherwise be alien to them and, on the other, it neglects the practicalities involved in the process of actually doing cosmopolitan research.

See also: *'Community Studies'; 'Ethnography'; 'Imaginary Communities'; 'Imagined Communities'; 'Political Community'; 'Postmodern Communities'.*

FURTHER READING

The idea of critical cosmopolitanism can be explored in further detail in a series of recent publications by Beck et al., identified below, especially the *British Journal of Sociology* special issue on cosmopolitanism (2006, Volume 57: 1). The theme of cosmopolitan ethics and the problems of that occur when communities feel the need to differentiate themselves from other social groups in order to achieve their sense of communal identity can be pursued in Appiah (2006).

REFERENCES

Appiah, K. A. (2006) *Cosmopolitanism: Ethics in a World of Strangers*. New York: Norton.
Bauman, Z. (1994) *Alone Again: Ethics After Uncertainty*. London: Demos.
Bauman, Z. (2004) *Wasted Lives: Modernity and its Outcasts*. Cambridge: Polity.
Beck, U. (2000) 'The Cosmopolitan Perspective: Sociology and the Second Age of Modernity', *British Journal of Sociology*, 51 (1): 79–105.
Beck, U. (2002) 'The Cosmopolitan Society and its Enemies', *Theory, Culture and Society*, 19 (1, 2): 17–44.
Beck, U. (2006) *Cosmopolitan Vision*. Cambridge: Polity.
Beck, U. and Sznaider, N. (2006) 'Unpacking Cosmopolitanism for the Social Sciences: A Research Agenda', *The British Journal of Sociology*, 57 (1): 1–23.
Benjamin, W. (1996) 'The Task of the Translator', in M. Bullock and M. W. Jennings (eds) *W. Benjamin Selected Writings, Volume 1, 1913–1926*. Harvard: Harvard University Press.

community as place

Bhabha, H. (1994) *The Location of Culture*. London: Routledge.

Blackshaw, T. (2005) *Zygmunt Bauman*. Abingdon: Routledge.

Delanty, G. (2006) 'The Cosmopolitan Imagination: Critical Cosmopolitanism and Social Theory', *The British Journal of Sociology*, 57 (1): 24–47.

Foucault. M. (1972) *The Archaeology of Knowledge*. London: Tavistock.

Marx, K. (1888, 1979) *Theses of Feuerbach*, quoted in the 3rd edition of the *Oxford Dictionary of Quotations*. Oxford: Oxford University Press.

Nairn, T. (2006) 'History's Postman', *London Review of Books*, 28 (2): 26th January.

Said, E. W. (1978) *Orientalism: Western Conceptions of the Orient*. London: Penguin.

Said, E. W. (2004) *Power, Politics, and Culture*. Edited by Gauri Viswanathan. London: Bloomsbury.

Viswanathan, G. (2004) 'Introduction', in Edward W. Said, *Power, Politics, and Culture*. Edited by Gauri Viswanathan. London: Bloomsbury.

LIMINALITY, COMMUNITAS AND ANTI-STRUCTURE

These three interrelated concepts are central to understanding the sense of community that emerges when individuals come together spontaneously to experience an intense and/or sharpened sense of being taken out of themselves and transported into a place of movement 'in and out of time', where it is argued they are united through some ostensibly higher power that is profoundly revelatory of the egalitarian/community spirit which feels something like the true essence of the human condition.

Section Outline: This chapter begins by outlining and discussing each of the three concepts. Thereafter, it discusses what they tell us about the ways in which men and women have historically connected with each other by subverting prevailing societal norms through shared liminal experiences at carnivals, feasts and popular festivals and how these experiences have been transformed in modern day leisure forms such as holidays, rock concerts and spectator sports. This is followed by an extensive critique of the literature on liminality, communitas and anti-structure, which it is suggested is limited by its interest in the borders of everyday existence at the expense of accounting for the problems that remain at society's centre.

The triumvirate of liminality, communitas and anti-structure appears in the seminal work of Victor Turner (1973) on pilgrimage processes.

The concept of liminality, derived from the Latin word *limen* (meaning literally a 'threshold'), connotes the idea of the 'betwixt and the between' or a place of movement 'in and out of time'. As expounded in the work of Turner, liminality describes the indefinable social and spiritual locations involved in religious rites of passage. This is also a perennial concept in the study of leisure, where it is most usually identified with rituals common to shared experiences, such as those found at carnivals, rock concerts and sports events, that signal a 'spatial separation from the familiar and habitual' and which in the process open up channels of communication to create cultural domains that transcend the limitations of class, gender, race, nationality, politics, religion or even geography. Insights gleaned from the work of Turner suggest that liminal domains may well have a powerful cosmological significance, conveyed largely through the emotions to affirm an alternative (dis)order of things, which stress 'generic rather than particularistic relationships'.

Turner describes the shared experiences of liminality through the concept of communitas, which not only entertains cultural and social differences, but also 'strains towards' an openness that provides a 'return' to the social group denied by the manifest inequalities inherent to bourgeois society. In much the same manner of Maffesoli (1996), Turner insists that the concept of *communitas* surpasses and subverts the utilitarian and rationalistic structures of society, finding expression in 'a very concrete and communal unmediated communication between people, which it is suggested, arises spontaneously within groups sharing a similar commitment or position' (Thompson, 1981: 6). The philosopher James Carse (2008) distinguishes this concept from *civitas*, this being an unbending and defensive kind of community, while *communitas* tends to be much more open-minded and borne out of collective delight. Communitas is captured within situations of liminal 'margin' and 'remains open and specialized, a spring of pure possibility as well as the immediate realization of release from day-to-day structural necessities and obligatoriness' (Turner, 1973: 217), and often involves a startling plunge into collective sensuality that invokes mysterious depths, where the world is reflected upside down. Here Turner, in common with Ehrenreich (2007), is concerned with a clearer and much more powerful sense of belonging than anything implied by the idea of community which, 'with its evocations of coziness and small-town sociability', more often than not disappoints even as it is being pursued.

Turner identifies three types of communitas. *Existential communitas* represents an explicit, total and authentic coming together of a social group, which undermines the capitalistic commodification of relationships encountered in an unequal world founded on economic alienation and class, gender and racial inequalities. Participation in existential communitas involves, for the individual, a total dependence on the dialectic of the self in relation to others and, when this occurs, it is liable to provide those experiencing it with a return to the unfettered social group of 'homogeneous unstructured, and free community'. Existential communitas is something astonishing and, for this reason, is always likely to be transient. However, this need not necessarily always be the case, and Turner defines *ideological communitas* as 'a label one can apply to a variety of utopian models or blueprints of societies (*see* 'Imaginary Communities') believed by their authors to exemplify or supply the optimal conditions of *existential communitas*'.

Normative communitas is what develops where *existential communitas* persists and the social group develops a need to organize and make its position more secure. Turner stresses, however, that this more durable form of communitas should not be confused with utilitarian social togetherness, such as Durkheimian mechanical solidarity, which is likely to have structural antecedents and be built on bourgeois–rational, *gesellschaften* foundations. For Turner, *communitas* type social groups tend to have non-utilitarian, enchanted and primordial origins and, in this sense, invariably surpass 'the utilitarian and functionalist aspect prevailing in the surrounding economic order' (Maffesoli, 1996: 79).

According to Turner, the third concept in the triumvirate, social 'anti-structure', evinces most fittingly the sense of interpolation experienced in thresholds of liminality. This concept is useful because it connotes the dispensation with definite pattern and structure associated with day-to-day existence which are achieved during liminal communitas experiences, giving the go-ahead to 'the whim of the moment' (Thompson, 1981), and signalling at the same time an abrogation of the dominant social order of things.

Where Turner offers a *specific* model of liminality, communitas and anti-structure in relation to religious pilgrimage processes, Ehrenreich (2007) offers a *general* discussion of 'the history of collective joy' by tracing emergence of carnivals, feasts and popular festivals in the fifteenth century, which came about as a result of the suppression within the churches of the more exuberant forms of worship and popular forms of piety. She argues that it was from this point onwards that men and women, at regular and officially approved intervals, deserted the hard day-to-day drudge of work to make collective sites of 'ordered disorder', which not only provided them with the opportunity for generating collective joy and a warm sense of cohesion through engaging together in hedonistic rituals of costume, song and/or dance, but also allowed social rules to be temporarily broken and subverted so that disputes and, most importantly, the 'otherness' of what it means to be human (and what would otherwise might remain incommunicable), could be safely explored without any communal sanctions.

The crux of Ehrenreich's thesis is that liminality, communitas and anti-structure are no longer what they once were. In her view, there has since the seventeenth century been a slow but profound shift in the way that we experience communitas: one which has altered, deeply, our entire view of these collective rituals. By this time the modern civilizing process (Elias, 1994) was in full swing, and capitalism and its handmaiden, Puritanism, was also on the rise, as Weber (1930) famously argued in his classic studies of the *Protestant Ethic and the Spirit of Capitalism*, affirming the significance of an ethic of hard daily work with a strong, disciplined work force. By the nineteenth and twentieth centuries, the carnival centred on collective joy had been superseded by the spectacle – namely through the 'sportization' of pastimes (Elias and Dunning, 1986), the commodification of festivals and the militarization of nationalist rituals – in which the producers of what were once collective rituals had been turned into consumer audiences.

These observations notwithstanding, Rojek (1995), in his discussion of liminality in relation to leisure spaces, leisure practices, configurations of association and identity formation, suggests that liminal conventions and practices continue to be appealing in modern societies because individuals recognize in them the promise of freedom and the opportunity to really be themselves. Liminal zones continue to offer this 'because they appear to be 'free spaces' beyond the control of civilized order' (Rojek, 1995: 88). A good example of this is Shields' (1991; 1992) work which explores the significance of leisure experiences 'to thresholds of controlled and legitimated breaks from the routines of everyday, proper behaviour' (1991: 7). In the light of Shields' work, it is possible to see that liminality abounds in leisure situations: from the beach to the dance floor, from the massage parlour to sports arena, offering innumerable betwixt and between spaces where the 'normal' social order can temporally be subverted.

Notwithstanding this important work in leisure studies, Thompson argues that the concepts of liminality and communitas are in themselves problematic. He hypothesizes that they evince little more than the commonsensical point that social collectivity can generate a sense of 'community spirit' and that this is more likely to occur when people are relieved from the structural constraints of day-to-day existence, such as when they are at their leisure. Consequently, for Thompson, liminality and communitas remain rather unsubstantial concepts, because they appear to be without any conceptual 'content', in the sense that they leave undisturbed the normative order of things.

What Thompson is suggesting here is that the work of Turner and others takes on an essentialist sensibility, in that it presumes necessary features of 'essential and universal human spirituality', which are magically set free at the 'threshold' of the liminal stage of 'margin'. This inherent tendency towards essentialism remains a given to such analyses. The upshot of this, for Thompson, is that what is 'released' when the structural constraints of day-to-day existence are broken or suspended ultimately remains *untheorized*. In the case of Turner's work, this is because the explanation for what is 'essential and universal human spirituality' relies on the religious experience of the process of the pilgrimage itself. For Thompson (p. 10), this renders Turner's thesis tautologous, in the sense that, to establish what is – in the case of Turner's study – a religious liminal experience remains wholly contingent upon the study of 'religious' experience to provide an explanation. Other critics have also suggested that the idea of liminality is ultimately an empty concept. Fulgham (1995) argues that, paradoxically (and contrary to the assertions of Turner), the most powerful dimension of liminality is its solitariness; the way it emphasizes, not so much a sense of coming together, but the individual's existential separateness from others.

If we turn to the ontological position of Turner's account, we can identify further problems with the concepts of liminality and communitas. Turner's account is blind to the metaphysical problem of what constitutes social reality. Indeed, in common with other proponents of structural functionalism, Turner makes the mistake of identifying social reality as a reified structural entity, and in this sense is clearly positivistic. The ontological position of positivism presumes that there is a world or reality out there waiting to be discovered or known, and the aim of positivist research is to reveal *the* truth about the world, and in so doing, learn how to measure, control and predict it. Constructivists (*viz*. Guba and Lincoln, 1994) find this not only unconvincing, epistemologically speaking, but morally and ethically wrong, that we should try to pretend that we are outside reality, looking in. Turner's work is manifestly unenlightened about such criticisms.

Notwithstanding its critique of Durkheimian understandings of community, Turner's anthropological account is also underpinned by structural functionalism that understands society as a 'social system', which can be analysed by investigating social phenomena with regard to the way they function for each other and for society as a whole; that is, the way in which the social system 'needs' each part of society to fit together in order to maintain overall social stability. Communitas brought about through liminal situations contributes to the functional equilibrium of the social system in two senses: on the one hand, liminal experiences remain just that, only a liminal experience, and on the other, those liminal moments that give rise to social conflicts and which challenge the status quo do not survive the return to 'normality'. As Merton (1973) points out, social patterns have many consequences and a complex society such as ours is ultimately affected by them in myriad ways, often, and sometimes paradoxically, benefiting some social groups more than others. Consequently, those who benefit most from the maintenance of the status quo, ultimately benefit more from communitas relations brought about in liminal situations, because their powerful social positions remain radically unaltered.

The other equally pressing issue with regard to liminal situations is that they have a tendency to undermine society's moral universe. This might be more often than not only be on a temporary basis, but liminal situations are nonetheless open to possibilities of disorderly activities that affect some social groups disproportionately more than others. This raises a number of ethical questions. For example, ecstatic manifestations of communitas such as parties are often associated with excessive drug or alcohol, which raises questions about people's health. Equally, such manifestations are often also fraught with the possibilities of disruptive violence, which also raises questions about the effects of unlicensed revelry on vulnerable groups such as minority ethic communities and women.

See also: *'Imaginary Communities'; 'Imagined Communities'; 'Liquid Modern Communities'; 'Postmodern Communities'; 'The Symbolic Construction of Community'.*

REFERENCES

Carse, J. P. (2008) *The Religious Case Against Belief*. London: Penguin.

Elias, N. (1994) *The Civilizing Process: The History of Manners and State-Formation and Civilization*, Integrated Edition. Oxford: Blackwell.

Elias, N. and Dunning, E. (1986) (eds) *Quest for Excitement: Sport and Leisure in the Civilizing Process*. Oxford: Basil Blackwell.

Ehrenreich, B. (2007) *Dancing in the Streets: A History of Collective Joy*. London: Granta.

Fulgham, R. (1995) *From Beginning to End*. New York: Ballantine Books.

Guba, E. G. and Lincoln, Y. S. (1994) 'Competing Paradigms in Qualitative Research', in N. K. Denzin and Y. S. Lincoln (eds) *Handbook of Qualitative Research*. Thousand Oaks: Sage.

Maffesoli, M. (1996) *The Time of the Tribes: The Decline of Individualism in a Mass Society*. London: Sage.

Merton, R. (1973) *The Sociology of Science: Theoretical and Empirical Investigations*. Chicago: Chicago University Press.

Rojek, C. (1995) *Decentring Leisure: Rethinking Leisure Theory*. London: Sage.

Shields, R. (1991) *Places On the Margin*. London: Routledge.

Shields, R. (1992) (ed.) *Lifestyle Shopping*. London: Routledge.

Thompson, G. (1981) 'Holidays', in *Popular Culture and Everyday Life*. Milton Keynes: Open University Press.

Turner, V. W. (1973) 'The Center Out There: Pilgrim's Goal', *History of Religions*, 12 (3): 191–230.

Weber, M. (1930) *The Protestant Ethic and the Spirit of Capitalism*. London: Unwin Hyman Ltd.

LOCALITY, PLACE AND NEIGHBOURHOOD

In community studies, the terms 'locality', 'place' and 'neighbourhood' all refer to conceptions of geographical space in which face-to-face relations dominate. It is often assumed that such delimited spaces are associated with the formation and maintenance of communities due to their ability to foster feelings of security, commitment and belonging.

Section Outline: This chapter begins by suggesting that neighbourhood is an ideological concept in the sense that the way it is commonly used is in the process of the production of meanings and ideas in relation to geographical locality and place. After exploring neighbourhood in relation to community, the chapter considers the ways in which notions of locality and place are linked with mutual aid and belonging to facilitate cooperation and how neighbourhood relations are negotiated by people living in various communities. At the same time, it discusses contemporary changes to

> *work and home life and how these have weakened local bonds and neigh-bourhood affiliations while also, paradoxically, strengthening people's desire for local contact, belonging and attachment to place.*

Nowhere is the ideology of neighbourhood better demonstrated than in the long-running Australian television soap opera 'Neighbours'. Centred on a quiet suburban cul-de-sac called 'Ramsay Street' in 'Erinsborough' (an anagram of 'Neighbours') near Melbourne, the soap's plot lines revolve around the daily encounters of a close-knit community. Little attention is paid to life outside the neighbourhood, as if to confirm what Philip Abrams said, that propinquity is the essential and key quality of being a neighbour (Bulmer, 1986). The spatial distance between neighbours might vary, but this is always within the limits of the neighbourhood, suggesting that being a neighbour is a matter of locality or place.

In common with the word 'community', 'neighbourhood' tends to be associated with positive connotations which are suggestive of 'a sense of belonging based on shared experiences, a common language, kinship ties, and above all of inhabiting a common spatial life world' (Delanty, 2003: 55). Neighbourhoods are in this sense best seen as 'situated communities characterized by their actuality, whether spatial or virtual, and their potential for social reproduction' (Appadurai, 1996: 179). In other words, neighbourhoods are already existing social formations in which community relations can be seen as the accomplishment of skilled actors. This is what distinguishes them from localities which are 'primarily relational and contextual, a phenomenological aspect of social life, categorical rather than either scalar or spatial' (Amit, 2002: 3).

The idea of neighbourhood is also often portrayed as promoting a welcome sense of familiarity, trust and commonality in an uncertain modern world that provides its members with security, ownership and safety in accordance with the popular perception that 'particular places are repositories of distinct sets of values' (Clarke et al., 2007: 94). Indeed, the notion of belonging to a neighbourhood would seem to signify the idea that not only is it the social formation that comes closest to community in the modern world, but also that neighbourhoods matter because they are spatially delimited and small-scale. For example, in their study of two southwestern cities in England, Clarke et al. (2007) found that notions of 'the British community' had little resonance for their respondents, who instead identified the smaller-scale local institutions of their

community as place

97

neighbourhood (e.g., schools, church, youth clubs) as more salient to their collective sense of identity and belonging.

Sociologists working in the 'Chicago School' (a group of scholars at the University of Chicago interested in urban studies) in the 1920s and 1930s, posited that the city was the natural manifestation of modern 'community' because it represented human social order (Delanty, 2003). As Redfield (1955) was to subsequently argue, community might always be under threat in the city; it is possible, but only when it is small-scale. Others, such as Knox (1987), have also since argued that community is prominent within city life. Knox in his review of work in the 1960s demonstrated that territory-defined communities have clearly been identified within cities and are commonly focused on local institutions such as the local public house and pool hall. However, there are those who have argued that that modern city life is not conducive to community, because of industrialization and, more recently, the twin threats of globalization and postmodernity (Delanty, 2003). Yet, the conclusions that a large number of urban sociologists seem to draw is that (see, for example, Gans, 1982; Harvey, 1990) community is safe in the locality, but is always threatened in the city. In other words, the sheer size and diversity of cities polarize their inhabitants, leaving them with no meaningful relationships with their environment. What this also suggests is that neighbouring can only be meaningful and salient in smaller localities.

This argument is certainly borne out in one of the earliest conceptions of community based on locality, which is that of the traditional working-class community. Also referred to as 'occupational communities', given the limited range of industry (such as mining) that is typical of such localities and central to their shared meanings, it has been argued that members of working-class industrial communities have historically been found to enjoy a high degree of social solidarity. This was often facilitated by the physical isolation of these communities and the lack of geographic and social mobility of their members, which also limited their contact with other communities. However, such communities began to decline as a result of the 'slum' clearance policies originating from the end of World War I when large-scale social housing was first introduced (see 'Community Regeneration'; 'Community Studies'). Together with the widespread economic restructuring that led to the decline of manufacturing industries such as mining and steel, these working-class communities were geographically dispersed, typically to the borders of industrial towns and cities. While one might assume that a sense of community can be re-invigorated if it can be based on a shared experience of place, Abrams argues that in the light of the welfare legislation that led to slum clearance and the building of large anonymous local authority council estates and the subsequent growth of local authority social and health services, neighbours have, in fact, become less reliant on each other in times of crisis and are therefore rarely strongly bonded to one another (Bulmer, 1986).

As Abrams noted in the light of his own research, conducted in the field of study some 20 years ago, neighbourhood is no longer capable – if it ever was – of sustaining community (Bulmer, 1986: 98). Some more recently published survey research, which at the beginning of this year appeared in the West Yorkshire property press in the United Kingdom, confirms Abrams' conclusions, suggesting that home owners typically baulk from communal association, shunning their neighbours in pursuit of 'more privacy and personal space'. The survey also found that more than half (53%) of home owners 'prefer to keep themselves to themselves and do not want nosey neighbours knowing their business', and almost three out of five of those asked (59%) said that they would prefer to buy a home that was private and not overlooked by neighbours, whereas more than 1 in 3 (37%) admitted that they often went for weeks without so much as seeing or speaking to their neighbours. What such evidence suggests is that, despite commonsense assertions modernity has undoubtedly led towards less neighbourly association.

To achieve any sense of 'neighbourhood', it is imperative that within any shared experience of place, inhabitants feel that they are in control of that place (Power, 2007) and are able to enjoy frequent contact with their neighbours. This, as Hanley (2007a) found in her autobiographical account of the history of council housing in the United Kingdom, is the common failing of many estates which often lack social amenities, such as social clubs, play areas, pubs and meeting places that are vital in generating feelings of belonging to a community (Knox, 1987; Clarke et al., 2007). It would seem that the greater geographical space on these estates which was assumed to be preferable to the cramped, close-proximity conditions of the city has actually led to greater isolation and loneliness of their inhabitants (Hanley, 2007a) as they endure less human contact and subsequently feel less bonded to, and less trusting of, those who shared the same locality. In the 1980s, this process was exacerbated by the Right-to-Buy policy introduced by the Thatcher administration in the 1980 Housing Act which, as Hanley (2007a) concludes, served to divide working-class communities living on council estates between those who could afford to buy their home and those who could not, effectively isolating the poorest groups, not only from the rest of society, but also from each other.

Abrams explains this move away from the most traditional forms of neighbourhood, where members are strongly bonded and rely on each other in times of crisis, towards the ideology of neighbourhood and its relationship with the contemporary search for local understanding in the discussion of what he calls 'modern neighbourhoodism' (Bulmer, 1986). According to Abrams, the increasing local levels of mobility and choice that are symptomatic of industrialization have led to the formal organization and politicization of neighbourhood. Modern neighbourhoodism creates what Abrams calls 'a local social world', where attempts are made to explicitly mobilize inhabitants' attachment to their locality by calling for the protection of amenities and enhanced resources and negotiating control of the locality between 'outside authorities' and local people (Bulmer, 1986: 95).

Certainly, a dominant theme in many sociological understandings of locality, place and neighbourhood has been the defence of community in the face of external threats. While such commonalities can enhance the bond between community members (Delanty, 2003), they can also lead to exclusion of outsiders who are perceived to be inferior in some way, but most typically in terms of their social class or ethnicity. To draw on the soap opera example again, the neighbours of 'Ramsay Street' are not just people who live near one another, they are uniformly homogenous: middle-class and white. In recent years, this trend has been exemplified by the privatized isolation of suburbia and, in particular, the rise of 'gated communities'. Such neighbourhoods offer their residents a 'private community' (Delanty, 2003) where they are separated (and therefore 'protected') from outsiders and associated threats (e.g., crime) by a never-before-seen level of surveillance involving high gates, 24-hour CCTV and often the employment of private security firms. Such division into the 'us' and 'them' is the contemporary manifestation of what Elias and Scotson (1994) termed the 'Established' and the 'Outsiders' in their infamous study of community relations between a group of inhabitants with long-term ties to the locality and a group of newcomers to the locality.

What Elias and Scotson found was that neighbourhood communities are able to exclude others as inferior, even if that classification is based on the most tenuous of differences. Indeed, social class differences are not as salient as they once were, given the rising living standards of much of the Western world and allegedly increasing opportunities for upward social mobility. Thus, we must find other resources by which to derive our communities' sense of self, which can only be done in relation to others (Cohen, 1985; Jenkins, 1996). And, as we have seen, neighbourhood and geographical place have dwindling significance for the formation of communities and their boundaries, thereby leading to what Cohen (1985) contends is the need to re-assert community though symbolic means. We can see that the gates of the gated community are more than a physical boundary that prevents others from entering; they become a symbolic boundary that exists 'in the minds of their beholders' (Cohen, 1985: 12) and enables those on either side to 'think themselves into difference' (*ibid*: 117). The gates come to symbolize the existence of a shared understanding and belonging between the residents behind them, in that they hold that same symbol in common.

Yet, such symbols of unity are often built on shaky ground as their meanings (e.g., the gates of gated communities) are not necessarily the same for all members (Cohen, 1985) and the 'community' behind the gates is likely to be disparate and shifting with members who are largely strangers to one another. As Blandy and Lister (2005) found, relationships within gated communities are most often centred on thin or weak ties, with residents placing far more importance on security and the value of their 'property' as an investment rather than on feeling strongly bonded to their neighbours. Yet, those excluded from the privileged community are similarly uncohesive, leaving them weakened and 'unable to close ranks and fight back' (Elias and Scotson, 1994: xxii), thereby preserving the superficial efficacy of the symbol.

It is by now frequently argued that the temporality and mobility of contemporary life that typifies modernity has been instrumental in the weakening of social ties (Clarke et al., 2007) and social cohesion. For example, people are now much more likely to be employed on fixed-term contracts and expect to change jobs and careers frequently, thereby necessitating an increasing degree of geographic mobility. The increasing reliance on private cars rather than public transport, and on out-of-town shopping malls rather than local stores, also means that we have less and less contact with our neighbours. As Hanley (2007b) laments, 'fewer chance encounters take place on the streets where we live, reducing a sense that the space around our houses is public and shared, or co-owned by the people who live there'. Furthermore, contemporary discourses around home ownership are now based on commodification and purchasing 'property' as a form of temporary investment rather than seeking a permanent home. Combined, these factors mean that many people no longer see the point in establishing strong communal ties with those who live around them and as a result do not rely on their neighbours for their sense of identity and belonging. In other words, there is no longer the state of permanence that is needed to foster locality-based neighbourhood community.

Because the attachments between neighbours are now often based on little more than proximity, neighbourhoods do not 'constrain their inhabitants into strongly bonded relationships with one another' and as such are too narrowly framed to sustain meaningful relationships (Bulmer, 1986: 87). Indeed, it could be argued that having strong ties to your locality may even be a disadvantage, as this ultimately constrains your upward mobility in an increasingly individualized, consumer society. As Bauman (2001: 38–39) points out, 'the degradation of locality' has meant that immobility 'is today the main measure of social deprivation'. Rather, the contemporary aim is to 'travel light' and 'avoid lasting attachment' (*see* 'Liquid Modern Communities').

We may even argue that the decline of traditional neighbourhood communities, and the concomitant decline of its ideology, has the potential to actually empower city communities within the 'global village'. The rapid development of information and communication technologies (ICTs) would seem to suggest that a loss of neighbourhood community is no great loss at all, as previous limits of time and space are of decreasing relevance. Research suggests that the Internet can be used as a supplementary form of community where geographical location is less important than shared interests and desires (Castells, 2000). As Castells (1999) points out, globalized city life serves to empower its inhabitants and stimulate citizen participation in new social movements, because communities in the global village are elective communities whose members have actively chosen to join up because of their individual desires and beliefs, rather than feeling any obligation due to traditional ties of locality and culture. This had led Richard Florida (2008) in his book *Who's Your City?* to the conclusion that globalization has made, and is making, place matter more, rather than less. According to Florida, it is the economic unit of the mega-region that is the driver of the global economy.

What this suggests is that it is also too early to say that the ideology of neighbourhood itself has entirely faded away. Not least because it can still be used as an important tool for defining people's position in an increasingly uncertain and shifting world that paradoxically strengthens their attachment to place (or at least our longing for such an attachment). Thus, there still remains a strong desire for 'geographic' community – particularly in times of crisis (Procopio and Procopio, 2007). As Sennett argues:

> One of the unintended consequences of modern capitalism is that it has strengthened the value of place, arousing a longing for community ...

the uncertainties of flexibility; the absence of deeply rooted trust and commitment; the superficiality of teamwork ... impel people to look for some other sense of attachment and depth (1998: 138).

Indeed, it would seem that it is the uncertainty of contemporary working life that is the very reason why we might still be strongly attached to the question of 'where am I from?'. Indeed, the assurance and security that the residents of 'Ramsay Street' appear to enjoy in 'Erinsborough' is certainly an attractive solution to lives that are increasingly characterized by the pressure to be (upwardly) mobile and constrained by nothing and no one. However, as Bauman suggests, the assuagements of locality, place and neighbourhood are only really possible (and only often desired) temporarily before we move on, unwilling and unable to provide the commitment to locality that any real sense of 'community' would necessitate. As he concludes, communities must now be flexible and amenable to change so that they can be displaced when they cease to satisfy or when more preferable alternatives arise. Thus, whilst the pull of locality, place and neighbourhood remain powerful, their much-sought-after comforts are likely to remain unfulfilled.

See also: *'Community Studies'; 'Hermeneutic Communities'; 'Imagined Communities'; 'Imaginary Communities'; 'The "Dark Side" of Community'; 'The Symbolic Construction of Community'.*

Co-authored with Beth Fielding-Lloyd.

FURTHER READING

Neighbours: The Work of Philip Abrams (Bulmer, 1986) is the classic book on neighbour studies, while Crow and Allan (1994) provide a more basic introduction.

REFERENCES

Appadurai, A. (1996) *Modernity at Large: Cultural Dimensions of Globalisation.* Minneapolis: University of Minnesota Press.
Amit, V. (2002) Reconceptualizing Community', in V. Amit (ed.) *Realizing Community.* London: Routledge.
Bauman, Z. (2001) *The Individualized Society.* Cambridge: Polity.
Bell, C. and Newby, H. (1971) *Community Studies: An Introduction to the Sociology of the Local Community.* London: George Allen and Unwin.
Blandy, S. and Lister, D. (2005) 'Gated Communities: Ne(gating) Community Development?', *Housing Studies*, 20 (2): 287–301.

Bulmer, M. (1986) *Neighbours: The Work of Philip Abrams*. Cambridge: Cambridge University Press.

Castells, M. (1999) 'The Culture of Cities in the Information Age', in I. Susser (ed.) (2002) *The Castells Reader on Cities and Social Theory*. Malden, MA: Blackwell.

Castells, M. (2000) (2nd ed.) *The Rise of the Network Society: The Information Age: Economy, Society and Culture Vol 1*. Oxford: Blackwell.

Clarke, S., Gilmour, R. and Garner, S. (2007) 'Home, Identity and Community Cohesion', in M. Wetherell, M. Laflèche and R. Berkeley (eds) *Identity, Ethnic Diversity and Community Cohesion* (pp. 87–101). London: Sage.

Cohen, A. P. (1985) *The Symbolic Construction of Community*. London: Routledge.

Crow, G. and Allan, G. (1994) *Community Life: An Introduction to Local Social Relations*. London: Harvester Wheatsheaf.

Delanty, G. (2003) *Community*. London: Routledge.

Elias, N. and Scotson, J. L. (1994) (2nd ed.) *The Established and the Outsiders*. London: Sage.

Florida, R. (2008) *Who's Your City?* New York: Basic Books.

Gans, H. (1982) *The Urban Villagers*. New York: The Free Press.

Hanley, L. (2007a) *Estates: An Intimate History*. London: Granta.

Hanley, L. (2007b) 'My new old neighbours', *The Guardian*, 24th May http://society.guardian.co.uk/comment/story/0,,2086609,00.html (accessed 20th August 2007).

Harvey, D. (1990) *The Condition of Postmodernity: An Enquiry into the Origins of Cultural Change*. Oxford: Blackwell.

Jenkins, R. (1996) *Social Identity*. London: Routledge.

Knox, P. (1987) (2nd ed.) *Urban Social Geography: An Introduction*. Harlow: Longman.

Power, A. (2007) *City Survivors: Bringing Up Children in Disadvantaged Neighbourhoods*. Bristol: Policy.

Procopio, C. H. and Procopio, S. T. (2007) 'Do You Know What It Means to Miss New Orleans? Internet Communication, Geographic Community, and Social Capital in Crisis', *Journal of Applied Communication Research*, 35 (1): 67–87.

Redfield, R. (1955) *The Little Community*. Chicago: University of Chicago Press.

Sennett, R. (1998) *The Corrosion of Character: The Personal Consequences of Work in the New Capitalism*. New York: Norton.

VIRTUAL COMMUNITIES

This term is commonly used to refer to the social networks mediated by information and digital technologies. Virtual communities are extraterritorial and do not necessitate the face-to-face contact, which is conventionally seen as central to community relations.

Section Outline: This chapter explores the implications of virtual communities – where social networks are not limited by the constraints of place or proximity – for conventional conceptions of community. In addition to examining the capacity of virtual worlds to generate community relations, it considers the ability of virtual communication to empower people by generating unrestrictive social networks that allow them to experiment with their identities based on their own individual choices and desires. In the light of this discussion, the chapter then considers virtual communities with respect to what are commonly considered to be 'real' communities and what this implies for traditional social, cultural and economic divides based on class, ethnicity and gender. Finally, the chapter assesses the argument that virtual communities exist only for virtual people, and that precious few of them manage to make it into 'real' communities, because their social networks are ultimately based on thin or weak ties.

The first thing to say about virtual communities is that they are best understood as social networks or *network communities* rather than as communities in the orthodox sociological meaning of the word. Arguably, it is the lack of community that makes these alternative cultures of belonging attractive. Virtual communities exist for virtual individuals, and they are highly personalized, meaning that their 'users' are able to search various 'communities' to fulfil their own particular individual needs. For example, virtual communities enable individuals to connect with each other through discussion groups and e-mail listings through which they can search for consumer advice on the most suitable products; support for emotional, physical or relationship troubles; or to engage with like-minded individuals around our shared work and leisure interests (e.g., sports teams, automotive clubs, music genres). Such help and support can be provided in the virtual world in the absence of any physical proximity, shared history or demographic similarity (Constant et al., 1996). This is in clear contrast to the ways in which individuals previously had to rely on the broad systems of support and reciprocity associated with traditional, village-type communities that we may be nostalgic for, and can be seen as symptomatic of a wider shift from communities based on locality and kinship ties to those based on specialized functions (Wellman and Gulia, 1999). The personalized communities available in cyberspace clearly manifest the move away from primary relationships (e.g., family) and secondary relationships (typical of association membership) towards *tertiary relationships*, which are centred on the individual's choices and have thus arguably led to 'the privatization of sociability' (Castells, 2001: 128). In other words, information technology is used to communicate between individuals rather than with a community.

This primary focus on individual choices means that it could easily be argued that virtual communities are not really communities at all because they largely consist of only thin or weak ties and require no lasting commitment. Certainly, anonymity is encouraged in virtual reality (i.e., by the use of avatars, alter egos or limited profiles). Therefore, it appears that we are rather disembodied from our contact with others in cyberspace and as participants in virtual 'communities' are essentially strangers who need not share social characteristics (such as gender, ethnicity, nationality and religion) and are not bound by conventions of reciprocity. Thus, 'community' members can easily withdraw from situations of conflict (Castells, 2000) without concern for the responses of others, as would be necessitated by face-to-face contact.

Yet, the lesser significance of social characteristics in these virtual contexts also means that the constraints of the 'communication audience' that are typical of real-life interactions are lessened. Furthermore, rapid technological developments (from the telephone to the Internet) have enabled us to 'transcend the confines of neighbourhood and kinship' (Wellman, 1996: 348), thereby increasing the potential empowerment of otherwise disenfranchised social groups (Wellman and Gulia, 1999). What this suggests is that, rather than dismissing the thin ties that are typical of virtual contact, we should in fact be embracing these as they appear to have the potential to promote egalitarian links between people of different backgrounds and circumstance. Thus, in an increasingly individualized world, our sociability is not constrained to seeking those who we recognize as similar to ourselves (Castells, 2000), but can be expanded to include those who we might conventionally define as Other.

Information and digital technologies help foster participation in multiple and partial communities, with varying degrees of involvement in each (from the committed, active member to the 'lurker') (Wellman and Gulia, 1999). Individuals are thus permitted to experiment with their identities; promoting some aspects as more salient than others and projecting their fantasies and ideas (Turkle, 1995) whilst being free from the constraints of their day-to-day identities. Certainly, some commentators have argued that advanced modernity is characterized by a sense of heightened reflexivity (Giddens, 1991) which allows individuals to spend more time considering who they are and who they want to be within the multiplicity of choices, ideas and information available to them (Bell, 2001). For example, the virtual world of *Second Life*, the MMORPG-cum-social networking site, gives its inhabitants the freedom to create their own 'avatars' to represent their chosen identities, enabling them to change their 'real' (i.e., offline) gender, ethnicity, occupation and sexuality, and develop friendships and love affairs based on this online persona (Smith, 2006). Moreover, in other social networking sites such as *Facebook*, notions of community are organized around the individuals' self-portraits (i.e., hobbies, social life, interests) which members are encouraged to continually modify (and inform others of these modifications via 'status updates' and 'news feeds'). It is in these ways that fragmentary and performative identities that are said to typify postmodern life are exemplified in virtual communities (*see* 'Postmodern Communities').

Rheingold (1993), a particularly vociferous proponent of the empowering and transformative potential of the Internet, argues that a new kind of community is now achievable in virtual reality, where people can be brought together by their shared interests and values, and that this may extend *into* face-to-face contact, thus promising unbound sociability. For Rheingold, virtual communities are a natural response to the enduring human desire for community, now that its traditional manifestations (i.e., communities defined by place, kin, or occupation, etc.) have disintegrated. Thus, he contends that the 'real' and the 'virtual' should be conceived as distinct and separate, with the latter being created as 'an alternative reality in a world gone wrong' (Robins, 2000: 87). Clearly, Rheingold is optimistic for the possibilities of virtual contact as fulfilling the nostalgic search for an ideal of community which may have been lost with the advent of modernity (*see* 'A Theory of Community').

However, what Rheingold fails to consider is that whilst the apparent freedoms of the Internet enable people to establish contact with those who are different from them, those freedoms paradoxically also make 'spaces for deliberating enclaves, consisting of like-minded individuals' (Sunstein, 2001: 193). Indeed, the freedom of individual choice that the Internet provides appears to be perhaps the most significant problem for notions of community because, as Sunstein continues, 'a communications system granting individuals an unlimited power to filter threatens to create excessive fragmentation', meaning that the Internet can serve to strengthen the position of all kinds of particular groups who might otherwise have limited opportunity to be heard. For example, the seemingly indiscriminate possibilities of virtual community may actually engender difference and conflict by supporting extreme political views. Whilst the potential for contact across social and cultural divisions exists with virtual community, it would be a mistake to assume that these possibilities are consistently fulfilled, or that they are always democratic.

This early optimism has been further critiqued by writers such as Castells who, whilst supporting Rheingold's empowerment thesis, contends that the Internet's effects on sociability have been less dramatic than originally envisaged. Whereas Rheingold sees the 'real' and the 'virtual' as distinctly different social spheres, the same problems of real life (difference, exclusion, conflict) unavoidably spill into the virtual. For example, access to new information technology is still restricted to those with the necessary economic, education and cultural resources, meaning that it has the potential to only 'empower' those within dominant social networks (Castells, 2000). As Wellman and Gulia (1999: 170) contend, on-line interactions are no different from offline interactions in that we bring our 'baggage' (such as our gender, cultural expectations, and socio-economic status) to both.

This is exemplified by the virtual community that is *Second Life* where members can be seen dealing with the same social problems as in 'real' communities (Dell, 2007). For example, at the time of writing, *Second Life* is experiencing widespread conflict as it struggles to negotiate between those users who subscribe to its founding ideals of liberty and self-expression and those users who demand centralized governance and regulation in order to protect their, now very real, economic interests on-line (Krotoski, 2006). What this suggests is that the wider context of social networking sites such as *Second Life* is not so much community comfort, but consumer comfort, facilitated by free-flowing markets. What it also suggests is that it may be inevitable that the pressures of commercialization will transform the character and membership of originally supportive and empathetic communities (Zhou, 2000; cited in Castells, 2001).

It does appear that virtual communities are an extension of 'off-line' communities, in that 'on-line' identities, experiences and relationships are heavily shaped by those in the 'real' world and that we should now be sceptical of those critiques which suggest that virtual communities are somehow unreal. As Castells (2000) points out, dictionaries typically define 'virtual' as 'being so in practice though not strictly or in name' whereas 'real' is defined as 'actually existing' (p. 403). In contrast to Rheingold (1993), he argues that what we actually experience in cyberspace is a *real virtuality* since human communication has always been practised and experienced via symbols, be it dress or language itself. Therefore, it is misleading to conceive of new communication technologies as creating new virtual, and thus inferior, communities; uncoded, unambiguous communities never existed in the first place. This is best exemplified by Baudrillard (1983), who teaches us that there is no meaningful distinction between reality and its representation. Rather, we live in a world of simulation where we can no longer see the differences between truth and falsity, meaning that the existence of those differences becomes threatened. Accordingly, if we cannot know the differences between real or virtual identities and communities, then the distinction between the two becomes invisible and irrelevant. To borrow from Baudrillard's (1983) medical analogy, there is now no attempt to look beyond the simulated symptoms of the virtual world (i.e., networks, forums) for the community's 'truth'. To do so would be absurd, for it would reveal that there is 'nothing behind them' (p. 9). Thus, the symptoms are already the truth that community members accept. To return to Castells, rather than debating the differences between 'virtuality' and 'reality', we should instead be exploring our 'virtual reality' as:

> … a system in which reality itself (that is, people's material/symbolic existence) is entirely captured, fully immersed in a virtual image setting, in the world of make believe, in which appearances are not just on the screen through which experience is communicated, but they become the experience (2001: 404).

In the light of the growing acceptance of virtual reality, it would seem that nostalgic concerns for the decline of face-to-face contact with family and friends, and the subsequent increasing use of new media technologies to communicate a sense of belonging with others, are becoming increasingly outdated. It is more appropriate for us to accept that face-to-face community is not a realistic goal in modernity, with its concomitant individualism, increased mobility and multitude of choices. Indeed, the Internet does not provide a separate reality or necessarily detract from our social contact with others, but typically serves to *supplement existing* relationships. For example, social networking sites such as *Facebook* and *Bebo* enable friends to communicate in between the times when they meet up, and are often used to organize face-to-face meetings, just as the telephone has always supplemented already existing relationships between those who are unable to meet frequently due to geographical location.

Accordingly, Wellman and Gulia (1999) argue that virtual and physical communities do not have to be positioned as opposites as this places too much focus on the medium rather than the relationship. Rather, they are just different forms of community with their own rules and dynamics. Thus, Wellman's chosen nomenclature is 'personal communities' which reflect our chosen relationships that can operate on- and offline, ranging from a handful of thick, intimate affiliations to potentially hundreds of thinner, less intimate ties (Wellman and Gulia, 1999). Personal communities are perhaps best exemplified by the phenomenon of *Facebook* where members collect 'friends' ranging from family members and intimate, long-term friends to past acquaintances with whom no face-to-face contact has taken place in decades. The thin or weak ties that are central to social networking sites can certainly be criticized as symptomatic of the narcissistic seeking of status rather than friendship (Rosen, 2007). However, as Granovetter (1983) contends, weak ties are commonly beneficial in that they enhance our mobility and ensure that we are not deprived of information and opportunities which could be inhibited within our narrow, 'strong ties' of neighbourhood and kinship.

Thus, it would appear that virtual communities organized around thin or weak ties are entirely appropriate if more durable notions of identity, place and community have been lost. Indeed, modernity would seem to *support* the indirect relationships that are facilitated in the virtual world. However, it would be incorrect to assume that thin or weak ties are only exemplified here. Our 'off-line', 'real-life' communities share the same problems as in their varying strength and commitment because they are often based on shared interests rather than loyalty to kin and locality. As if in a marketplace, we search for particular communities that serve our particular needs and dispose them off when we find more suitable alternatives (Bauman, 2001). But, perhaps it is just that, in the virtual context, the marketplace metaphor is more exaggerated as 'the very architecture of computer networks promotes market-like situations' (Wellman and Gulia, 1999: 186) where we shop for the human contact (via social networking sites, discussion boards, etc.) that fulfils our particular wants and desires.

This is not to say that the virtual world cannot still be a source of information, support and companionship (Wellman and Gulia, 1999). As Bell (2001) suggests, whilst our participation in virtual life has had a significant impact on the forms and functions of community, it has not led to an erosion of the *ideal* of community either. Therefore, we can conclude that the debates around the salience of virtual relationships as sites for building communities share many parallels with debates around the alleged decline of communities in all social contexts. The virtual world is simply another manifestation of the search for belonging in a world where previous certainties of identity and shared experience have been lost.

See also: *'Imaginary Communities'; 'Imagined Communities'; 'Hermeneutic Communities'; 'Liquid Modern Communities'; 'Postmodern Communities'; 'Social Network Analysis'; 'The "Dark Side" of Community'; 'The Symbolic Construction of Community'.*

Co-authored with Beth Fielding-Lloyd.

REFERENCES

Baudrillard, J. (1983). *Simulations*. New York: Colombia University.

Bauman, Z. (2001) *Community: Seeking Safety in an Insecure World*. Cambridge: Polity.

Bauman, Z. (2005) 'Identity for Identity's Sake is a Bit Dodgy', *Soundings*, 29: 12–20.

Bell, D. (2001) *An Introduction to Cybercultures*. London: Routledge.

Castells, M. (2000) (2nd ed.) *The Rise of the Network Society: The Information Age: Economy, Society and Culture Vol 1*. Oxford: Blackwell.

Castells, M. (2001) *The Internet Galaxy: Reflections on the Internet, Business, and Society*. Oxford: Oxford University Press.

Constant, D., Sproull, L. and Kiesler, S. (1996) 'The Kindness of Strangers: The Usefulness of Electronic Weak Ties for Technical Advice', *Organization Science*, 7 (2): 119–135.

Dell, K. (2007) 'Second Life's Real-World Problems', *Time Magazine*, Thursday 9th August http://www.time.com/time/magazine/article/0,9171,1651500,00.html (accessed 6th March 2008).

Giddens, A. (1991) *Modernity and Self-Identity: Self and Society in the Late Modern Age*. Cambridge: Polity.

Granovetter, M. (1983) 'The Strength of Weak Ties: A Network Theory Revisited', *Sociological Theory*, 1: 201–233.

Krotoski, A. (2006) 'Real Life Crashes into Second Life's Digital Idyll', *The Guardian*, Thursday 30th November http://www.guardian.co.uk/technology/2006/nov/30/secondlife.web20 (accessed 17th December 2007).

Rheingold, H. (1993) *The Virtual Community: Homesteading on the Electronic Frontier*. Reading, MA: Addison-Wesley.

Rosen, C. (2007) 'Virtual Friendship and the New Narcissism', *The New Atlantis*, 24: 15–31.

Robins, K. (2000) 'Cyberspace and the World We Live in', in D. Bell and B.M. Kennedy (eds) *The Cybercultures Reader*. London: Routledge.

community as place

Smith, D. (2006) 'How to Get the Life you Really Want', *The Observer*, Sunday 9th July http://www.guardian.co.uk/technology/2006/jul/09/secondlife.web20 (accessed 6th March 2008).

Sunstein, C. (2001) *Republic.com*. Princeton: Princeton University Press.

Turkle, S. (1995) *Life and the Screen: Identity in the Age of the Internet*. New York: Simon & Schuster.

Wellman, B. (1996) 'Are Personal Communities Local? A Dumptarian Reconsideration', *Social Networks*, 18: 347–354.

Wellman, B. and Gulia, M. (1999) 'Virtual Communities as Communities: Net Surfers Don't Ride Alone', in M. A. Smith and P. Kollock (eds) *Communities in Cyberspace* (pp. 167–194). London: Routledge.

Community as Identity/ Belonging

COMMUNITY AND IDENTITY

The root of the term 'identity' is 'sameness'. The 'problem' of identity in psychology is generally seen as the problem of personal identity ('who am I?'), while the vexing issue of what precisely constitutes the identity of a particular individual through time and how this forms as a result of social interaction is generally taken up by sociologists. The term arises in community studies especially in connection with the issue of belonging ('to what do I belong?').

Section Outline: This chapter begins by distinguishing the relationship between community and identity as an enduring modern problem that we yearn to solve in a world that is always on the cusp of change. Thereafter, it considers how our efforts to define ourselves via appeals to community lead to the seemingly unavoidable construction of difference. It is argued that what is problematic about the use of the term 'community' as it is used in this way is that it seems to understand social relations through what

Amartya Sen calls a 'solitarist' perspective, which tends to assume that our identities are formed by membership of a single community, when the reality is that we more often than not belong to many other communities as well. Paul Ricouer's ipse and idem-identity strategies are then explored in some detail to explain how notions of singular, ostensibly fixed identities are achieved and maintained. The chapter concludes by raising some issues about the tangled relationship between community, identity and individualization.

The word 'identity' is derived immediately from the sixteenth-century word *identitās*, itself a derivative of the Latin *idem*, meaning 'same'. As Jenkins (1996) points out, however, implicit to the idea of 'sameness' (a commonality with others) is that of 'distinctiveness' (signifying a difference from others that is continuous over time). What this suggests is that if identity is irrevocably social (it can only be constructed alongside, and in relation to, others), difference is also irrevocably implicit to social identity formation.

The notion of identity is, of course, also central to the vocabulary of everyday life and beyond the central issues concerned with personal identity ('who am I?). Here, its meaning is often understood both as something that we share with others ('to what do I belong?') and as something that is defined explicitly as a lasting possession. However, contrary to what this lay perspective suggests, identities are not so much possessions, as 'projects', that need to be worked on, which in their realization can never be completed (Bauman, 2004), meaning that they are best seen as 'practical accomplishments (Jenkins, 1996: 25). What this suggests is that it is important that we recognize that the idea of identity is very much a modern idea, and as such it is destined to remain a problem to be 'solved'. Indeed, it can be argued that it is precisely because of the uncertainties and changes that are the basis of modern life, and which often appear to us as both disconcerting and disorienting, that identity has become so important, particularly if we see it as refuge or an escape route from the vicissitudes of modern life (Bauman, 1996).

Whilst our identities are always in flux, this is not to say that we cannot 'feel' that we can or have achieved durable, clearly defined ways of being in the world (Brah, 2007), for when considered over a period of time, our identities take on the appearance of being fairly stable. Moreover, that we tend to search for some sense of stability in our lives suggests that fixed conceptions of identity are appealing precisely because they offer individuals a way of 'understanding one another as they understand themselves' (Young, 1990: 309). As Jenkins (1996: 5) points out, the verb 'to identify' means to classify things or persons and 'human social life is unimaginable without some means of knowing who others are and some sense of who we are'. What this suggests is that in order to define ourselves as being anyone, we must simultaneously define what we are not. This has led some commentators to argue that the 'sameness' that is at the root of identity unavoidably invites 'difference' and necessitates that social distinctions be firmly maintained by generating borders against, and subsequently conflict with, others (Young, 1990). As Melucci (1989: 46) argues, human conflicts are always conflicts of identity where individuals and groups 'struggle to affirm what others deny'.

As Julia Kristeva recently put it, we are at that moment in human history when men and women seem less inclined to the question 'Who am I?', and are most interested in 'To what do I belong?' (Kristeva cited in Wajid, 2006). In the event, identity is today more and more confused with belonging. The trouble with belonging, Kristeva argues, is that it is not about questioning. This view is reinforced by Young (1990) in her discussion of the problematic relationships of identity that form the basis of communities. Young argues that what always comes with the desire for community is the grounding of two metaphysical essences: on the one hand the metaphysics of *presence* and on the other the logic of *identity*, or what she calls a 'metaphysics that denies difference'. What this amounts to is nothing less than the commingling of a fetishism for an ideal that cannot help but be *absent* in a modern world with a putative *identity*, which needs to be preserved at all costs and often through the depredations of others – if that is what it takes (*see* 'The "Dark Side" of Community').

In a critical response to this state of affairs, Sen (2007) argues that it is only by acknowledging the multiplicity of human identities, and accepting the futility of seeking a singular identity, that can we avoid the problems of 'difference' and reach some kind of harmony through our diversity. Rather than reifying ostensibly putative differences – for example, the Western 'war on terror' versus the atrocities of the 'suicide bombers' representing the Middle East – we need to better empathize with each others' identities and, most importantly, identify what we have in common. Notwithstanding the ethical persuasiveness of this argument, the 'problem' of identity is likely to remain a stubborn one and particularly so for those communities with fragile identities and whose collective mission it is to overcome their collective ontological insecurity and establish for themselves a more secure existence.

One of the main strategies by which communities try to make themselves more ontologically secure is by telling themselves stories about themselves and others. The *hermeneutical* philosopher Paul Ricoeur offers a compelling explanation of this process of narration, which suggests that two complementary manoeuvres are always the basis of communal attempts to preserve ontological security: the *ipse-identity* strategy and the *idem-identity* strategy. A good application of Ricoeur's ideas is Tony Blackshaw's (2003) book *Leisure Life*, which explores the dialectic of self and Other that constitutes what he calls the leisure life-world of 'the lads', a group of men who live in Leeds, England, who spend their leisure time together in the pubs and clubs in the city.

Blackshaw begins his analysis by arguing that the *idem-identity* strategy seeks to secure for identity a sense of permanence by ensuring that the process of identity making itself is straightforwardly uncomplicated. What this involves is the idea that identity itself has a rigid immutability that transcends time and space. 'The lads', he argues, are able to find the essentialist support for such a strategy in the discourse of the leisure life-world. Blackshaw argues that the idem strategy developed 'lad style' is a performative procedure which draws on the Kantian category of *Einbildungskraft* – literally, the 'transcendental power of the imagination' – to construct the Others' 'true face' and 'schematize' its shape with concrete features (Žižek, 2002).

In relation to the leisure life-world, this strategy enables 'the lads' to attach ready-made versions of the Other to those who are not part of the leisure life-world, like 'resplendent images more real than the actual bodies they obscure'. For example, the narration of the leisure life-world describes women all the same, but variously as 'good women', 'slags, 'fanny' and so on. 'The lads' hand out these identities precisely because it helps them to attach to the Other a sense of immutability, of sameness. The 'universal' truth of this rationality is what enables 'the lads' to divide themselves and others into two categories: 'us' and 'them'. 'The lads' know that these mutually constructed stories of *idem-identity* are but allegories, but what others make of them is neither here nor there. The key point is that Other litters what is otherwise an orderly place and must be dealt with accordingly. What prompts 'the lads' to deal with the Other is the search for some order in a world of endemic disorder, and it is in 'their' leisure lives where 'the lads' perceive that a kind of utopia can be achieved (*see* 'Imaginary Communities').

The *idem-identity* strategy, then, is always polysemic, in Ricoeur's terminology: a polysemy of Otherness. These Others are never persons; they are merely characters in the plot, which is a story of leisure written by 'the lads'. Moreover, these characterizations do not have to be 'real'; 'the lads' simply have to be convinced that they are. What is important for 'the lads' is the *meaning for them* of these characterizations to their version of truth, which is something that enables them to form what they perceive *is* the world when they are at leisure together. Indeed, it makes sense to 'the lads' that they populate their leisure life-world with these, their very own characterizations of the Other.

These processes of narration also draw on the counter strategy of *ipse-identity* making. This strategy involves, for Ricoeur, the occasioning of self-identity making proper, which is always occasioned in the flux of everyday life, achieving through the process of its narration a 'mythic stability', which in this case enables 'the lad' to perpetuate their own world as distinct from others. The *ipse-identity* strategy works through the discourse of the leisure life-world in the following way: the figure of 'the lad' is always understood as a character in the leisure life-world's very own story line and is never imagined as anything other than through his experiences in the leisure life-world. In this leisure world, each one of 'the lads' shares the condition of, to use Ricoeur's expression, a 'dynamic identity' that is specific to the story which is recounted each time 'the lads' come together. In this sense, the leisure life-world has its own discursive and contingent temporality outside common sense notions of time and space, which constructs the identity of each of 'the lads', that is what can be called 'his own particular narrative identity, in constructing the story told' (Ricoeur, 1992). It is then the meta-identity of the discourse of the leisure life-world that makes the individual *ipse-identities* of each of 'the lads' as well as their collective desire to conform to the discourse of the leisure life-world that perpetuates the constancy and sameness confirmed by *ipse-identity*.

In Ricoeur's terminology, the leisure life-world is ultimately 'the lads'' very own epistemology of 'attestation' that works in two ways which are mutually dependent. First, the discourse of the leisure life-world operates as 'the lads'' very own truth about the world, which is defined through the certainty of an identity that enables 'the lads' to give assurances to one another that it is in their leisure that they 'really' can be themselves. Second, it is through the selfsame certainty of this discourse that 'the lads' can certify that their leisure world is 'free' from those that this discourse has created through its narrative.

Yet, in his review of Bauman's work, Blackshaw (2005) concludes that the ambivalence central to modernity is that most people do not, in fact, seek the ontological security of singular identities, but actually identities that help to ease the simultaneous loneliness and overwhelming demands that individualism creates. The truth is, we expect our communities to be our like identities: flexible, disposable and amenable to change – and whenever they cease to satisfy are displaced by more attractive alternatives (Bauman, 2001). Thus, in common with Blackshaw's 'lads', most of us use the contingent and short life-span of neo-tribes – what Scott Lash (2002: 27) calls 'post-traditional' *Gemeinschaften* of 'mobile and flexible groupings – sometimes enduring, often easily dissoluble – formed with an intensive affective bonding – to our advantage, not least because they enable us to pay 'lip-service' to feelings of togetherness and belonging without the necessary commitment. This is perhaps why Rutherford (2007: 30) concludes that the conception of identity is an expressive desire of both freedom and security through which we 'desire to experience our individual life as unique and meaningful to ourselves, but we equally feel a need to belong to, and define ourselves through, broader collectives. It is in our relationships with others that we attempt to reconcile this paradox and find self-fulfilment'.

See also: *'Setting the Record Straight'; 'Imagined Communities'; 'Hermeneutic Communities'; 'Liquid Modern Communities'; 'The "Dark Side" of Community'; 'The Symbolic Construction of Community'; 'Virtual Communities'.*

Co-authored with Beth Fielding-Lloyd.

FURTHER READING

Jenkins (1996) provides an excellent introduction to social identity and its relationship with community.

REFERENCES

Bauman, Z. (1996) 'From Pilgrim to Tourist – or a Short History of Identity', in S. Hall and P. Du Gay (eds) *Questions of Cultural Identity*. London: Sage.

Bauman, Z. (2001) *Community: Seeking Safety in an Insecure World*. Cambridge: Polity Press.

Bauman, Z. (2004) *Identity: Conversations with Benedetto Vecchi*. Cambridge: Polity.

Bauman, Z. (2005) 'Identity for Identity's Sake is a Bit Dodgy', *Soundings*, 29: 12–20.

Blackshaw, T. (2003) *Leisure Life: Myth, Masculinity and Modernity*. London: Routledge.

Blackshaw, T. (2005) *Zygmunt Bauman*. London: Routledge.

Brah, A. (2007) 'Non-Binarized Identities of Similarity and Difference', in M. Wetherell, M. Laflèche and R. Berkeley (eds) *Identity, Ethnic Diversity and Community Cohesion* (pp. 136–145). London: Sage.

community as identity/belonging

Jenkins, R. (1996) *Social Identity*. London: Routledge.

Lash, S. (2002) *Critique of Information*. London: Sage.

Melucci, A. (1989) *Nomads of the Present: Social Movements and Individual Needs in Contemporary Society*. London: Hutchinson Radius.

Ricoeur, P. (1988) *Time and Narrative Vol. III*. Chicago: University of Chicago Press.

Ricoeur, P. (1992) *Oneself as Another*. Chicago: University of Chicago Press.

Rutherford, J. (2007) *After Identity*. London: Lawrence and Wishart.

Sen, A. (2007) *Identity and Violence: The Illusion of Destiny*. London: Penguin.

Wajid, S. (2006) 'Murder, She "Wrote"', *The Times Higher Education Supplement*, 24th March, p. 20.

Young, I. (1990) 'The Ideal of Community and the Politics of Difference', in L. J. Nicholson (ed.) *Feminism / Postmodernism*. New York: Routledge.

Žižek, S. (2002) 'Are We in A War? Do We Have an Enemy?', *London Review of Books*, 24 (10): 3–6.

IMAGINED COMMUNITIES

The idea of 'imagined communities' is taken from the work of Benedict Anderson, who developed it in order to examine the rise of the modern nation-state. Anderson's work suggests that although the nation-state is an entity that is very much taken for granted by most people, the process by which its rise occurred was the outcome of an extraordinary set of events that involved a recasting of the ways that societies both thought about themselves and communicated with the outside world. What this suggests is that not only is connection where modern community lies, but also that territory becomes important when it registers with the collective imagination.

Section Outline: As Anderson observed, the nation is the ultimate 'imagined' community because it signifies the idea of a cohesive entity with an ostensible common history, a shared culture and apparent sense of purpose. After outlining and discussing the genesis of the 'imagined community' of the nation-state, this chapter explores why the concept has such a ubiquitous presence in community studies and, in this regard, focuses its attention on the ways it has been applied to the sport of football. In so doing, the chapter also offers a critique of the concept which evinces both its strengths and weaknesses for community studies.

The starting point of Anderson's thesis is that with the substitution of the modern liberal state for feudalism there was a profound shift in social stratification: one which altered, deeply, our entire view of the nation's past, present and possible futures. If feudalism was a closed system of social stratification based on land ownership and legal inequalities which worked through a process of vertical organization based on hierarchal 'estates' (the first estate [the monarch, aristocracy and landed gentry]; the second estate [the church]; and the third estate [merchants, artisans, serfs]), modern liberal states are open societies with no legal or religious restrictions on the movement of individuals from one social group to another. Modern individuals (in a modern liberal state, a person is an individual first and all the rest after) are 'citizens', rather than 'subjects' of the monarch, and this necessitates a social order based on horizontal association and a sharing of identity between (formal if not informal) equals.

The modern nation-state came to be represented as such an entity, first through its political constitution and second through its ability to supersede hitherto fragmented traditional agencies of association, which was facilitated by new technologies of mass communication. It is in relation to this second feature that Anderson offers his model of 'imagined communities', which was not only able to offer a form of sharing that transcended all the partial viewpoints of these hitherto fragmented traditional agencies of association, but was able at the same time to enter emphatically into any of them. In the words of Anderson himself, the development of new technologies of mass communication, particularly the print media, is the precondition of all modern 'imagined communities' which 'are to be distinguished not by their falseness/genuineness, but by the style in which they are imagined' (1991: 6). In other words, with the advent of the appropriate technology, people were not only now able to learn about the same events in the same manner, but as a result it became possible to predicate the nation as a mental construct and the idea of nationhood as a collective state of mind. Contrary to what that major philosopher of the Enlightenment Jean-Jacques Rousseau believed, it was no longer necessarily by knowing each other that individuals could be a community; they could now know community by collectively imagining it.

To take one good example, think about the ways in which the English population react when its football team is playing in an international competition such as the World Cup. What is important is not just the enormous numbers of people wearing white or red England football shirts, the symbolic adoption of the cross of St. George flag by white-van drivers and face-painters, or the full-on chats of 'In-ger-land, In-ger-land, In-ger-land ...' in pubs and bars across the land, but the fact that each one of those individuals involved knows that there are other people like them celebrating their national identity in the same ways. It is through this kind of conviction that the process works; belief in the collective dimension of the imagined community is the individual belief of each of its members.

What this suggests is that there is more 'imagined' than 'community' in these communities, which makes the idea of 'imagined communities' something of an oxymoron; that is, it is a conceptual contradiction in terms because it is difficult to tell what is 'real' and what is not, and what is swinging in the hammock of imaginative supposition strung between the two parts. Unperturbed, Anderson suggests that the idea of the nation-state is the ultimate 'imagined community' because it is a cohesive entity that provides its adherents with a common history, a shared culture and an apparent sense of purpose. This is perfectly summarized by Bauman (2006: 37), who points out that '[t]he state needed subjects of the state as patriots of the nation, ready to sacrifice their individual lives for the sake of the survival of the nation's "imagined community"; the nation needed its members as subjects of a state empowered to conscript them to the "national cause" and, in case of need, to force them to surrender their lives in the service of the nation's immortality'. In other words, it was only with the emergence of 'imagined communities' that 'the question of nation at the level of creaturely pain and vulnerability and fear of the grave' (Clark, 2006: 6) becomes conceivable.

If, as far as Anderson was concerned, the nascent nation-state was the first major modernizing attempt to provide collective answers to the questions that previously religions had been capable of making their own (Clark, 2006), he also purposely developed in his work an understanding of community which did not have its base in social relations, and it is not unreasonable to suggest that he merely 'appropriated the idea ... as a vehicle for explaining the affective loyalties invested in nationalism' (Amit, 2002: 6). In other words, he developed a concept that had close affinities with Hobsbawm and Ranger's (1983) idea of the 'invented tradition'. According to Amit, Anderson was not really concerned with the social interaction that compelled ostensibly diverse groups of people to conceive themselves as 'imagined communities', as ready-made nations, but used the concept instead to demonstrate how one particular version of history manages to be tacitly accepted by particular nation-states and how contemporary circumstances emerge as a result.

However, the assumption that Anderson merely used the idea to theorize how 'imagined communities' could be mobilized by nation-states to predicate the idea of nationhood as a collective state of mind is surely over-simplistic. Still, with the publication of the first edition of his book in 1983, it 'wasn't long before imagined communities of one kind or another were popping up almost everywhere' (Amit, 2002: 8). As Anderson puts it in the preface to the third edition: 'Aside from the advantages of brevity, [the idea of the 'imagined community'] restfully occludes a pair of words from which the vampires of banality have by now sucked almost all the blood' (quoted in Clark, 2006: 6). To return once again to the example of football, it has indeed so often been in the case of the sociology of sport that scholars have tended to use the idea in this rather lazy way to suggest that if groups, such as football supporters, believe they are a community – even if it is for only 90 minutes or so – then they are a community. However, what these kinds of applications of Anderson's concept largely fail to recognize is that if football 'communities' are imagined, they are imagined, not just because their members will never know most of their fellow-members, but also because the demands and opportunities required by modern living mean that 'imagined communities' are all the time in the process of disembedding and re-embedding, to use Tony Giddens' apt expression (*see* 'Liquid Modern Communities').

As Sandvoss (2003: 92) shows, if football communities are *imagined in structure*, they are also *imagined in content* as football fans claim their individual membership through their putative readings of the values and attributes of the game and their inculcation in its cultural habitus. However, because football fandom today is perhaps more transplantable and more transferable than it used to be in the past, fan communities are increasingly less likely to be bound by propinquity and are more likely to form deterritorialized groupings. As Sandvoss points out, this does not make some football fans 'authentic' and others 'inauthentic'; some fans will come, some will stay, and others will go, because today they inhabit a modern consumer culture, and not only that, they live in a time when it is the liberty of the individual, not the collective, that is the overriding value (Bauman, 1997).

These observations notwithstanding, when Anderson said that in the minds of each member of an 'imagined community' lives the image of their communion, which can be conceived as a deep-felt mutuality, he was surely onto something else that was useful to scholars of football studies, who have always pointed out the cathartic, breathtaking intensity of the shared experience of supporting your football club. What he also said about 'imagined communities' being limited by their strictly demarcated, though elastic boundaries, beyond which lie various threats and uncertainties, he was also saying something that was obviously pertinent to understanding the dynamics of football rivalry, which Sandvoss again demonstrates is no longer confined to localities as football's communities have undergone the transformation from territory to the semiotic space of the global 'imagined community'.

The most compelling use of Anderson's understanding of community in the sociology of football literature, however, has featured in the work of Anthony King (*see* 1995; 1997a; 1997b; 2000; 2001), who clearly recognizes that in a global world which is no longer institutionally enclosed within the framework of the nation-state as it was conceived in early modernity, it was perhaps inevitable that sport, and particularly football, would come to play such a pivotal role in allowing individuals to express their cultural identities through local, national and international versions of collective expression. As he puts it:

> the use of the term 'invented tradition' or 'imagined community' to describe ... [football fans] ... should not be interpreted as claiming that they are a specious social group whose political claims can therefore be dismissed. Rather ... [it] highlights the actual process by which this group has come into being. Despite its appeals to a working-class tradition, this group's formation is not primarily determined by objective and prior social facts such as class location but rather the group arises out of the frequent interaction of quite socially diverse individuals at football games. Following these interactions in which these individuals come to recognize each other and form relations with each other, appeals to notions of 'tradition', 'the working class' and 'Manchester' [and we might add community] become the key ways in which a common identity between them is established and the group comes into being. The putatively long-standing traditions to which fans appeal, in fact, refers to the practices of those individuals who are currently present in this group (whatever their social origins and history of support), and the appeal to tradition serves to highlight their shared contemporary experiences and understandings (King, 2001: 708–709).

What also makes King's analysis all the more convincing is that it provides evidence of an applied sense of Cohen's (1985) *symbolic construction of community* in which both dedicated football fans and less committed consumers of football alike can shelter under the same umbrella.

However, what King perhaps fails to take sufficiently into account is that if the 'imagined communities' surrounding football are sovereign, it is not because they exist at that particular stage in history when freedom is only a rare and much cherished ideal *vis-à-vis* Anderson's 'imagined communities', they exist because fans *choose* to support their football teams. In marked contrast to Anderson's nation-state 'imagined communities', football's 'imagined communities' do not make totalizing claims on the individual – nor could they even if they wanted to – and are by contrast never fully guaranteed. Football, as the great Liverpool manager Bill Shankly famously said, 'isn't a matter of life and death, it's more important than that'. But, what he failed to point out is that there is a gap between what people actually believe and the way they live, and when all is said and done we all know that football is, after all, only a game.

What this last criticism overlooks is the point that supporting your local or chosen club is not the same as supporting your national team. The significance of this distinction is captured by Debray (2007) in his observation that, even in an increasingly globalizing and cosmopolitan world, the national remains ineradicable, and the battle of historical memory against forgetting is fought on many fronts: 'History as tradition, language, even the clothes you wear (and we might add football shirt, scarf and flag), will always take precedence over ideas'. Any analysis that fails to take on board this important observation about the power and particularities of national culture is surely lacking. However, in order to develop a fuller understanding of the significance of 'imagined communities' in football, or for that matter, of understanding other ways in which this concept might usefully be applied, we also need to do what most scholars have failed to do, and that is mapping out the social conditions which explain *why* community has become the natural noise of our contingent present. A good starting point for doing this would be to turn to the chapters on 'Liquid Modern Communities' and 'Community and Identity'.

REFERENCES

Amit, V. (2002) 'Reconceptualising Community', in V. Amit (ed.) *Realising Community: Concepts, Social Relationships and Sentiments.* London: Routledge.

Anderson, B. (1991, 1983) (2nd ed.) *Imagined Communities: Reflections on the Origin and Spread of Nationalism.* London: Verso.

Bauman, Z. (1997) *Postmodernity and its Discontents.* Cambridge: Polity Press in association with Blackwell.

Bauman, Z. (2006) *Liquid Fear*. Cambridge: Polity Press.

Clark, T. J. (2006) 'In a Pomegranate Chandelier', *London Review of Books*, 28 (18): September.

Cohen, A. P. (1985) *The Symbolic Construction of Community*. London: Tavistock.

Debray, R. (2007) 'The Religion of Revolution: An Interview with Gerry Feehily', *The Independent Review*, 13th April.

Hobsbawm, E. and Ranger, T. (eds) (1983) *The Invention of Tradition*. Cambridge: Cambridge University Press.

King, A. (1995) 'Outline of a Practical Theory of Football Violence', *Sociology*, 19 (4): 635–651.

King, A. (1997a) 'The Lads: Masculinity and the New Consumption of Football', *Sociology*, 31 (2): 329–346.

King, A. (1997b) 'The Postmodernity of Football Hooliganism', *British Journal of Sociology*, 48 (4): 576–593.

King, A. (2000) 'Football Fandom and Post-National Identity in the New Europe', *British Journal of Sociology*, 51 (3): 419–442.

King, A. (2001) 'Abstract and Engaged Critique in Sociology: On Football Hooliganism', *British Journal of Sociology*, 52 (4): 707–712.

Sandvoss, C. (2003) *A Game of Two Halves: Football, Television and Globalization*. London: Routledge.

THE SYMBOLIC CONSTRUCTION OF COMMUNITY

To say that community is symbolically constructed is neither to suggest that it has deep meaning to which only certain privileged individuals have access, nor is it to suggest that communities are formed by the imagination of something akin to a collective consciousness that is confident and clear about its own ontological existence. On the contrary, it is to recognize that communities are not only the outcome of the unconditioned agency upon which their existence depends, but also that they do not exist without imagery, boundary marking processes, customs, habits, rituals and the communication of these. What this suggests is that community is made manifest through people's – outsiders as well as insiders – repeated and deep engagement with it, at an analytical as well as an imaginative level.

Section Outline: This chapter begins by exploring Anthony Cohen's idea that symbolic communities depend on boundaries as much as they are imagined by insiders and outsiders. Thereafter, it provides a critical assessment

> *of Cohen's model based on both its theoretical efficacy and empirical applications. It is suggested that although this idea has much to offer community studies, it would appear that under its terms of reference, every kind of social and cultural relation is potentially or actually a community.*

Symbols, Paul Ricoeur once wrote, both provoke us and provide us with the information for thinking. In other words, they are not so much consciously elaborated rhetorical devises – like metaphors or analogies which we use to make language in magical and enlivening ways – that are formed by the imagination of individuals who are already quite clear about what they want to say about the world and need only a better way of expressing it. On the contrary, symbols are things without which thought, and concomitantly the world itself, would not be possible. It is this sense of the term 'symbolic' that is the starting point of Anthony Cohen's (1985) theory of community: without symbols and their communication, community would not be possible.

Cognizant of the limitations of the orthodox sociological way of defining its key ideas, Cohen points out that it took the genius of Ludwig Wittgenstein to alert philosophy to the efficacy of exploring the ways in which concepts are used in everyday life, rather than simply relying on normative definitions. This is the starting point for Cohen's own theorization of community, drawn from his own empirical research, mainly on the island of Whalsey in the Shetland Isles (*see* Cohen, 1987), which leads him to argue that imagery, boundary-marking processes, such as customs, habits and rituals and the communication of these, are vital defining features of community membership, because they not only gesture at a shared sense of reality, but they also shape that reality, even though they are on the face of it merely the imaginary social constructs of both insiders and outsiders. This is a sense of community that cannot always be seen but is always known – a topography of community imagined from both the inside and outside. What this also suggests is that the symbolic and the actual are impossible to prise apart, and, as a result of this, we are insistently forced to acknowledge that there is no solid ground of unassailable truth on which any community can rest.

At one level, Cohen's conception is essentially that of an 'imaginary' sense of community encapsulated previously in what orthodox sociologists meant when they talked about 'common affective union' (*see* Bell and Newby, 1971). However, in Cohen's hands, this union is not merely assumed, it is confirmed empirically. Indeed, the 'imaginary' in community is something that is constructed symbolically, and although the 'sense of belonging' associated with it does not necessarily have any spatial significance, its putative membership is subject to shared meanings and tacit, local knowledge. The great virtue of Cohen's idea is its merging of a sense of place and space with local customs, habits and rituals – the regular, repetitive and rule-determined patterns of social life used to signify shared and common experiences. As he suggests, 'whether or not its structural boundaries remain intact, the reality of community lies in its members' perception of the vitality of its culture. People construct community symbolically, making it a resource and repository of meaning, and a referent of their identity' (p. 118).

There are two basic criticisms that can be levelled at this ostensibly empirically grounded understanding of community. The first of these is that, notwithstanding his argument that our concern should be the idea of community as it is used in everyday life (rather than simply relying on normative definitions), what Cohen fails to acknowledge is that even if they are empirically informed, concepts have their genesis in the heads of social scientists and can just as well be used to distort social phenomena as they can be said to represent them. This leads to the second criticism of Cohen, which is that the problem with his own account is that it begins with an alternative, applied way of understanding community, but in the event ends up 'proving' that theory by referring to *pro tem* events, such as the annual Notting Hill carnival in London, or in the main, small, atypical anthropological cultures consisting of the kind of community life that is the world small groups and small-minded places into which are crushed ready-made mores, cultures and moral ties that make them feel even smaller and tighter (see, for example, Cohen (1987)), rather than demonstrating that community is still a useful basic concept for interpreting social and cultural life associated with the modern lives of the majority of people.

Contrary to this second criticism, Cohen's work has generally been welcomed as an important addition to the theoretical domain of community studies, precisely because it offers a general model of community that can be applied empirically to a variety of social and cultural formations. A good application of Cohen's ideas is Brown, Crabbe and Mellor's (2006) research on football and its communities. These authors argue that not only does Cohen provide a compelling model with which to understand football clubs as symbols around which the customs, habits and rituals of communal activity are acted out, but it also provides a theory which enables us to see communal symbols (e.g., football clubs, the different stands inhabited by fans in football stadia, etc.) as contested phenomena, which mean different things to different people, and that these meanings can change over different historical periods. As they point out:

> In this regard, Cohen's theory allows us to move beyond geographically deterministic understandings of football supporter communities which see functional and inevitable relationships emerge between people and sports clubs in set spatial areas. Instead, Cohen allows us to identify individual actors' agency in creating their community formations, and their different interpretations of them. For some people, football supporter communities may be (and may have always been) entirely geographical affairs. That is simply the way that they choose to define them. However, even these communities can be read as symbolic or 'performative' as people within them seek to 'display' *their* geography through their football support. For others, football communities may represent an entirely different type of bonding. The key point is that Cohen allows us to see football communities as fluid and always open to change (p. 170).

These observations notwithstanding, the major obstacle with following Cohen's line of argument is that it would appear that every kind of social and cultural relation is potentially and actually a community. As Jenkins (1996: 112) points out, though, one of the key strengths of this theory of community, which is built on a framework that importantly incorporates similarity and difference, is that it 'emphasises that the "belonging" of "community" is symbolically constructed by people in response to, even as a defence against, their categorization by outsiders'. To stay with the example of football and its communities, it might have become something of a cliché to suggest that nothing unites football fans like a common enemy, but to paraphrase Jenkins, it is against such a foil that difference is asserted and similarity symbolically constructed in football; it is in the face of the Other that communal identity is necessary. Gregory Bateson's (1958) idea of anti-types is useful in this regard, because it helps us recognize that, in the realm of football rivalry, the opposition fans are not merely represented as Other; rather, two opposing sets of supporters polarize and become each other's Other: United as anti-City and City as anti-United. In this way, football rivalry can be seen not merely as a clash of opposites, but also as an oppositioning around a clash.

Putting these important insights aside for a moment, another key problem with Cohen's understanding of community, constructed as it is through a theory which puts so much emphasis on inclusion *in spite of* members' ostensible differences, is that it took as its basis Victor Turner's *specific* model of *liminality, communitas, anti-structure* as it was applied to pilgrimage processes and turned it into a *general* model. There is, of course, no doubting the efficacy of drawing on Turner's work for understanding the shared rituals associated with the ephemeral social and cultural drama of football spectatorship, for example. However, in adapting a *specific* model which is 'open and specialized' as well as being attuned to 'the immediate realization of release from day-to-day structural necessities and obligatoriness' (Turner, 1973: 217), as a *general* model, Cohen is essentially bringing together what were hitherto separable conventions of the imaginary and the real, the symbolic and the material, the needs of the individual and the collective, as well as similarity and difference, all of which he argues makes community real in its consequences in any given context. In doing so, he is surely exaggerating, like Turner, the extent that these opposing conventions can be so easily fused together like an umbrella under which ostensibly anybody, whatever their putative social, cultural, political and economic differences, can potentially shelter.

On the face of it, Cohen's model might appear to be a seductive alternative to classic sociological conceptualizations of community, but it is still in the main an academic rendering of an ideal of community. Indeed, as the history of 'community' relations in football shows, if difference is pivotal to community ways of being in the world, it is always invariably as a response to the incongruity between same and other; that is, the *difference* between *our* club and *theirs*. According to Young (1990), what is a permanent fixture with the 'desire' for community is the grounding of two metaphysical essences: on the one hand, the metaphysics of *presence*, and on the other, the logic of *identity*, or what she calls a 'metaphysics that denies difference', which to draw on our football example once again, means that it always seems necessary for community to have to define itself by way of frontiers and borders, as Fredric Jameson (2003) recently put it: 'by way of a kind of secession: it must always, in other words … posit an enemy'.

Arguably, it is largely due to Cohen that community theorizing has become such a vague and ambiguous activity, and it is not unfair to suggest that his contribution to the literature is undoubtedly part of the reason why community has become such an overworked, catch-all concept. We can conclude that what Blackshaw and Crabbe (2004) said of that other highly contested concept in sociology, 'deviance', is true of Cohen's arbitrary use of community; its habitual 'naming' is not really a reflection of some reality, it is rather ideological in that it tends to 'fix' a particular kind of meaning to different and diverse practices and activities and identities, and kinds of belonging, which might otherwise be accompanied by a multitude of other possible meanings and under-standings.

As Jacques Derrida (1991) might have put it, the 'name' community, as it is used by Cohen, is so powerful and pervasive that it is its own signature word. And, like all other signature words, it comes with the promise to consign the present to the future and with it limit the possibilities of choice concerning anything from geographical spaces to social identities, from cultural differences to political exigencies. For example, calling the populace of a poor inner city locality who live in the vicinity of a professional football club a 'community' is not evidence that it *is* a community, but its 'naming' invariably acts as a kind of 'thinking-without-knowing [which] *decides*, precisely, that it is going to know after all in any case. So it *pronounces*, about various matters of which it is ignorant' (Jarvis, 2003: 45).

In the end, Cohen's idea of community simply exceeds the possibility of its own representation. Indeed, using the word in such a catch-all way means that it tends to be defined not by its ability to transcend the immutability of its orthodox sociological counterpart – in an applied way – but rather by the confirmation of 'community's' immanence, the sense in which its users tend to make putative assumptions about diverse socio-cultural interaction and institutional orders (and disorders) which are forced to remain within the ontological trajectory of the originary concept of community itself, but which if they cared to look at through an alternative lens would tell them a good deal more about people's ability to render for themselves imaginative cultural identities and ways of being together somewhere between 'reality' and its representation.

See also: *'A Theory of Community'; 'Community Studies'; 'Imaginary Communities'; 'Imagined Communities'; 'Liminality, Communitas and Anti-Structure'; 'Postmodern Communities'.*

REFERENCES

Bateson, G. (1958) (2nd ed.) *Naven*. Stanford, CA: Stanford University.

Bell, C. R. and Newby, H. (1971) *Community Studies*. London: Allen & Unwin.

Blackshaw, T. and Crabbe, T. (2004) *New Perspectives on Sport and 'Deviance': Consumption, Performativity and Social Control*. Abingdon: Routledge.

Brown, A., Crabbe, T. and Mellor, G. (2006) 'English Professional Football and Its Communities', *International Review for Modern Sociology*, 32 (2): 159–179.

Cohen, A. P. (1985) *The Symbolic Construction of Community*. London: Tavistock.

Cohen, A. P. (1987) *Whalsey: Symbol, Segment and Boundary in a Shetland Island Community*. Manchester: Manchester University Press.

Derrida, J. (1991) 'Ulysses Gramophone: Hear Say Yes in Joyce', in P. Kamuf (ed.) *A Derrida Reader: Between the Blinds*. New York: Columbia University Press.

Jameson, F. (2003) 'Pseudo-Couples', *London Review of Books*, 25 (22): November.

Jarvis, S. (2003) 'Thinking-Cum-Knowing: A Book Review', *Radical Philosophy*, 117: 43–45.

Jenkins, R. (1996) *Social Identity*. London: Routledge.

Turner, V. (1973) 'The Center Out There: Pilgrim's Goal', *History of Religions*, 12 (3): 191–230.

Young, I. M. (1990) 'The Ideal of Community and the Politics of Difference', in L. J. Nicholson (ed.) *Feminism/Postmodernism*. London: Routledge.

Community as Ideology

COMMUNITARIANISM

Communitarianism is both a philosophy and ideology operational-ized as a model of political organization, which stresses communal solidarity, kinship ties and other collective obligations based on nor-mative social relations and traditional values.

Section Outline: This chapter begins by outlining the philosophical and ideological context of communitarian thought. After identifying the central tenets of political communitarianism, it offers a rigorous critique, sug-gesting that in the hands of communitarians not only is the function of community to carry out a kind of moral criticism of modern life, but also that it places some unacceptable limits on individual freedom.

In the majority of discussions, the philosophical position of communi-tarianism is usually cast as the binary opposite of liberalism. Its starting point is that the majority of liberals make the mistake of not recognizing the proper value of community for social and political solidarity. As Charles Taylor has argued, the major complaint by communitarians of liberal thought is that it not only presupposes an atomistic conception of the individual and holds the view that human agency is to all intents and purposes a matter of freedom of choice, but it also ignores the fundamentally *dialogical* character of human life (Taylor, 1994). This argument conforms to the well-rehearsed debate in philosophy which leads liberals and communitarians into an ontological and epistemological dispute based on a futile argument: the individual-as-socially-independent (liberal individualism) versus the individual-as-socially-embedded (communitarianism).

From a critical sociological perspective, it can be argued that liberalism and communitarianism are twins of a kind (even if they are ideological opposites): Both positions are promulgated by charismatic political extremists who want to remake the world in their own understanding because they believe they know what makes human-kind tick; and both understand the power of culture as a political weapon. The simplicity and coherence of each of these political ideologies is similarly seductive, but the principles on which they are based rarely stand up to the already existing social reality. In the place of social reality, we are instead treated to merely a bluster of political motives.

Also, moving beyond the fatuous debate about metaphysical first-principles, the pragmatist philosopher Richard Rorty (1991) sidesteps the expected and discusses two common sense and ultimately more politically useful communitarian objections towards liberalism. The first is the empirical argument that the already existing liberal sociality and its extant political order cannot continue to sustain the relentless effects of its principled individualism. The second is the moral objection that socially embedded individuals, and the neo-liberal polities that they continue to elect to represent them, cannot go on neglecting humanity's collective responsibilities for its social and cultural (and we might add, natural) environment.

This political version of communitarianism is opposed to what it sees as the inadequate morality of 'until further notice' relations entered between any miscellany of individuals lacking the binding commitment that should be mainstay of any interacting community. In the hands of communitarians, the function of community is to carry out a kind of moral criticism of modern life. In this sense, communitarianism is nothing less than a heartfelt plea for a different politics which takes into account local ways of knowing in order to mobilize individual responsibility. If there is a maxim for political communitarianism, it is 'small is best'; 'Only when an individual and family cannot do something should a local group, a school or church take responsibility. Only if it is beyond the local group should responsibility be passed up to city, state or federal government' (Smith, 1996). In a nutshell, communitarians mobilize the community concept as a peg on which to hang a pointed response to how far people's lives have become privatized and detached from their mutual responsibilities by their individualized adherence to liberal ideal of self-interested competitiveness.

The most extreme political communitarians, like some of their philosophical counterparts, imagine that what was once a more socially and politically informed collective life has collapsed into a self-consuming Hobbesian world. However, it might be argued that, at the very least, all political communitarians are of the belief that too many of our universal values have been steadily rubbed away. This nostalgia for an imagined past is reflected in the writings of US communitarians such as Robert Putnam (2000), who argues that too many people today 'bowl alone' and Michael Sandel (1996), who laments the disappearance of the 'proud craftsmen' of the Jacksonian era (*see* 'Social Capital'). Arguably, the major ideological idea of communitarianism, then, is that we need to return to the quotidian of a golden age that nonetheless remains concertedly in the present.

Accordingly, political communitarianism has managed to yoke its adherents' nostalgia for the past to an active political consciousness in the works of writers and political activists such as Amitai Etzioni, whose idea of the 'responsive community' is promulgated larger-than-life on his personal web site (www.amiati-notes.com). Etzioni imagines contemporary Western culture as one in which a more itinerant, anonymous life has taken shape and where people no longer know or care about their fellow citizens. The contemporary world is one in which individuals find themselves oppressed and detached from the local communities of which they are a part. What these actively political communitarians do is not just make community their window on the world but mobilize it as a damning critique of individualized dreams and delusions, and in particular those descendents of the feckless and wasteful age of 1960s affluence. Etzioni's critics suggest that this is not a world which actually existed, of course, but intimations of a fictional world that are meant to spool through the mind like an American feel-good movie, which political communitarians hope will end up unfurling, ideologically intact – tales of allegorical certainty: of well-mannered children;

father at work and mother in the kitchen; and all the family resting on the Sabbath (*see* Etzioni's web site for more details).

There is no questioning the sparkle and the pleasure these communitarian tales give their adherents in need of a retro sugar fix. However, this retro version of community also provides a template for those communitarians who imagine that the majority have neither the social capital nor the moral instruction manuals to go about their day-to-day lives – the same people who have no commitment to mutual solidarity and demand too many rights as opposed to meeting their obligations to the community at large.

Since the 1990s, communitarianism has become one of the main exemplars of the 'Third Way' (Giddens, 1998) political aesthetic, embraced by academics, think tanks and policy makers alike for its discourse of pulling-togetherness and its social control function, as well as its ability to operate between state control and the free market (*see* 'Setting the Record Straight'; 'Political Community'). In both the United States and the United Kingdom, this 'Third Way' has also been adopted by both the political Left and the Right, who it might be argued have mobilized the idea of community to reconceive the social class inequalities associated with dreary old Marxism and re-wardrobe them as social inclusion agendas which in their manifestos emphasize responsibilities as well as rights but without any commitment to the economic redistribution of wealth – an idealized ideology of community, an object of belief requiring no apparent party subscriptions, only a commitment to some inclusivist but ultimately essentialist communitarian ideal. Left or Right, the recipe is repetitive, additive, more community, just like the imagined past, impressing 'Third Way' adherents with its inexhaustible quality of power and plunder. The basic line is: more community – and more – still more community – still more.

There are no indications that this ersatz 'brand' of community sloganeering is running out of energy, and it continues to be formulated by an overwhelming and accelerating epidemic of nostalgia for the certitudes of the past. Yet, as Zygmunt Bauman, one of communitarianism's major critics, has suggested, this is hardly an adequate political agenda for dealing with contemporary social and economic problems which have their roots in global not local contexts:

> Communitarianism is unlikely to mitigate, let alone eradicate, the pains it promises to cure, though it accumulates its emotional capital and

creams off political profits on the strength of that promise. A deep flaw resides in its endemic inadequacy to the task it was conceived to resolve – insofar as that task consists of eradicating the causes of the misery which prompted its constituency to seek remedy in the first place, so made them wish 'to do something about globalization'. Rather than bridling the globalization forces and staving off the dire consequences of their free rein, the political fragmentation, profusion of hostilities and breakdown of solidarity, which communitarianism is capable of generating (perhaps bound to generate), would only pave the way to yet more absolute, unchallenged domination of the forces it meant to tame and keep at a distance (Bauman, 2002: 85).

Bauman's other crucial point is that communitarianism tries to indemnify the future by proffering a version of community that represents certain kinds of choices and selectivities – with inevitable exclusions and inclusions – which set limits and restrict individual freedom. Bauman rejects the naïve liberal position and knows that we are all part of a shared human world. But where communitarians suggest that liberal individual aloofness is nothing short of a profanation, Bauman alerts us to the point that modern lives have become, more than ever before, the fruit of freedom and contingency: of existential subjectivity and chance associations and as such we must respect people's individual differences as well as their cultural differences.

In developing this critique, Bauman argues that the watchword of communitarianism is this: 'choose but choose wisely'; and what this implies is 'choose what others have chosen and you can't go wrong'. For Bauman, communitarians do not really believe in freedom, then, only a circumscribed and simplified version of community which:

> means a lot of sameness and a bare minimum of variety. The simplification on offer can only be attained by the separation of differences: by reducing the probability of their meeting and narrowing the extent of communication. This kind of communal unity rests on division, segregation and keeping of distance. These are the virtues figuring most prominently in the advertising leaflets of communitarian shelters (Bauman, 2001: 148).

In a nutshell, communitarians speak from their ideologically and traditionally formed Anglo–Saxon values rather than from the varied and authentic experiences of cultural diversity. The more communitarianism is unpacked, the more it becomes apparent that its use of the idea of community is less a respecter of cultural difference and more an ambiguous returning fiction. In Bauman's terminology, communitarians legislate the future by re-imagining the past and use it to maintain hegemonic ways of seeing. In other words, communitarianism-made policy becomes a staged reality, while reality itself seems increasingly to dissolve into discourse. In Bauman's view, such discourses are always likely to turn into the flipside of the warm and cosy community which ultimately see forlorn hopes and dreams replaced by the foolproof unifying traditions of 'us' and 'them', 'same' and 'other'.

As Bauman goes on to point out, when communitarians refer to an emancipatory politics of 'difference', they are speaking about something very different to liberals. For liberals, 'difference' is *external* to individuals, in the sense that it refers to that realm of choices concerning the manifold ways of being human and of living one's life. For communitarians, however, 'difference' is instead a 'refusal to the contrary' and very much a duty-bound form of 'difference' to be *internalized* by individual members of the group. As a result, Bauman's disdain for communitarianism is severe. This is because, whatever happens, when it comes to freedom, it is inevitable that communitarian 'difference' will always stand for the power of the community to *limit* the freedom of social actors (Bauman, 1997: 188). Communitarianism is ultimately repressive because its top–down ideology does not permit or make room for proper involvement of those lives it purports to represent. It cannot because its solutions are always guaranteed in advance and, in effect, it silences the Other it claims to represent because its certainist discourse depends on the Other's silence.

This criticism is best illustrated in Etzioni's suggestion that, in order to remedy the current discrepancy between social order and freedom in US society, responsibilities should wax towards rights and rights should wane towards the responsibilities. However, such a strategy compounds rather than addresses the problem of extant social inequalities, such as those built on gender differences. This criticism is reflected in the feminist challenge to communitarianism which argues that 'communities' often make claims on their members which are based on extant and often insidious hierarchies of patriarchal domination and subordination and that units of social relations invoked by communitarians, such as the family, neighbourhood and nation, are themselves often found to be 'troubling paradigms of social relationship and community life' (Friedman, 1989: 279).

The foregoing critique suggests that communitarianism is politically constrained by its commitment to re-write the same old verses while the world itself continues to move on in ever new ways. Indeed, we have seen that if communitarian policy agendas are obsessive for an imagined, imaginary or unimaginable golden age, they are also unable to deal with individuals and social groups that slip between the cracks of postulated communities. Ultimately, we can conclude that political communitarianism suffers from being intellectually diminutive in its certainties, when what a world as culturally diverse as our own demands is a politics so large in its openness to being absolutely sure about nothing.

See also: *'Cosmopolitanism, Worldliness and the Cultural Intermediaries'; 'Political Community'; 'Social Capital'.*

REFERENCES

Bellah, R., Madsen, R., Sullivan, W., Swidler, A. and Tipton, S. (1987) *Habits of the Heart*. Berkeley: University of California Press.

Bauman, Z. (1997) *Postmodernity and its Discontents*. Cambridge: Polity Press in association with Blackwell.

Bauman, Z. (2001) *Community: Seeking Safety in an Insecure World*. Cambridge: Polity Press.

Bauman, Z. (2002) *Society Under Siege*. Cambridge: Polity Press.

Beck, U. (2002) 'Zombie Categories: Interview with Ulrich Beck', in U. Beck and E. Beck-Gernsheim (eds) *Individualization*. London: Sage.

Delanty, G. (2003) *Community*. London: Routledge.

Festenstein, M. (1997) *Pragmatism and Political Theory*. Cambridge: Polity Press.

Friedman, M. (1989) 'Feminism and Modern Friendship: Dislocating the Community', *Ethics*, 99 (2): January.

Giddens, A. (1998) *The Third Way*. Cambridge: Polity Press.

Putnam, R. D. (2000) *Bowling Alone: the Collapse and Revival of American Community*. New York: Simon & Schuster (Touchstone).

Rorty, R. (1991) *Objectivity, Relativism and Truth: Philosophical Papers 1*. Cambridge: Cambridge University Press.

Sandel, M. (1996) *Democracy's Discontent*. Cambridge: Cambridge University Press.

Smith, G. (1996) *Community – arianism*. http://homepages.uel.ac.uk/G.Smith/community-arainism/gsum.html

Taylor, C. (1994) 'The Politics of Recognition', in A. Gutmann (ed.) *Multiculturalism: Examining the Politics of Recognition*. Princeton: Princeton University Press.

IMAGINARY COMMUNITIES

Not to be confused with 'imagined communities', this is the term employed by Phillip E. Wegner (2002) in his attempt to identify, describe and analyse communities that are always a fantastical projection. In other words, these are communities that offer alternative ways of conjuring, narrating and making the world. To this extent, imaginary communities are interpretive or hermeneutic and have their essence in Romanticism (life as an act of artistic and inventive creation), which can be contrasted with the Technologism (life as a technological problem to be solved): imagination in opposition to reason and goals means rationality, subjectivity in opposition to objectivity, and poetic, private introspection against prosaic, social institution.

Section Outline: The starting point of this chapter is the argument that community has the ability to fire the imagination like no other idea – to pursue an ideal, to embody a dream, to struggle against loss. With this in mind, it suggests that the idea of imaginary community is in one sense another expression of utopia, or in other words, a paradise on earth whose vista shimmers in a rose-tinted haze and is always accompanied by a home (or some other form of habitat) at its centre. After making the distinction between abstract *and* concrete *utopias and the differences and similarities between the concepts of ideology and utopia, which are all discussed with the aid of a good range of examples, the chapter concludes with a detailed discussion of Foucault's imaginary community of heterotopia, a fallen paradise, which is associated with deviance, is decentred and found in no place in particular.*

Imaginary communities are not so much real (they rarely reflect actual places in the world), but 'have material, pedagogical, and ultimately political effects, shaping the ways people understand and, as a consequence, act in their worlds' (Wegner, 2002: xvi). What tends to unite the adherents of imaginary communities is the seduction of a life path not as yet travelled, and that seduction takes its force from their instinctive (e.g., religious, philanthropic, nostalgic, etc.) and collective political belief (usually leftist, anti-capitalist and/or ecological) that the present world is simply not good enough. Yet, we should not ignore the fact that imaginary communities also tend to found their impetus in the partial editing of the everyday, or what Hegel called the 'prose of the world', implying that there is something important about the world that is very ordinary and which defies orchestration, ideology and indoctrination.

In one sense, the idea of imaginary communities is an alternative description of utopianism. Utopianism is a form of political thinking which presents an ideal model of an imaginary way of living, its aim being to relativize the world of the present, and to show that the reality we inhabit is not inevitable and that human imagination can provide an opposition to dominant ideologies, such as capitalism. What unites utopians is the seduction of a not-as-yet-travelled path, and that seduction takes its force from their instinctive sense that the present does not live up to their aspirations. To this extent, utopianism is a way of galvanizing action, a way of making a dream a reality, with the intention of changing history. As Manguel and Guadalupi (1999: 675) put it, in characteristically leftist utopian terms, in that essential companion to imaginary communities *The Dictionary of Imaginary Places*:

> Politically, Utopia is a republic in which there is no private property and in which everyone takes seriously his duty towards the community. No one is rich, but there is no poverty and no one risks going short of anything. The public storehouses are perpetually full, thanks to the efficiency of the economy and rationally planned distribution of national resources. The abolition of private property and money has wiped out the passion for property and money; it also led to the disappearance of all crimes and abuses connected with the desire for wealth and superiority, and for the same reasons, poverty itself has vanished.

What this quotation suggests is that it is the description, rather than the actual making, of utopia that has hitherto enchanted the human spirit. This should not surprise us since, as Bose (1997) points out, the word 'utopia' is itself a play on the two Greek words *outopia* (meaning 'no place') and *eutopia* (meaning 'good' or 'fortunate place'). Since the publication in 1516 of Thomas More's (1997) classic political fantasy *Utopia*, the term has come to refer to an ideal or longed-for life which paradoxically cannot exist.

Notwithstanding this last observation, the literature does nonetheless distinguish between *abstract* utopias, which tend to be contented with expressing their desire of another world, and *concrete* utopias, which carry with them the hope that another world is achievable (Levitas, 1990). A good example of an abstract utopia is leisure time, which might be understood as an oppositional response, or at least an attempt to escape the drudgery of work through 'the right to laziness' (Wegner, 2002: 21). While a good example of a concrete utopia is the Kantian model of cultural discourse, which might take place around a dinner table: where the enjoyment of good food and drink is accompanied by the mutual contentment of social sociability through conversation. Agnes Heller suggests that such instances of cultural discourse effectively constitute 'other worlds' – what we might call *virtual communities*, because they are fictions shared among friends and it this that makes them concrete. In other words, they are realities in which virtuality and actuality come together. It is here that utopia is made tangible – if 'only under the condition of the partial suspension of the pragmatic, the theoretical, and the practical pursuits in life' (Heller, 1999: 133).

Another good example of a *concrete* utopia is Charles Taylor's (2004) idea of the 'social imaginary'. This concept is concerned with the ways in which modern men and women imagine their social existence, how this fits together with what other people imagine, how these sorts of connections impact on social relations between people, the expectations that follow and how these are met. To this extent, Taylor is also concerned with the 'deeper normative notions and images' – narratives such as fables, myths, poetry, stories, songs, etc. – which provide the basis of any social imaginary. These not only provide members of imaginary communities with the sort of mutual understanding that makes common practices possible, but they also give them their shared sense of legitimacy. As Taylor points out, social imaginaries can linger on the margins of a culture or society for many years without being concretely realized, but they can also arrive with a shock and move like a shot towards the centre. An excellent application of the way in which a marginal social imaginary can move to the centre of politics is *The May Day Manifesto*, Williams (1968) cited by Chris Rojek as being 'one of the fullest expressions of the New Left's social imaginary', this 'demanded a 'socialist national plan' that would not only tackle necessary economic reforms, but establish the strategy for changing the culture of private competition and possessive individualism' (2003: 157).

The distinction between *abstract* utopias and *concrete* utopias can also be understood through the work of Karl Mannheim (1936). Preempting Levitas, Mannheim distinguishes between ideological thought, which he depicts as an idealized version of the current reality, and utopian thought, which always seeks a new kind of society. However, Mannheim argues that the concept of utopia is generally used to convey both of these interpretations and he compared and contrasted it with ideology. From Mannheim's perspective, both *concrete* utopias and *abstract* utopias might express unattainable ideals, but whereas the former outlook effectively inspires hopeful political activity in the direction of some cherished ideal, the latter is merely ideological in the sense that it serves the interests of the status quo. On this account, 'the right to laziness' as an oppositional leisure response to the drudgery of work is nothing less than the unrealizability of a utopian ideal, because although the individuals involved might temporarily escape the clutches of work, capitalism continues to strip them of the creativity that is their human potential. What Mannheim's work suggests is, although utopian ideas can generally be distinguished from ideologies because they possess a potentially transforming capacity, we should also bear in mind that every utopia is also potentially an ideology which offers its own set of beliefs or true ideas about what constitutes the world.

There are other ways in which it might be said that imaginary communities are actualized. The evidence for this lies in Bauman's (2003) observation that, however conceived, utopias have throughout history been associated with and as rule confined to clearly defined places or territories. In this regard, he points out that the utopian imagination has historically been fundamentally architectural and its concrete expressions have usually been found in urban environments. What Bauman is referring to here is the legacy of ideological utopian experiments that emerged with the onset of modernity, offering visions of a life from above in which freedom was by 'necessity understood and obediently, willingly, and gratefully accepted' (p. 16) by the poorer denizens of society, which are charted by Darley (2007) in her book *Villages of Vision*. Darley traces more than 400 of these imaginary communities in Britain, all planned from scratch with the designated mission of placating the excesses of modern living and founded with the aim of realizing an ideal form of society. Examples of these are Titus Salt's purpose-built industrial village established to house mill workers near Shipley in West Yorkshire; Ebeneezer Howard's 'Garden Cities', such as Welwyn and Letchworth built in the early twentieth century to solve the twin problems of the congested city and of the 'undeveloped' countryside; and the Bourneville Village Trust, built in 1900 by the Cadbury family to improve the living of working men and women through the provision of houses with gardens and open space.

In his recent photography collection *Sweet Earth: Experimental Utopias in America*, Sternfeld (2007) shows that there is also a utopian impulse deeply engraved in the history of urban geography of the United States. As Dyer (2007) points out, Sternfeld identifies three distinct periods in which these utopian experiments flourished. The first of these occurred between 1810 and 1860. This was a result of the reaction to the dehumanizing effects of the factory work. Subsequently, concrete imaginary communities emerged at irregular intervals, but it was not until the 1960s and the burgeoning hippy counterculture that there was another expansive growth in utopian activity. The third phase, underway since the beginning of the 1990s, has seen the spread of gated communities, eco-villages and co-housing communities.

Another application of imaginary communities which demonstrates this ability to meld the material and immaterial, in ways that are located outside of the places we generally take for granted as the already existing reality, is the concept of heterotopia. This concept is found in the work of the philosopher Michel Foucault, who defines it by contrasting heterotopias with utopias, which as we have seen often present themselves as alternative ways of living in a perfected form. According to Foucault (1984), while this ultimately renders utopias 'unreal' places or spaces, it nonetheless means that they can be contrasted with heterotopias, which are 'real' places 'without geographical markers' found in all societies and cultures. These heterotopias effectively constitute liminal 'counter-sites' (*see* 'Liminality, Communitas and Anti-Structure') of concrete utopia, which, in the forms they take paradoxically, lie outside all other places in any given society or culture, while nonetheless being actually localized in the already existing reality.

Foucault identifies two main categories of heterotopia. There are the pre-modern heterotopias of crisis, otherwise known as 'elsewhere' places which tended to be relegated to the margins of modern societies. Foucault has in mind here privileged places such as single-sex boarding schools where young boys are taken through a particular rite of passage; sacred places such as pilgrimage sites; and forbidden places such as brothels, where people visit prostitutes for sex. In assessing the ways in which these 'elsewhere' places have been transformed in modern societies, Foucault offers his second category of heterotopia, which at their most basic are the places of deviance, such as prisons and mental asylums, where those considered abnormal by the standards of modern norms can be spatially isolated.

In developing a more elaborate conception of this second category of heterotopia, Foucault's analysis suggests that these places of deviance must be understood in relation to the kind of society in which they occur. In modern societies, Foucault suggests, heterotopias have the ability to juxtapose what might conventionally be seen as several contradictory spaces into a single real place. In common with *liquid modern communities*, they also exist in *pointillist* time, which means they are experienced as episodic. Heterotopias also contain, within these sequestered spaces, their very own systems of 'opening and closing' that both isolate them from the rest of society and operate to exclude those who do not have the necessary credentials to enter (*see* 'The "Dark Side" of Community'). Last but not least, heterotopias, like all other communities, function by way of opposition; that is, they have a tendency to unfold 'between two extreme poles'. However, heterotopias offer spaces of compensation (rather than the illusion of utopia) that function in relation to the way that their (deviant) populations understand they are imagined by the rest of society.

Foucault's work raises the question as to why some men and women seem to want to abandon the centre and the real for the remote and the imaginary. What his analysis suggests is that a sense of recompense for a life that is not being lived in the confines of a modern society leads people down the track of heterotopia: reality and rationality are not on their menus, since what they are after is an unmediated immediacy of something altogether out of the ordinary. What it also suggests is that if imagining community often invests in the pursuit of the ideal and embodies particular dreams, it is also given to the melancholic as well as the optimistic, the toxic as well as the beatific. In Foucault's concept of heterotopias, these 'positive' and 'negative' imaginings get mixed up with one another.

A good example of some recent research which illustrates to good effect how heterotopias operate in modern societies is Blackshaw and Crabbe's (2004) discussion of car cruising. They argue that car cruising is a 'deviant' leisure activity with its own kind of detached existence, of being 'in' but not 'of the space it temporarily occupies', and which is capable of transforming ordinary life into a form of theatre. They also contend that car cruising is a 'deviant' leisure activity as much without a history as it is one without a future and that car cruises are imaginary communities, whose inspiration tends to spring from the performativity of individual cruisers: they are both events for consumption and things to be consumed by. The affiliation found at cruises is not really one of friendship, or of a community proper, but one of symbiosis and its only glue is cruisers' insatiable appetites to connect with like-minded others.

Consequently, Blackshaw and Crabbe assert that car cruising is unequivocally *not* about community in the orthodox meaning since its narrative structure is effectively sustained by the collective imaginations of cruisers, manufactured only for the time being, paraded as a performative community aching to be credible. Cruising is merely about performing modified cars, performing bodies. Yet, despite its apparent simplicity as a leisure activity, cruising is difficult to locate. First, in its disorganization, the culture of cruising is dislocated in no place in particular; it is always on the move and the theatre for its performativity is always at an improvised stage set. There are 'official' cruises and 'unofficial' cruises, and the latter tend to be 'deviant'.

Blackshaw and Crabbe's research also suggests that the majority of cruisers are working-class young men who are players who play out their own kind of magic, which they find with cars and women. Cruising has its own vernacular which is misogynist. As well as being sexist and fraternal, cruising is also a hedonistic feeling of freedom and irresponsibility. Cruisers attend cruises in search of a familiar truth, nothing mysterious as such, just something which can be made tangible with something on four wheels. Indeed, as Blackshaw and Crabbe point out, the discursive field in which cruising constitutes itself allows for the deconstruction of taken-for-granted hegemonic norms. It is in the process of this deconstruction that individual cruisers are able to perform, not only an augmentation of their existential capacities for the affectual and the imaginative, but also experience an atmosphere of intensified engagement with other like-minded people.

On the face of it, cruising has no apparent hierarchies, only aesthetics, everyone included, nothing excluded, not even the fumes from the engines and burning tyres, which pervade the cruise scene as surely as a security blanket – just the amazing reality of an ephemerally flowing magical leisure world played out with a creative intervention. Yet, when you begin to look a little closer, Blackshaw and Crabbe argue, car cruising is a flat and featureless leisure activity, with few distinguishing characteristics or points of difference, a harsh mechanical environment in which it is easy for men to be sexist and obtuse towards women. Cruising is in the final analysis an ephemeral optative heterotopia, which is, on the face of it, determined by choice, but is to all intents and purposes

dictated largely by gender, age and ability to afford the right performance kit. It is also a mode of performance that swaggers with an uncomplicated capitalistic atmosphere: a cultural mix of heady marketeering
combined with trappy commercialism and personal aspiration; it is mass
similitude dressed up as individual preferences.

What this discussion of heterotopia demonstrates is that what people
are often looking for in imaginary communities these days are simply
places where they can, for the time being, express 'deviant' interests and
identities with similarly minded others. It also confirms Bauman's argument that if the meaning of utopia used to lie in the future, in the contemporary world men and women seem intent on living it in the now.
Indeed, utopia today often manifests itself in no place in particular, is
hardly ever a one-off act, tends to be imagined 'from below' rather than
'from above', and is more often than not found 'homeless and floating,
no more hoping to strike its roots, to 're-embed' (Bauman, 2003: 22). It
was perhaps with this kind of observation in mind that Foucault (1984)
said that 'the ship is the heterotopia par excellence. In civilizations without boats, dreams dry up, espionage takes the place of adventure, and the
police take the place of pirates'.

See also: *'Imagined Communities'; 'Hermeneutic Communities'; 'Liquid Modern
Communities'; 'Political Community'; 'The "Dark Side" of Community'; 'The Symbolic
Construction of Community'; 'Virtual Communities'.*

FURTHER READING

The essential companion to imaginary communities is the *The Dictionary
of Imaginary Places* (Manguel and Guadalupi, 1999). Wegner (2002)
explores the utopia literature in a great deal of depth and as such provides an excellent bibliography.

REFERENCES

Bauman, Z. (2003) 'Utopia with No Topos', *History of the Human Sciences*, 16 (1):
    11–25.
Blackshaw, T. and Crabbe, T. (2004) *New Perspectives on Sport and 'Deviance':
    Consumption, Performativity and Social Control*. Abingdon: Routledge.
Bose (1997) 'Foreword', in T. More (1997) *Utopia*. Ware: Wordsworth.
Darley, G. (2007) *Villages of Vision: A Study of Strange Utopias*. Nottingham: Five
    Leaves.
Dyer, G. (2007) 'Look Right, Then Left', *The Guardian*, 6th January.
Heller, A. (1999) *A Theory of Modernity*. Oxford: Blackwell.

Foucault, M. (1984) 'Of Other Spaces (1967), Heterotopias'. Translated by Jay Miskowiec. http://foucault.info/documents/heteroTopia/foucault.heteroTopia.en.html

Levitas, R. (1990) *The Concept of Utopia*. Syracuse: Syracuse University Press.

Manguel, A. and Guadalupi, G. (1999) *The Dictionary of Imaginary Places*. New York: Hartcourt, Inc.

Mannheim, K. (1936) *Ideology and Utopia*. London: Routledge and Kegan Paul.

More, T. (1997) *Utopia*. Ware: Wordsworth.

Rojek, C. (2003) *Stuart Hall*. Cambridge: Polity Press.

Sternfield, J. (2007) *Sweet Earth: Experimental Utopias in America*. Göttingen: Steidl.

Sternfeld, J. (2008) *Sweet Earth: Experimental Utopias in America*. London: Steidl.

Taylor, C. (2004) *Modern Social Imaginaries*. Durham: Duke University Press.

Wegner, P. E. (2002) *Imaginary Communities*. London: University of California Press.

Williams, R. (1968) (ed.) *The May Day Manifesto*. Harmondsworth: Penguin.

NOSTALGIA

As the great Czech novelist-cum-philosopher Milan Kundera (2002) points out in his novel *Ignorance*, the word 'nostalgia' is derived immediately from the Greek *Nostos* (return) and *Algos* (suffering). In its primary sense, therefore, the idea is suggestive of the sort of anguish that is caused by 'an unappeased yearning to return'. Full of the ache and melancholy of reminiscence for home, its meaning freighted with implication, 'nostalgia' is the word for what will always be yet never quite was. Raymond Williams once remarked that we also need to understand community in a similar way; that is, as a special way of being together that 'always has been'. What this suggests is not only that community is always accompanied by its own conflicting and ambivalent tug of territory – the need to get away from home, the ache of wanting to return – but that it is indelibly linked to nostalgia.

Section Outline: After outlining and discussing the relationship between nostalgia, community and the contemporary ways in which individuals relate to one another and the world, this chapter goes on to explore in some depth how, according to Blackshaw (2003), the link between community and nostalgia is ineradicable in sustaining what he calls the leisure life-world of the 'lads' in his book Leisure Life: Myth, Masculinity and Modernity.

The two concepts of nostalgia and community are indelibly connected as they simultaneously evoke the idea of a past that is committed to memory on the basis of both enchantment and appetite. As is suggested in the chapter 'Hermeneutic Communities', even if it was thought that, as a matter of principle, or definitional consistency, that the two should be kept apart, this would be out of the question, since the modern use of community is hermeneutical, and hermeneutics is burdened by a romantic sensibility, which by its very nature evokes feelings of nostalgia (Heller, 1999). What the two concepts also have in common is that they are enjoined by the idea of home. If 'community' is another word for 'home', the word 'nostalgia' is used in modern ways of thinking which understand the human relationship to the world as one of permanent homesickness. What this suggests is that, in this coming together of community and nostalgia, there is a strong connection between the themes of loss, longing, regret and suffering, all of which are accentuated as a result of the undeviating changes and transformations that are the hallmark of modern living.

Kundera argues that we tend to think of nostalgia as something that concerns modern men and women more as we get older, and that as such it is the preserve of the old: 'the more vast time the amount of time we've left behind us, the more irresistible is the voice calling us to return to it' (2002: 77). This is really a facade. The truth is that, as we get older, each moment of our lives becomes more and more precious, and we are more likely to stop wasting our time over recollections about the past. According to Kundera, this is the 'mathematical paradox' of nostalgia; it is at its most powerful in our youth, when the amount of our lives passed is somewhat small.

What Kundera is suggesting here is that we live in an age when even nostalgia is not quite what it used to be! This theme is taken up by Zygmunt Bauman (2000) in his books about *liquid modernity*, where he argues that just as our contemporary age is one of rapid technological advancements, it is also one when social *relationships*, including communal ones, have become episodic, and in some cases, merely mechanical ways of *relating* built on speeded-up separations (*see* 'Liquid Modern Communities'). Bauman also suggests that the overriding ethos of the *Zeitgeist* is the preservation of youth combined with an obsession for specificity, for 'really' *feeling* what you do and living life to the full. What all this suggests is that not only are we constantly trying to authenticate our realities in going about our everyday lives, but in this beginning and ending formula of experience and expectations, we are all also inevitably drawn to loss, to nostalgia.

Bauman's ideas can be seen in the way that *virtual communities* operate on the basis of nostalgia, where men and women are always on the lookout for shared *identities* that connote past encounters, as well as those spurned or not acted upon. High on the familiarity of it all, we log on to *eBay* to bid for old albums and childhood comics and toys, download clips of concerts and pop videos from *YouTube* we never got around to seeing, sign into *Friends Reunited* or *Classmates* and reconnect with people we never much liked in the first place, and join *Second Life* as 'avatars' (hot chicks, rock chicks, chick magnets, sporty types and so on) of what we have always wanted or could not be, or were too embarrassed to make the effort.

The relationship between community and nostalgia is also explored in some detail by Tony Blackshaw in his book *Leisure Life: Myth Masculinity and Modernity*. It is often said that each generation creates its own brand of nostalgia, and in this book, the author explores the leisure lives of a group of working-class men intent on making pilgrimages into their own shared past. Here, community is imagined as a double movement: back in time and back a particular place. Drawing on Bauman's distinction between solid modernity and liquid modernity (*see* 'Liquid Modern Communities'), the crux of the thesis is that 'the lads" collective leisure experiences are animated by their belief in an *imagined community* which is perceived as the cornerstone of their shared masculine working-class existence. 'The lads' only feel 'real' in relation to this leisure life-world. There is a warmth, a particular feeling of home about this life-world, which offers 'the lads' a protective cocoon where they are 'naturally' safeguarded from the uncertainties of liquid modern change. They close its shutters to guard against their mutual homemade models of themselves losing credibility and the intricate cogs of their masculine realism from being damaged or lost. The leisure life-world enables them to keep these ready-made narratives alive in their collective memory, their own private gallery, which is the legacy of their youth.

Blackshaw's central argument is that it is this shared passion for a *solid modern* missing world, sometimes proudly resurrected and celebrated, sometimes merely borne out of the private burden of individuality, which gives this shared leisure life-world its weight and its depth. The book charts 'the lads" intermittent forays into Leeds city centre on Friday and Saturday nights, which constitute a memorable vindication of this missing world. Nights out with 'the lads' tend to spin themselves out into a familiar web which feels like one of those re-unions which famous rock bands have when the group gets back together after playing with other people. When 'the lads' are on stage together once again, it feels great and everything just clicks into place. They drink their beer faster than is good for them, and conversation moves from subject to subject. They finish each other's sentences, and communicate, more remarkably, without speaking at all. With a real affinity, and in the spirit of the communion that exists between them, they use gestures known only to them.

'The lads', in a collective act of nostalgic remembrance, conjure the leisure life-world, in the process restoring a past reality, if not in its entirety, as a form of resurrection, which is another expression for a life beyond death, but carrying with it a kind of immortality. Here, community closes the gap between the then and the now in the minds of 'the lads'. Near and far become elided, then is juxtaposed with now, and a version of community arises in the form of the leisure life-world, which gives 'the lads' a secular version of Tillich's (1952) 'power of being', which, as the philosopher Martin Heidegger would have said, enables them to overcome the threat of their non-being.

This leisure life-world operates in the cusp between imaginary reality and the really existing reality (*see* 'Imaginary Communities'), which pass through each other, their shapes muddled, not a perfect fit, but awfully close. Here, the virtual and the actual are hard to prise apart; as a result, we are insistently forced to acknowledge that there is no solid ground of unassailable truth on which this leisure life-world rests; it blurs the boundaries between the virtual and the real. It is a remarkable creation, not quite of the world. The gap, the slippage, the contingency of the discourse of the leisure life-world and the already existing reality itself is the point.

However, on these nights out, 'the lads' do not so much re-live their youth as recreate through their leisure its unheroic aftermath. In truth, the leisure life-world has, to use the rock band analogy once again, been turned into a sort of heritage museum for ageing lads, which Blackshaw argues in recent years has become more a duty than a pleasure, and whose nagging subliminal power reverberates only on the edges of individual lives lived in the main elsewhere. Indeed, although it is the ultimate experience of a *solidly modern* leisure life 'the lads' desire, but cannot really capture, it does not deter them from endeavouring to regain the power and certainties of its past, and seeking a realm of mutual happiness that was once upon a time theirs.

Outside the leisure life-world, resignation and disillusionment are the nearest things 'the lads' have to freedom, or so it seems. In the fluidity of *liquid modernity*, they have to watch powerless as the Other invades uninvited into their existential and material realms: women controlling their bedrooms and telling them what to do, women and black people taking their jobs, buying their houses, taking over their shops and their schools. But, in the leisure life-world, 'the lads' are in control. Here, they are determined to ensure that their leisure lives are unaffected by difference. In the leisure life-world, the features of the Other begin to elongate and liquefy, swell and then re-solidify; like Sartre's *le visqueux*, they are transformed into 'the lads'' own DIY custom-made creations.

Take, for example, women, who can never exist as cheerful subjects of their own lives in the leisure life-world, but exist merely as scaffolding for 'the lads' shared dreams – happy and loving shags without a single care except perhaps 'to go down on' working-class white blokes. That these characterizations are not 'real' is neither here nor there; 'the lads' simply have to be convinced that they are. What is important for 'the lads' is the *meaning for them* of these characterizations to their version of truth, which is something that enables them to form what they recognize *is* the world when they are at leisure together. Women have to be wiped out from a *solid modern* story in which they have no place, excluded from the leisure world that has created them. These characterizations of the Other become symbols of subjugation, power and knowledge, the luscious fruit of a *solid* leisure life lived in a *solid* version of truth. The 'universal' truth of the rationality which divides 'the lads' and Others into two categories: us and them, same and Other.

Aware of the utter contingency of their individual being-in-the-world, and aware too that collectively they are no longer really together, or at least are only intermittently so, 'the lads' are anxiously aware of their non-being, because their collective existence is threatened by it. In the leisure life-world, 'the lads' have the best of both worlds; they have their nostalgic myth and are able to relativize it as a *contingent* leisure experience which has its own monologic. Indeed, the *modus operandi* of 'the lads' leisure together always presumes this form of closure – the conformation of hegemonic masculinity and the restoration of disrupted stability, which provide intimations of the past world of communal bliss in a protected time space in which the leisure life-world attempts to impose the fixity of a masculinist, working-class myth on to the ostensible fluidity of contemporary everyday life.

Yet, 'the lads'' apparently granite authenticity is not at all what it seems. In common with other *liquid modern* men and women, they find it difficult to remain authentic for long because they simply have too many other choices in their lives. 'The lads' know that the weekend experience of this life-world is just a nostalgic leisure break; they understand this and are resigned to their fate.

There are some critics who would suggest that the nostalgia associated with this leisure life-world has another meaning that is less connected with loss, longing, regret and suffering, and more with an affecting indulgence. In other words, 'the lads' merely wallow in the nostalgia of a backward-looking gaze, remembering the snapshots rather than the long video clips of a past edited of the bits they would rather forget. Scholars of ideology would also add that there is a false consciousness associated with this leisure life-world, in the way that it is both at the same time something nostalgically remembered and magically recreated, but also something suppressed – a denial of the real. However, Blackshaw's reading suggests that it is only because of its own impossibility that the leisure life-world is possible at all. 'The lads' may be figures nostalgically carved out of the past, but their *identities* are maintained in the present, and, in common with other liquid modern men and women, they are *individuals* first and all the rest after. In the words of Bauman, it is this observation that represents the 'irreparable and irredeemable ambivalence' of the leisure life-world of 'the lads'.

See also: *'Community and Identity'; 'Imagined Communities'; 'Imaginary Communities'; 'Liquid Modern Communities'; 'Postmodern Community'; 'Virtual Communities'.*

REFERENCES

Bauman, Z. (2000) *Liquid Modernity*. Cambridge: Polity Press.
Blackshaw, T. (2003) *Leisure Life: Myth Masculinity and Modernity*. London: Routledge.
Heller, A. (1999) *A Theory of Modernity*. Oxford: Blackwell.
Kundera, M. (2002) *Ignorance*. Translated by Linda Asher. London: Faber and Faber.
Tillich, P. (1952) *The Courage to Be*. New Haven: Yale University Press.

key concepts in community studies

THE 'DARK SIDE' OF COMMUNITY

Where the trend is to proffer a wholly positive view of community, what is offered here is a critical deconstruction, a diagnosis of the darkness beneath the surface brightness. What this chapter demonstrates is that to think community is often to forget cultural difference and create hostilities, animosities and/or feuds, which operate as part of an elaborate classificatory symbolic realm of forced differentiation that engrosses some and horrifies others in the same measure – connections that turn simple understandings of good on its head, and ultimately imbue the Other with a history of evil, violence and misunderstanding.

> *Section Outline: After demonstrating that the bright and the dark sides occupy parallel universes in any community milieu, this chapter explores symbolic violence, the malicious conduct exercised on and against 'outsiders' through hostility, the denial of resources, of treating 'them' as inferior, and dealing with 'them' in duplicitous ways. In so doing, the chapter draws extensively on the work of Elias and Scotson to reveal how some populations always and inevitably seem to fail the 'authenticity test' and are cast in the role of 'outsiders' – intruders, trespassers and unwanted visitors – who have broken community's charmed mood. This discussion is extended to explore how in Mary Douglas's words these 'outsiders' are socially constructed by communities through the idea of 'pollution' or dirt. This theme of alienation through classification is thereafter discussed through the work of Zygmunt Bauman, who suggests that inclusivist and exclusivist strategies operate conjointly as part of the practice of any communal domination, however conceived. The final part of the chapter considers the implications of the dark side of community for popular cultural interests such as sport, as well as for understanding the morally abhorrent process of ethnic cleansing.*

What is often overlooked in the community studies literature is that community is always a double. In other words, all its warmth, charm and geniality, notwithstanding, there is much about community that is distinctly unsettling: if one side of its coin is inclusion and harmony, its companion side is always exclusion and oppression. Indeed, to rephrase what Jenny Diski (2008) has said about the family, community is, by its very nature, a breeding ground for both overt and covert operations, its very structure, its system of classification, composed as it is of frontiers and borders which operate by way of secession, tending to encourage animosity, conspiracy and duplicity. Demanding as it often does the faithfulness of its members, and faithful as it is in the way it conceives its enemies, it is regularly the case that 'us' and 'them' rub up against each other like tectonic plates, both within the community, and between the community and its necessary Others (outsiders, strangers, intruders, trespassers, exiles, aliens and other unwanted visitors), sometimes leading to intolerable and incurable conflicts. What this suggests is that the communal solidarity of this dark side is of a territorial army, born not of any generosity of spirit but of fear, sometimes manifesting itself as outright hatred and violence, while on other occasions subjecting the least powerful social actors in communities much more quietly to a form symbolic violence, which not only legitimizes the systems of meaning constructed in the interests of the powerful, but also maintains extant structures of social inequality.

Examples that fit the latter can be found readily in the community studies literature. For example, Elias and Scotson's (1965) classic study *The Established and the Outsiders: A Sociological Enquiry into Community Problems* demonstrates that, under community's ostensibly warm exterior, there are often to be found some old and familiar divides. Drawing on an approach to sociology that explores how communities operate in processual terms, by seeking to understand human relations as interdependent and evolving through the figurations or webs of attachment that the men and women form through their relationships with each other, Elias and Scotson explore the unintended social consequences of specific historical circumstance and how later social formations arise out of earlier ones.

Elias and Scotson's book is fundamentality about one question: Who is allowed to join the 'small community' of Winston Parva? This is the pseudonym they use for the suburb that was the basis of their research and is on the outskirts of the city of Leicester in England, where it was established at the end of the nineteenth century. On the face of it, the answer to this question is: anybody – or so it would seem. After all, Winston Parva is characterized by a wealth of different types of residences, inhabited by a diversity of social classes and social groups, who pursue a range of different interests. But as Elias and Scotson go on to show, community here is much more complex than it would seem on the surface, this is because, in the language of their process sociology, power both *constrains* and *enables* the cut and thrust of interdependent action in the established-outsider figuration in this 'small community' of Winston Parva.

According to Elias and Scotson, the suburb is made up of three residential zones: Zone 2, the oldest part of Winston Parva, which is the hub of the community, comprising various work places and local amenities as well as residences; Zone 1, the smallest area, built by degrees between the wars, and seen locally as a marginally superior residential area to Zone 2, notwithstanding the presence of some poorer 'working-class' housing in the vicinity; and Zone 3 comprising a rented housing estate built on marshy land on the other side of Zone 2. The authors argue that the social networks which operate between the inhabitants of Zones 1 and 2 are highly structured and organizationally far reaching, while Zone 3 is palpably lacking in structure and organization. To this extent, they argue that the inhabitants of Zone 1 and Zone 2 not only share close social ties but also see themselves as representing the community of Winston Parva, while the inhabitants of Zone 3 are imagined as the subsequent Other, the 'outsiders', to themselves, the 'established'.

In this respect, Elias and Scotson offer not so much as a snapshot of present-day community life in Winston Parva, but trace the figuration of a shift that has occurred historically in this suburb – local long-term developments in a particular locality that are largely unplanned and unpredicted. What they are suggesting is that once the residents of Zones 1 and 2 became the hegemonic social group, and with this the residential areas of Zones 1 and 2 the naturalized heart of the community, not only did the distinction between the 'established' and the 'outsiders' become synonymous with belonging and not belonging, respectability and roughness, but that this logic, with its own operations of selectivity, could easily be directed against those who threatened the stability of this putative socio-spatial arrangement. In other words, this figuration of power could operate with its own differentiating cultural logic, a way of suppressing other forms of group heterogeneity, in favour of a shared identity determined by the 'established'.

The upshot of this state of affairs is that it allows the 'established' to use their powerful *social networks* to situate the behaviours of the residents of Zone 3 symbolically 'outside' the community. For example, Elias and Scotson note how on the one hand the sporadic deviant behaviour of Zone 2 residents, though heavily sanctioned by the local community, is by and large overlooked by almost everybody in Winston Parva, while on the other the exploits of a handful of disruptive and badly behaved families in Zone 3 leads to the labelling of the whole estate as deviant. Not to be part of a community along these lines is to know what it is like to be under excluding eyes, to be an unwelcome presence meeting a collective gaze. Moreover, to be 'Othered' like so, is to be marginalized, to be rendered metaphorically placeless, 'outside' the local community. In effect, the 'established' force the 'outsiders' to live their lives in a *liminal* space.

What Elias and Scotson's research also suggests is that the social role of 'outsiders' in communities is to be feared. The work of Mary Douglas (1966) is instructive about understanding this phenomenon because it offers a general framework that can be used to demonstrate how 'outsiders' are often constructed by communities through the idea of pollution or dirt. Dirt is used here by Douglas in a cultural sense, meaning, not something that is inherently 'dirty', but something that is applied to 'outsiders' who take on the appearance of 'dirtiness' in communities where they do not fit, do not belong. Dirt in Douglas' sense is, therefore, an effect of socially constructed systems of classification, a culturally defined symbolic mapping of what belongs where. Through such systems of classification – when they are mobilized by communities – dirt is constructed as a foreign body, a pollutant which needs to be excluded because it does not have a place in 'our' symbolic mapping of what belongs where. Dirt and its population always come from somewhere else, invading the community from an alien zone. In other words, 'outsiders' must be dealt with because they offend order; they disrupt 'our' system of classification through their very Otherness.

The theme of alienation through classification is also taken up by Bauman (1995), who, also in common with Elias and Scotson, is concerned with the empirical truth that for social groups to exist collectively, they often need to differentiate themselves from other social groups in order to achieve their sense of communal *identity*. In bringing our attention to this most pernicious aspect of community life, Bauman also clarifies what divisions can be like when communities commit themselves to adhere to a set of values in an emphatic sense. And, as he suggests, the result of such tyranny and absolutism is *oppression*, which results from the 'pressure to keep the intended flock in the fold … the craved-for cosiness of belonging is offered as a price of unfreedom' (p. 277).

Bauman suggests that oppression is carried out through two complementary strategies, which not only stress the value of loyalty to community and punish any betrayal to it, but also work coextensively to exclude 'outsiders' while polarizing them. Borrowing from Lévi-Strauss, Bauman argues that, at every level of society, communities can be seen employing, conjointly, *anthropophagic* and *anthropoemic* strategies of oppression; the two strategies are only effective precisely because they are used in conjunction. Communities employing *anthropophagic* strategies, gobble up, devour and assimilate 'outsiders', who they perceive to carry 'powerful, mysterious forces' (p. 179). In marked contrast, those employing *anthropoemic* strategies (from Greek, meaning 'to vomit') towards 'outsiders' metaphorically throw them up, casting them into exile, 'away from where the orderly life is conducted … either in exile or in guarded enclaves where they can be safely incarcerated without hope of escaping' (p. 180). The two strategies work as one:

> The phagic strategy is *inclusivist*, the emic strategy is *exclusivist*. The first 'assimilates' the strangers to the neighbours, the second merges them with the aliens. Together, they polarize the strangers and attempt to clear up the most vexing and disturbing middle-ground between the poles of neighbourhood and alienness – between 'home' and 'abroad', 'us' and 'them'. To the strangers whose life conditions and choices they define, they posit a genuine 'either-or': conform or be damned, be like us or do not overstay your visit, play the game by our rules or be prepared to be kicked out from the game altogether. Only as such an 'either-or' the two strategies offer a serious chance of controlling the social space. Both are therefore included in the tool-bag of every social domination (*ibid*).

The pervasive theme emerging from each of the studies outlined above is the reminder that what often lurks beneath the friendly front-face of community is symbolic and emotional violence, to be callously acted out on 'outsiders' who have broken its charmed mood, but also that this often also has the potential to tip over into actual, physical violence through community's ready-made outlets for prejudice and excessive emotionalism, which are often located in vicious rivalries that define themselves largely as and by resistance to their bitterest opponents, blossoming whenever 'we' expunge 'them', achieving their sensual union through the depredations of their necessary Others – a sense of community that is essentially based on and stands for one-way or mutual hatred.

As Amartya Sen (2006) argues in his book *Identity and Violence: the Illusion of Destiny*, it is the illusion of a singular communal identity that is often the wellspring for such overt physical violence, leading to the impression that it is hate that is the glue that holds community together. To use a good example from popular culture, it has been observed by authors such a Blackshaw (2008) that most football fans have some knowledge of these violent versions of single-group community, built on the mutual identification and reciprocity that comes with supporting 'City', which expresses its violent solidarity in opposition to 'United': 'United' as anti-City and 'City' as anti-United. To use an even more horrendous example, so do those communities at the brunt end of ethnic cleansing, which is the systematic process used to eliminate minority communities on the basis of ethnic or nationalistic territorial claims to land. As Danner (1999) demonstrates, for example, in his critical discussion of ethnic cleansing in Bosnia and Kosovo by Serbians in the early 1990s, what cannot be overestimated with such violence is the extent to which it is premeditated, rationally planned and brutally routinized. In both of these cases, it is the assumption that every individual must be a member of a single cultural group, each belonging to a single community defined by the exclusion of others *and* the stubborn reluctance to either share or limit that identity for ideological and/or religious reasons that are the sources of communal violence.

See also: *'A Theory of Community'*; *'Community and Identity'*; *'Imagined Communities'*; *'Postmodern Communities'*.

FURTHER READING

Douglas (1996) and Bauman (1989; 1995) are the most instructive guides to the heart of the theoretical debates about the 'dark side' of community, while Elias and Scotson (1965) is the classic community study.

REFERENCES

Bauman, Z. (1989) *Modernity and the Holocaust*. Oxford: Blackwell.
Bauman, Z. (1995) *Life in Fragments: Essays in Postmodern Morality*. Oxford: Blackwell.
Blackshaw, T. (2008) 'Contemporary Community Theory and Football', *Soccer and Society*, 9 (3): 325–345.
Danner, M. (1999) 'Endgame in Kosovo', *The New York Review of Books*, 46 (8): 6th May.
Diski, J. (2008) 'Extreme Understanding', *London Review of Books*, 10th April.
Douglas, M. (1966) *Purity and Danger*. London: Routledge Kegan and Paul.
Elias, N. and Scotson, J. (1965) *The Established and the Outsiders: A Sociological Enquiry into Community Problems*. London: Frank Cass.
Sen, A. (2006) *Identity and Violence: The Illusion of Destiny (Issues of Our Time)*. London: W. W. Norton and Co. Ltd.

Community as Policy and Practice

COMMUNITY ACTION

Like many other concepts in community studies, 'community action' is a broad term that has various meanings depending on who is using it. Insofar as there is a commonly accepted formulation, it is used to describe the organization of direct, often localized, collective action, which sets out to achieve change through organization, mobilization and negotiation, in ways that can be both unconventional and unconstitutional. To this extent, community action can also be identified with four kinds of power relations with extant institutions and/or other forms of authority: conflict, co-operation, confrontation and change. What all of this suggests, not surprisingly, is that community action is a political process that presumes an active view of the participative citizen.

> *Section Outline: This chapter begins by distinguishing organic community action from that which is part of community development. After identifying and briefly discussing, with examples, the distinguishing features of community action, the chapter outlines one compelling theoretical approach to understanding how individual indifference can turn into radical mutual action, albeit often short-lived. Thereafter, the discussion turns specifically to social movements. Drawing on examples, it discusses those social movements inspired by both popular discontent and radical elites. The chapter closes with a concise discussion of the limits of community action.*

Community action has a number of variants which overlap to some extent, but also show some sharp differences. For example, community action is often regarded as being part of the *community development* process, and, in particular, attempts by disadvantaged groups (more often than not supported by a community development practitioner) to organize, mobilize and negotiate locally to achieve change within a community or neighbourhood. However, community action often arises from more general concerns rooted in communities of interest which turn into challenges to authority. These tend to emerge in situations when people collectively turn into activists because they feel that they can no longer go on with things as they are. The catalyst for action is usually repression or exploitation, and it tends to happen when issues relating to people's day-to-day existences are brought into sharp relief by change, or what the French Marxist–existential philosopher Sartre (1977) calls 'exterior exchange', which leads them to the realization that things could be different. This kind of community action has a long history in popular radical movements in Britain. For example, in the mid-seventeenth century, the Levellers, widely supported by some members of the army, yeoman farmers and tradesman, acted on radical ideas that had deep social roots with the explicit aim of establishing a republic based on a unicameral parliament, suffrage, religious toleration and other far-reaching social reforms.

Just as important as the visions that these challenges to the status quo, however, is the social strength of their communal relations, which often enable them to carry on resolutely and against all the odds for long periods of time. A good example of this is the Solidarity movement in Poland in the 1980s. Solidarity began its life as the first non-communist trade union in a communist country made up of shipyard workers, artists, intellectuals and the support of the Catholic Church. The Polish government initially attempted to destroy the union during a period of marshal law during the early 1980s. However, by the end of the decade, a Solidarity-led coalition government was formed, and its leader Lech Walesca was elected president of the country.

Few commentators have attempted to theorize the reasons why some communities mobilize themselves for change, but most of them do not, other than by the way of rational choice (action) theory (e.g., Olson, 1971). Sartre's (1977) discussion of the Maoists in France is an exception. Discussing the Maoist faith in the spontaneity of the masses, Sartre explicates their view that although men and women are born free and socialized into social formations which are collective in orientation (i.e., the family and the local community), they will eventually be alienated and atomized by the larger social forces that dominate capitalist society (i.e., work, private property and various other institutions such as the armed forces, universities, etc.). According to this view, these institutions end up reducing men and women to individuals who are not only 'other' than themselves, but are at the same time identical with all the others who are also 'other' than themselves.

What Sartre is suggesting here is that although we inevitably become members of different societal institutions which bring us into collective situations with other people (what Sartre calls 'collectives'), these address us, not as part of a community or any other kind of collective organization, but merely as 'a member of a series'. In the process, we become identical with all other members of 'the series' and differ from them only on the basis of our individual 'serial number' (student ID, payroll number, rank, etc.). When we are 'serialized' in this way, not only do we feel alone and resigned to our individual fate, but we also fail to register this thought in an identifiable form. This is because our critical faculties have been masked by 'serial thought', which atomizes us and justifies that separation.

Sartre goes on to explain that, in the light of this situation, men and women cannot become aware of their repression or exploitation without revolting against it collectively in a radical way. This only happens when an 'exterior exchange' occurs, because it reveals the actual conditions of people's existence, provoking in them a 'particular, concrete, and precise refusal' to carry on with the ways that things seem to be. At first, serial thinking opposes the practical unity of mutual organization, but as soon as concrete action calls for collective action – even if it is only temporary – it is soon replaced by a community of interest whose collective response expresses – though often without formulating it – a radical refusal to be repressed or exploited. Any barriers to the formulation of the group also quickly disappear the moment community action is taken. 'This happens', Sartre (1977: 168) points out, 'not because the mechanisms [of separatist thought] have been noticed, identified, and verbally denounced, but because they are facets of the separatist idea, which is no longer needed'.

What Sartre is describing here is reminiscent of what the one-time Maoist philosopher Badiou (2005) has more recently called the politics of the 'event', which involves the sudden transformation of the nothing of the world into something radical. According to Badiou, we today inhabit a world in which a wide variety of nineteenth century socio-economic phenomena are beginning to reappear at an alarming rate: poverty, social injustice and nihilism, which is particularly present amongst the young, and politics has 'dissolved into the "service of wealth"'. As Badiou puts it, it is only through the 'event' that we can break with this general situation:

This is our task, during the reactionary interlude that now prevails: through the combination of thought processes—always global, or universal, in character—and political experience, always local or singular, yet transmissible, to renew the existence of the communist hypothesis, in our consciousness and on the ground (2008: 42).

Also writing from a Marxist perspective, Castells (1983) argues that the 1970s saw the emergence of a new battleground for the 'urban problematic', involving a series of political struggles over housing, transport, redevelopment, leisure and recreation facilities, and so on. This, in Castells's (1976: 148) view, constituted a major part of the consumption of goods and services, whose site of reproduction is the city, and which is 'a unit of collective consumption corresponding more or less to the daily organisation of a section of labour power'. He argued that because the state is persistently unable to meet the costs of collective consumption, this often leads to cuts in provision, which as he saw it at the time were beginning translate into a new political struggle in the form of what came to be know as the 'new social movements'.

Social movements are groups, often connected by shared ideologies and *identities*, whose collective aim is to bring about change (and sometimes resist it) in the societies to which they belong, or in the world more generally. The 'new' in 'new social movements' refers not so much to the ways and means of a novel area of community action, but the shift from class politics to community 'issues', such as those concerning anti-capitalist and anti-globalization protesters, environmentalists, animal and human rights groups, and those formed around social divisions such as 'race', ethnicity, sexuality, age and disability. What is common to all social movements, however, is that they tend to be spontaneous grass-roots forms of community action, which have their basis in political struggles for control and resources and freedom from exploitation by powerful others. The 1932 mass trespass of Kinder Scout in the Peak District of England is a good example of social movement involving this kind of community action. The trespass, organized by the communist activist Benny Rothman, was in response to the power of rich landowners who wanted to keep the countryside for their own exclusive use and the laws that denied ordinary people access to what had historically been public rights of way. Looking back, the impact of this action has been enormous and was the impetus for the Access to the Mountains Act in 1939 and the establishment of the National Parks in the 1960s.

Leisure continues to play a key role in contemporary radical community action (*see* 'Leisure and its Communities'). As Laviotte (2006) demonstrates, extreme leisure presents an ideal means for developing creative forms of radical political subversion. Through his ethnographic research into 'surfing against sewage', Laviotte explores how a surfing community in Cornwall in the United Kingdom uses extreme subversion as part of its environmental campaigns to protect the ecological sustainability of coastal leisure pursuits. Another trend has seen the growing prominence of community action in sports such as football. A good example is the establishment of FC United of Manchester (FCUM), which saw a group of Manchester United fans withdrawing their support as a result of the corporate takeover by Malcolm Glaser to set up their own community-based club. FCUM is an Industrial and Provident Society (IPS), a one-member-one-vote organization where every member owns an equal share in the club and has an equal say in how it is run. Another is AFC Wimbledon. The club was formed by former Wimbledon FC fans after the decision to grant that club permission to relocate to Milton Keynes, moving the club from its London roots. The Dons Trust is a not-for-profit organization which now owns AFC Wimbledon and is committed to strengthening the voice of supporters in decision-making processes. The Trust and IPS models are reflective of a growing move to a community approach to governance and accountability in football.

What the Kinder Scout example discussed above shows is that community action often has its roots in the leadership of charismatic individuals and/or radical intellectuals. Perhaps one of the most famous charismatic exponents of community action is Mohandas Karamchand Gandhi, who came to be known as 'Mahatma', or the 'great-souled' one. Through the moral leadership of the Indian freedom movement, Gandhi not only attempted to improve the living conditions of low-caste Hindus stigmatized as the 'untouchables', but he also attempted to heal divisions between Hindus and Muslims. Encouraging members of his own community with the words 'you must be the change you wish to see in the world', he was a pioneer of non-violent resistance through mass civil disobedience.

A good example of an intellectual inspiring community action is the Italian Marxist thinker and activist Antonio Gramsci, who believed that 'ordinary men and women could be educated into understanding the coercive and persuasive power of capitalist hegemony over them' (Hoare and Nowell Smith, 1971: 49–50). Gramsci's counter-hegemonic approach to bringing about societal change can be contrasted with the work of Saul Alinsky (1972) who organized community action in the Back of the Yards area of Chicago and helped establish the Industrial Areas Foundation in the city. Alinsky's approach was not only more issue focused and pragmatically driven than Gramsci's, but it compelled activists never to go outside the experience of their own lives, emphasizing that social change could only be achieved by the mobilization and organization of people seeking change in their own lives through direct action. This realism, located in liberal individualism, was reflected in his belief that activists are not motivated by altruism, that they need to have their self-interest appealed to and that they must communicate within the experience of the people with whom they are working. However, redolent of Gandhi, Alinsky espoused a belief in universalism, and specifically the idea that individuals cannot be free unless they are willing to sacrifice some of their interests to guarantee the freedom of others. Like Gramsci, Alinsky also saw the need for organizers to agitate and create disenchantment with the status quo, and to generate a shared passion for change.

What the foregoing discussion indicates is that literature has a tendency to focus on mobilizations that have had some modicum of success. However, the evidence suggests that there are also some recurrent and pervasive problems associated with community action. Crow and Allan (1994) claim that, on the whole, community action is less effective for working-class groups than it is for the middle classes, as these groups often lack the organizational base and the necessary political know-how of their more affluent counterparts. Providing a more general critique, Saunders (1979) has suggested that much community action tends to be reactive and limited by its localized nature, holding little hope for the 'future transition to a qualitative different mode of organization of society'. Saunders's view reflects the other more general limitation of community action, which is that it often begins with a commitment to radical change but tends to drift back into more conventional politics, confirming Herbert Marcuse's (1968) astute observation of the way in which hegemony is maintained through a process of 'resistance through incorporation'. Basically, one of the major reasons why the *status quo* is maintained (and capitalism flourishes) is that it readily incorporates from dissenting movements those aspects which dovetail with its *modus operandi*, while being always successful in resisting the remainder.

See also: *'Community Development'; 'Cosmopolitanism, Worldliness and the Cultural Intermediaries'; 'Imaginary Communities'; 'Locality, Place and Neighbourhood'; 'Political Community'.*

Co-authored with Donna Woodhouse.

key concepts in community studies

FURTHER READING

A fuller commentary on social movements is provided by Crossley (2002) and McAdam, McCarthy and Zald (1998). Crossley also critically develops a number of other themes relating to social movements specifically, but which can also be applied to community action more generally.

REFERENCES

Alinksy, S. (1972) *Rules for Radicals: A Pragmatic Primer for Realistic Radicals*. London: Random House.

Badiou, A. (2005) *Being and Event*. London: Continuum.

Badiou, A. (2008) 'The Communist Hypothesis', *New Left Review*, 49 January/February: 29–42.

Castells, M. (1976) 'Theoretical Propositions for an Experimental Study of Urban Social Movements' in C. G. Pickvance (ed.) *Urban Sociology: Critical Essays*. London: Methuen.

Castells, M. (1983) *The City and the Grassroots: A Cross-Cultural Theory of Urban Social Movements*. London: Edward Arnold.

Crossley, N. (2002) *Making Sense of Social Movements*. Buckingham: Open University Press.

Crow, G. and Allan, G. (1994) *Community Life. An Introduction to Local Social Relations*. London: Harvester Wheatsheaf.

Hoare, Q. and Nowell Smith, G. (eds) (1971) *Selections from the Prison Notebooks of Antonio Gramsci*. London: Lawrence and Wishart.

Laviolette, P. (2006) 'Green and Extreme: Free-flowing Through Seascape and Sewer', *WorldViews: Environment, Culture, Religion*, 10 (2): 178–204.

Marcuse, H. (1968) *One-Dimensional Man. Studies in the Ideology of Advanced Industrial Society*. London: Routledge.

McAdam, D., McCarthy, J. and Zald, M. (1998) 'Social Movements', in N. Smelser (ed.) *The Handbook of Sociology*. London: Sage.

Olson, M. (1971) *The Logic of Collective Action*. Cambridge: Harvard University Press.

Sartre, J-P (1977) 'The Maosits in France', in *Life/Situations: Essay Written and Spoken*. New York: Pantheon.

Saunders, P. (1979) *Urban Politics: A Sociological Interpretation*. London: Hutchinson.

community as policy and practice

In its purist sense, the term 'community development' refers to the collective means by which the ideal conditions of freedom and security – human kindness, mutual respect and recognition, tolerance, care, solidarity and social justice – might be achieved. Community development thus refers to a process that involves people working together in productive and non-exploitative ways in order to remove inequality and oppression to improve their collective conditions of existence. That modern societies are predicated on relations based on social class, gender, ethnic and other differences which mitigate against individuals working collectively to make their own destinies under the conditions of their own choosing means that practitioners educated and trained with the composite knowledge and skills in community development are often required to play an important role in facilitating this process, so that it might fulfil its potential. Facilitator, enabler, sensitive guide, *animateur*, conduit, mediator, *cultural intermediary* – these are all terms associated with the community development practitioner.

Section Outline: This chapter is in the main concerned with community development in public policy. After outlining and discussing the central tenets of community development in this context, the chapter summarizes the skills and attributes of the ideal practitioner. The subsequent discussion explores the challenges that stand in the way of the accomplishment of effective and enduring community development work, which it argues in the main derive from three mutually reinforcing limits – namely, those of community development practitioners, existing practice and the policy context in which it is currently resides.

In the context of public policy, community development has most often been associated with projects that have their origins in grassroots activity aimed at benefiting local people and which more often than not are facilitated by a community development practitioner. These projects are, as a rule, concerned with social welfare, unemployment, health, education, crime and anti-social behaviour (or any combination of these), and they are also increasingly facilitated through art, leisure and even sport.

According to Glen (1993: 24), there are three conditions conducive to facilitating community development: the community in question gets to define its own needs and makes provisions for those needs; the processes of engaging that community involve fostering, creative and co-operative networks of people and groups; and the practitioner involved operates with community development skills in a non-directive way.

As this suggests, what characterizes community development is the value base from which it is undertaken; its overriding ethos being to promote self-help through egalitarian and participative relationships by 'starting where the community is at'. Mutual trust is the watchword of community development, and most initiatives take place on a local or neighbourhood basis. Its key aim is to encourage self-help and self-determination and a sense of mutual belonging by removing oppression and exploitation from existing social relations. It is to this extent a critique of existing social, political and economic arrangements, as well as the kinds of public service delivery they have historically fostered, which provides a frame of reference for a broad alliance of like-minded people committed to the belief that the resources needed for change are located in communities themselves. In the context of a failure of conventional public policy initiatives – both those based on market principles and bureaucratic paternalism – it might also be seen as an attempt to change the world through a counter-hegemonic strategy based on mutual aid.

The ideal community development practitioner is a facilitator or enabler rather than an expert, whose role it is to build community capacity, *social capital* and collective organization. This is supported by the adjunct role of *cultural intermediary*, whose responsibility it is to encourage individuals and communities to become more aware of their own circumstances and, importantly, those of others. What is recognized in this role is that conflict is not only an inevitable part of communities 'coming together', but also that society is torn by conflicting interests. It is in the light of the success of these twin objectives, whereby people have developed their own creative potential and have harnessed this for their own individual benefit and that of their local community, that projects then continue independently.

Community development is not a new approach in public policy. Taylor (2003) reminds us that it was used by departing colonizers in the 1950s in the context of preparing territories for independence by initiating health, education and other welfare projects, while stressing self-help and the promotion of indigenous leadership. In the United States and the United Kingdom, this top–down approach came to be applied to projects in the 1960s and 1970s focused on *restoring* community in the light of urban decline and the perceived social pathologies with which it was often associated (*see* 'Community Regeneration'). More recently, it has been seen as a way of tackling urban unrest, the putative power of restored community, a theme that has emerged strongly in an era where *communitarianism* is ostensibly a powerful public policy driver (*see* 'Political Community').

Stewart and Taylor (in Taylor, 2003) suggest that the objective of community development in the current policy climate in the United Kingdom is to develop confident communities, respected by the outside world, which become localities where people want to live and work. In order to achieve this objective, both *capacity* and *social capital* need to be built and existing strengths realized so that community members do not see themselves as failures. New relationships with outsiders also need to be constructed, in addition to those that empower people as service users, consumers and workers, and to help erase any negative images that may exist. Finally, there also needs to be the development of jobs and assets that encourage people and resources into the locality, creating stronger links between the community and the mainstream economy, in the process empowering the community as co-producers and which help to build new forms of governance that also empower them as citizens.

The increased interest in community development since the 1980s can be explained largely in the context of global economic restructuring and the emergence of neo-liberalism (*see* 'Setting the Record Straight'), which has signalled an ideological shift towards welfare as the responsibility of the individual, the family and community, rather than the state. As a result of this, some agencies have become more involved in the day-to-day regulation of people's lives, in the name of, or under the guise of, community development as an ideological force. Across the political spectrum, there is a fear of social disintegration and concomitant calls for the recovery of community. However, these calls are more often than not conservative, in that the stress on self-help and social responsibility merely assists in the maintenance or reproduction of already existing social inequalities with the wider, more global, causes of social and economic disintegration being kept firmly at a distance. What compounds this situation is that locality today is, for many people, less important for community life than religion, ethnicity or lifestyle. This often serves to further complicate attempts to develop communities, rather than offer new hopes of re-building social relations on the basis of shared interests and mutual concerns.

Also discussing the UK context, Henderson and Glen (2006) claim that community development as a profession by and large kept a low profile until the election of New Labour in 1997. From this point on, self-help initiatives won the backing of many agencies, but at the same time, campaigning, or attempts to influence policy, was considered much less palatable by those very same agencies. Their research also shows that relatively small amounts of time is still spent by community workers in direct contact with communities, which militates against workers generating the kind of credibility necessary to operate successfully in community settings, with practitioners often having wider locality responsibilities and favouring consensual, rather than challenging, activities. Coupled to the structural constraints that may steer workers away from a focus on direct, bottom–up work with communities, there is often also a skills deficit amongst staff who are used to more didactic, top–down ways of working with 'clients'.

Henderson and Glen also highlight concerns over the continued fragility and insecurity of funding and casualization of the profession. Many posts are not highly paid, there is little uniformity in terms of the experience and qualifications employers' expect, and often a rapid turnover of staff, especially of young staff members, which has the effect of creating an ageing profession. Although acknowledging their small sample size, Henderson and Glen say that unpaid workers are gaining skills traditionally associated with paid workers. Whilst this may, on the one hand, be seen as positive, there is concern that the motivation of poorly funded, short-term projects using volunteers may have more to do with financial stricture than with community development aims.

Notwithstanding evidence which shows that self-help may provide a substitute for, or accompaniment to, community services *and* challenge mainstream ways of working, it would appear that it is often the case that this provides some local authorities with an excuse to under-invest in services. The upshot is that many grants or service-level agreements between statutory agencies and community groups tend to be short term and conditional. There is also the problem that, on the basis of the competitive culture that accompanies bidding for funds, one community organization may receive resources at the expense of others. Often inexperienced in terms of planning, community groups may also suffer from overambition in terms of what and how quickly they hope community development may achieve the changes they desire. Agencies need effective community development strategies, but creating these is difficult when those developing them often struggle to grasp what exactly constitutes effective practice.

If community development is not embedded in an organization's culture, then this, along with the difficulty of measuring outputs and outcomes in order to argue that it provides value for money, makes community development difficult to establish and vulnerable to attack where it already exists. Banks and Orton (2007: 97) conclude that there is the 'uneasy relationship between community development work and the local state', which means that although it can challenge aspects of local authority policy and practice, it can also create tensions.

This overall state of affairs has led critics such as Ledwith (2005: 19) to comment on the general lack of critical thinking on the part of some community development practitioners, noting a tendency towards what she calls *thoughtless action*, which signals the failure to acknowledge the underlying causes of community issues, and *actionless thought*, wherein such issues are recognized but no plans are made to address them. Ledwith encourages a more radical approach to community development work, stating that 'there will be no sustainable change unless communities themselves are given the power and responsibility to take action'. However, as Glen (1993: 25, 26) points out, too much reliance on such 'a "felt needs" approach may neglect those needs of which communities are unaware or prefer to ignore', such as HIV and Aids work; and it might also even lead to less pressure for public authority investment in local services.

Perhaps the most piercing criticism of community development *per se*, rather than focusing on the difficulties it faces embedding itself as a way of working in an era which is risk averse rather than experimental, is that it seeks to ameliorate, rather than change, social divisions. Ingamells (2007) suggests that development goals are often couched within the values and ideals of privileged groups, so, even within nominally egalitarian framework, power relations are uneven, with workers and policy makers likely to influence the direction and minutiae of community development initiatives. In the current political climate, which has seen resurgence in conservative moral agendas, 'problematic' community members may be excluded from the development process, not just by agencies, but also by peers, who aspire to conservative values.

Overall, Henderson and Glen (2006) describe the infrastructure of community development today as 'worryingly weak'. One of the upshots of this is that, in comparison to established professions, such as social work, community development practitioners may suffer from being viewed by other practitioners as anti-professional. This situation is exacerbated by the preferred ways of working of community practitioners, whose ultimate aim is to render their own presence unnecessary. In Banks and Orton (2007: 109), one worker portrays community development colleagues as 'the grit in the oyster', a description which conveys the discomfort and invisibility of their work, whilst also illustrating the opportunity it creates to produce valuable outcomes. Despite tensions between the centralizing push of managerialism and the decentralizing pull of governance, there is the potential for community development to change existing social processes and inequalities. If such changes are aided by sensitive community engagement, it may make possible the creation of a new, more progressive consensus which includes the active participation of the poorest members of society in making their own destinies under the conditions that are of their own choosing.

See also: *'Action Research'; 'Community Action'; 'Community Regeneration'; 'Cosmopolitanism, Worldliness and the Cultural Intermediaries'; 'Leisure and its Communities'; 'Locality, Place and Neighbourhood'; 'Political Community'; 'The "Dark Side" of Community'.*

Co-authored with Donna Woodhouse.

FURTHER READING

Ledwith (2005) offers a critical and detailed discussion of community development. Glen (1993) provides succinct outline of community development and it relationship with *community action* and community services.

REFERENCES

Banks, S. and Orton, A. (2007) '"The Grit in the Oyster": Community Development Workers in a Modernising Local Authority', *Community Development Journal*, 42 (1): 97–113.

Glen, A. (1993) 'Methods and Themes in Community Practice', in H. Butcher, A. Glen, P. Henderson, and J. Smith, *Community and Public Policy*. London: Pluto Press.

Henderson, P. and Glen, A. (2006) 'From Recognition to Support: Community Development Workers in the United Kingdom', *Community Development Journal*, 41 (3): 277–292.

Ingamells, A. (2007) 'Community Development and Community Renewal: Tracing the Workings of Power', *Community Development Journal*, 42 (2): 237–250.

Ledwith, M. (2005) *Community Development: A Critical Approach*. Bristol: Policy Press.

Taylor, M. (2003) *Public Policy in the Community*. Basingstoke: Palgrave.

Community partnership working involves the coming together of organizations which actively require the assistance of each other in pursuing their individual goals. On the face of it, the rationale of independent community organizations for combining is either one or all of the following: pooling resources to avoid the duplication of effort; to improve community participation and take-up of services; and to achieve better representation and social and political prestige. However, in the current political climate, partnership working is hardly a choice, and more of a requirement. You might say that it is now the *only* way of delivering services in communities.

Section Outline: After outlining the central tenets of community partnership working, this chapter critically discusses the advantages and disadvantages which ensue when organizations combine. This discussion looks particularly at the issue of power and conflicts in partnerships which can be submerged and never really resolved. What is most striking about community partnerships, it is also suggested, and this is examined in some detail, is that, while the rhetoric of interdependent working foregrounds 'community' in the partnership process, the reality is often the case that the 'community' is seldom seen as a meaningful partner.

key concepts in
community studies

170

In community studies, the term 'partnership' is used to refer to the ways in which community organizations exist interdependently. Community organizations can be interdependent in different ways, and the term is used to describe both informal and formal community partnerships. The Audit Commission (1998) uses the term 'partnership' to refer to two or more agencies coming together to achieve a common goal. It describes such partnerships as joint working arrangements where partners can be identified on the basis of the following criteria: they are otherwise independent bodies; they agree to co-operate to achieve a common goal; they create a new organizational structure or process to achieve this goal which is separate from their own individual organization's; they plan and implement a jointly agreed programme, often with joint staff or resources; they share relevant information; and they agree to pool risks and rewards. Wilson and Charlton (1997: 10) define partnerships rather more succinctly as 'three or more organisations, from public, private and voluntary sector, acting together by contributing their diverse resources in the furtherance of a common vision with clearly defined goals and objectives'.

There are a number of obvious advantages that partnership working has over the efforts of single organizations or agencies, which can be summarized as follows: it promotes economies of scale; it lends itself to rational and efficient use of resources, and, ultimately, improved take up of services; it overcomes duplication and fragmentation through co-ordination and shared responsibility; and it promotes wider consultation on issues beyond immediate organizational interests, lending itself to maximum feasible participation.

Historically, getting community organizations to combine has often proved very difficult, not least because of their stereotyped views of one another. However, in the current political climate, partnership working is hardly a choice any longer, and is more of a requirement. Today, there is enormous pressure from central government and external funders, such as the European Union and Regional Development Agencies, as well as rising public expectations around service provision, which impels organizations and agencies to work interdependently. Since the 1990s, partnership working has become the *sine qua non* of community development in the United Kingdom, although such a cross-departmental and multi-agency approach to working had been happening on an ad hoc basis for a number of years. Such working emerged as recognition that the functional divisions of policy leads to silo working and incoherence, but also because it was increasingly being recognized that independent ways of working had hitherto failed to address a number of key issues. Partnership was seen as a way of boosting sustainability; improving facilities and services; generating the critical mass needed to drive through initiatives; making services relevant to the whole community; and drawing in complementary services. In the event, central government introduced legislation to reduce some of the legal barriers that had historically impeded partnership working. Good examples of these are the 1999 Health Act, which enabled the NHS and local authorities in England and Wales to provide and commission more integrated services; and the Compact on Relations between Government and the Voluntary and Community Sector in England (1998), which set out principles for effective working relationships and encourages local authorities to establish compacts with third-sector groups, such as informal partnership agreements, often essential in terms of accessing funding.

Such legislation and policy provide a clear demonstration of the centrality of partnership working to central government around the delivery of effective public services, which it sees as having five main objectives: improving the user experience of services; dealing with difficult 'wicked issues'; promoting citizen involvement in shaping services; ensuring easy and timely access to services; and making the best use of available resources (www.joint-reviews.gov.uk/money).

The first of these objectives, improving user experience of public services, it is imagined, can be achieved through streamlining systems to make access easier, including joint assessments, reducing overlap and duplication in the process, and creating economies of scale. Dealing with 'wicked issues' is about addressing cross-cutting challenges, such as social exclusion, which are complex, chronic, require long-term strategies and have not responded to previous initiatives. Promoting citizen involvement in the planning and delivery of services, it is argued, can help create cohesive communities and will, in the event, it is claimed, ensure that services are designed and delivered to meet local need. The key to such community involvement is consultation, participation and empowerment, which should be properly resourced; learning from people's experience of what is needed and what works is presented as making this a cost-effective investment. The fourth objective, trouble-free and timely access to services, is based on the premise that establishing integrated services makes it easier to develop a holistic approach to assessing need and delivering services, reducing the likelihood of 'buck passing', and allowing for the development of common documentation and records. Finally, it is argued that partnerships should make for better use of available resources, responding to the government's 'Best Value' approach by, for example, pooling budgets, creating joint posts and sharing facilities, and then reinvesting the savings made in additional or new services. Partnership working, overall, it is claimed, 'adds value', including allowing agencies to access social groups, which otherwise might have been difficult to reach.

Partnerships are made up of stakeholders; that is, those who have a stake or interest in the partnership. Wilson and Charlton (1997) argue that there are four categories of stakeholders: people or organizations needed as a resource; those who will be affected by the initiative; those who may not be directly involved but have an interest; and those who feel that they have a 'right' to be involved. Kotter (1996) suggests that partnerships function best if they operate on the basis of the following criteria: openness, integrity, accountability, selflessness, honesty, leadership and objectivity. It is vital that, if partners are to 'own' issues and solutions, then all stakeholders must play an active role in partnerships.

This is a challenge, even for those genuinely committed to partnership working, as stakeholders can be numerous and the issues being addressed can be complex. It is interesting to note that, apart from 'community' regeneration schemes, the business 'community' is rarely involved as a visible stakeholder, which may engender cynicism with regard to the perception of the commitment of the business to partnership working.

Although the discussion thus far has outlined the 'theory' of interdependent working, in reality there are multiple barriers both to the establishment and functioning of effective partnerships. Central to the failure of partnerships to operate successfully is the issue of power. Some local authorities have found sharing control and resources, both with other agencies and members of the public, difficult, the 'greater maturity and self-confidence … to encourage a move towards a state of "interdependence" with others' (www.joint-reviews.gov.uk) rarely being achieved. The justification for not involving community representatives in partnership working is often that they will fail to grasp the issues around policy creation and implementation because these are too technical to understand. This tells us much about professional power, the power relations that exists in organizational structures, and about the ways in which individuals and organizations use technical expertise to legitimize themselves and exclude others from their fields of work.

In developing a critique of partnership approaches to the problems of neighbourhood crime, Hope (1995) suggests that the idea that the solutions lie with corporate 'joined up' thinking in order to promote self-help in local 'communities' is flawed. He argues that what is really required is a fundamental investment in the institutional infrastructure in order to offset the destabilizing tendencies of the free-market economy. Indeed, it might also be argued that the current corporate management approach to partnership working tends to centralize power, which, crucially, works against consultation and community involvement, and that when local authorities do attempt to consult with communities, they do so because consultation is obligatory, it is used to quell or deter *community action*. Indeed, critics argue that community consultation is often cursory and does not inspire significant levels of participation. When the community does not 'join in', some local authorities blame apathy, rather than their own lack of skills with regard to consultation. Crucially, many agencies are still to come to terms with the fact that one of the key reasons why communities do not join partnerships is that they can often see partner agencies as part of, or as *the* problem being addressed, rather than as the solution.

Community participation is, ultimately, still a 'minority sport' (Thake in Pearson and Craig, 2001: 130), with serious doubts over whether many 'community reps' are representative at all, and with the potential for communities to reach saturation point in terms of their capacity to engage with all the schemes that require their involvement. Much reticence among officers and councillors towards a genuine community participation in local politics is underwritten by a fear that many who currently hold power may lose it or may have to share it if communities become involved in policy creation, delivery and monitoring and evaluation. Despite the rhetoric of empowerment, relatively little in the way of resources is made available for communities to improve their knowledge so that they can challenge expert power. Power, or a community's lack of it in relation to agencies, is rarely foregrounded, and is underplayed in the work of authors such as Putnam (1999), whose work is currently so influential in US and UK community policy circles (*see* 'Social Capital'). Some critics argue that partnerships, in reality, are more often than not used to legitimize the preferred actions of agencies, with community goals couched within the values and ideals of the privileged group. Any positive outcomes are then attributed to the intervention, and thus the status of the privileged partner is enhanced, reinforcing already unequal power relations, contra-genuine *community development* which is as interested in the value of *process* as it is in outcomes.

The claim that partnerships 'add value' must also be carefully examined. Whilst partnerships are *de rigueur*, they do not automatically aid policy implementation, the Audit Commission making the observation that 'complicated partnership arrangements confuse lines of responsibility and accountability and hamper successful delivery at a local level' (in Banks and Orton, 2007: 100). The failure of partnerships, either to form or to deliver, can be due to a number of factors: the absence of a common framework and clear decision-making processes; uneven levels of commitment; shifts in wider strategy by one or more partners; tension between outcomes required by some organizations which may be seen as counter-productive for others, as well as conflicting loyalties and under-management. Such lack of leadership, needed to make partnerships democratic, claim Rowe and Devanney (in Ingamells, 2007: 246), means partnerships may end up as 'little more than key players suppressing mutual loathing in the interest of mutual greed'. Lack of clarity about accountability can result in 'finger pointing' when things go wrong; and there can be a reluctance to share information and a desire not to relinquish responsibilities, if agencies or individuals see a function as 'their job'. Another significant barrier to good partnership working is a lack of understanding of the cultures of other organizations, including communities, or the desire of one organization to dominate the process. If partnerships fail to function, resources can actually be wasted by squabbles and inertia; overall, a preoccupation with process and bureaucracy can lead to losing sight of the ultimate espoused aim of improving outcomes for service users.

Kotter (1996) suggests that an effective vision for a partnership is one which is: imaginable, desirable, feasible, focused, flexible and communicable. If they are to maintain momentum and achieve positive outcomes, partnerships need to set priorities, targets and timescales. However, the 'success' of partnerships is often evaluated using performance management concepts (meaningless to some agencies and community groups), and which instead pay heed to the three 'E's – economy, efficiency and effectiveness – in measuring inputs, outputs and outcomes. Targets are usually governed by agency key performance indicators, rather than arrived at via negation with local communities. Where partnerships do not appear to be 'achieving', either in relation to their key performance indicators or locally negotiated outcomes, this can lead to a lack of commitment by partners, particularly if joint working has been unsuccessful in the past, or if previous community involvement is viewed by local people as having lacked genuine commitment or did not lead to change.

The most effective partnerships may be those which evolve organically and give themselves time to transform the ways of working of those involved. Moss Kanter (1994) uses the analogy of the development of a personal relationship that leads to a successful marriage in order to develop a five-stage model of effective partnership working. Firstly, the partners meet, are attracted and discover some compatibility. Secondly, they start going steady and agree to draw up plans for the future. Thirdly, like couples setting up house, partners discover that they have different ideas about how things should be done. In the penultimate stage, the partners settle down, developing ways of coping with their differences so that they can continue getting along. Finally, the partners grow old together, recognizing the important changes each has made as a result of accommodations made to keep the relationship functioning effectively. Whilst this may be a useful analogy where partnerships have time to evolve, if, as is often the case, when partnerships are imposed from the top–down, perhaps even bound by contract to protect the lead agency's interests, the analogy loses much of its value. A domineering partner, driven by its own priorities, or those of its family, is hardly conducive to a happy, 'productive' marriage, and in such cases, a divorce is often in the offing.

Encouraging partnership working, the government urges that 'we need to marshal the contributions of the public, private and voluntary sectors, and of communities themselves. We will not achieve genuinely citizen-centred services unless service deliverers work well together' (Section 2.30, 2001). Such an approach to working, particularly if one acknowledges the cross-cutting nature of key contemporary social issues, seems logical. However, what reality suggests is that the territoriality of experts and expert power means that agencies have struggled to fully embrace genuine partnership working, even when compelled (or perhaps because of such compulsion) to do so. As with community development, agencies have found ways of incorporating what some perceive as threatening ways of working, rather than adapting their own working styles to function co-operatively, utilizing what Marcuse (1968) refers to as absorbent power, which assimilates the antagonistic, and seeks a harmonizing pluralism. Most disappointingly, partnership working is often still marked by an unwillingness or inability to meaningfully involve communities in ways that move beyond cursory consultation.

See also: *'Action Research'; 'Community Action'; 'Community Development'; 'Community Regeneration'; 'Political Community'; 'Social Capital'.*

Co-authored with Donna Woodhouse.

REFERENCES

Audit Commission (1998) *A Fruitful Partnership: Effective Partnership Working.* London: Audit Commission.

Banks, S. and Orton, A. (2007) ''The Grit in the Oyster': Community Development Workers in a Modernising Local Authority', *CDJ*, 42 (1): 97–113.

Government White Paper (2001) *Strong Leadership – Quality Public Services.* London: HMSO.

Home Office (1998) *Compact: Getting it Right Together. Compact on Relations between Government and the Voluntary and Community Sector in England.* London: HMSO.

Hope, T. (1995) 'Community Crime Prevention', in M. Tonry and D. Farrington (eds) *Building a Safer Society: Strategic Approaches to Crime.* Chicago: Chicago University Press.

Ingamells, A. (2007) 'Community Development and Community Renewal: Tracing the Workings of Power', *CDJ*, 42 (2): 237–250.

Marcuse, H. (1968) *One-Dimensional Man. Studies in the Ideology of Advanced Industrial Society.* London: Routledge.

Kotter, J. (1996) *Leading Change*. Harvard: Harvard Business School Press.

Ministry of Housing and Local Government (1969) *People and Planning: Report of the Committee on Public Participation and Planning*. London: HMSO (the Skeffington Report).

Moss Kanter, R. (1994) 'Collaborative Advantage', *Harvard Business Review:* July–August.

Pearson, S. and Craig, G. (2001) 'Community Participation in Strategic Partnerships in the United Kingdom', in J. Pierson and J. Smith (eds) *Rebuilding Community. Policy and Practice in Urban Regeneration*. Palgrave: Hampshire.

Putnam, R. (1999) *Bowling Alone*. New York: Simon & Schuster.

Wilson, A. and Charlton, K. (1997) *Making Partnerships Work: a Practical Guide for the Public, Private, Voluntary and Community Sectors*. York: Joseph Rowntree Foundation (www.joint-reviews.gov.uk/money/partnerships/files/partnerships-HardCopy.pdf).

COMMUNITY REGENERATION

'Community regeneration' is a new phrase used to refer to an old phenomenon in government policy – urban renewal, or the social, economic and environmental rehabilitation of neighbourhoods, towns, cities and conurbations understood to have fallen below normal standards of public acceptability. This observation notwithstanding, community regeneration differs from urban renewal in two ways: on the one hand, a key aspect of its remit is to involve a range of private agencies beyond those public bodies normally associated with urban renewal and, on the other, it is explicitly aimed at encouraging participation from all sections of the general public.

Section Outline: *After outlining the central focus of the regeneration process, this chapter offers a thumbnail sketch of the six main phases of its evolution in the United Kingdom. Thereafter, it discusses the successes and weaknesses of community regeneration programmes and initiatives in more detail, paying particular critical attention to current phase which is marked by a reliance on the market and ostensibly aimed at encouraging community participation, but which often has unintended consequences for those poorer groups in society who tend to be at the mercy of social, cultural, economic and political forces over which they have little control.*

As the above definition suggests, 'community regeneration' is used for current ways of thinking about how to deal with the urban disintegration that raises problems such as inadequate housing, schools and transport, limited employment and leisure opportunities, ground, water, air and noise pollution, traffic congestion, conflicting and/or non-conforming land uses, and the destructive psychological, social and environmental impacts these have on the well-being of individuals and communities. Whereas urban renewal was, by and large, pursued by public bodies because conventional wisdom had it that urban disintegration was in many ways attributable to market failure and the view that public intervention could improve on market outcomes, community regeneration is based on the view that public bodies are neither best placed nor sufficiently well informed as private agencies and communities to effect optimal solutions. The result has been a switch of policy in favour of competitive tendering, which allowed for regeneration schemes to be considered in terms of their effectiveness (i.e., the best-quality output, irrespective of the input costs) and based on greater community involvement (*see* 'Political Community').

Six main phases in the evolution of community regeneration can be identified in the United Kingdom. Each phase is characterized by both a particular reason or set of reasons for urban disintegration, and a corresponding policy solution.

The 1930 Housing Act initiated a number of slum clearance and new building schemes across the United Kingdom by local authorities, but interventions were both extemporary and variable. However, the period directly after World War II saw regeneration better co-ordinated and planned, with the scope and scale of both private and public house building extended. There were three main reasons for this: the need to tackle the shortages brought about by war damage; the emergence of town planning; and the new driving force of nationalization. The 1946 New Town Act authorized the implementation of the administrative and financial structures for the building of 14 new towns in both new and already existing settlements between 1947 and 1950. However, by 1949, there was an explicit shift from redevelopment to regeneration as the problems of accelerating costs and the implications of social upheaval became clear.

The second phase, from 1968 until 1977, was dominated by the focus on the problems of people as well as place. These urban aid programmes were radical when contrasted with the current consensus on approaches to regeneration. However, they were inspired by ideological assumptions about the efficacy of self-help and sociological theories such as the cycle of poverty thesis which meant that they had a tendency to pathologize the behaviours and attitudes of the poor. As a result, the urban aid programmes tended to be experimental and assumed that interventions could be successful in removing deprivation by changing the cultural aspects of people's behaviours. Despite this, some of those involved in implementing policies locally sought to identify community assets and to unearth structural processes which caused social malaise and problems such as delinquency, racial tension and low levels of educational attainment. This paved the way for the Home Office Community Development Project (CDP).

These twelve projects set up in neighbourhoods of between 10000–20000 people were essentially experiments to find inexpensive and alternative ways of dealing with urban malaise. These projects shifted the emphasis of regeneration from social pathology and laid the blame for deprivation squarely at the foot of economic inequalities, which paradoxically highlighted the limitations of experimental palliative cures of which they were clearly a part. Despite the fact that support for the CDP was not sustained, during their short lifetime, some of them were successful in campaigning on a number of issues, especially employment. Some of the workers involved were also successful in challenging the limitations imposed by *place* and moved local debates to a more radical critique of structural inequality (Henderson and Armstrong, 1993). However, these early attempts at regeneration were also marked by another explicit contradiction, in the sense that calls for more local intelligence and co-ordination were often not backed by the necessary strategic vision, something which helped to cause an increase in resistance towards the programmes by some of those at whom they were expressly targeted.

Phase three, which ran from 1978 to 1987, was prompted by the publication of the White Paper for the Inner Cities (DoE, 1977) which acknowledged the sheer scale and interconnectedness of urban disintegration and deprivation. The Paper recommended that *mainstream* policies which could impact on regeneration be changed, predicting a rise in bitterness and alienation amongst the poorest groups in the inner cities (the ill-defined term that was now being used to describe urban areas marked by multiple deprivation) if nothing was done. The Inner Urban Area Act was passed in 1978 and Urban Aid resources quadrupled. The year 1979 saw the election of the first Thatcher Government and a reorientation of the welfare state towards the market, competitiveness and social cohesion. There was also a formalizing of partnerships during this phase, with private sector partnership increasingly encouraged, for instance, via Enterprise Zones, which had planning exemptions and offered grants to induce private sector investment. Quasi Autonomous Non Governmental Organizations (QUANGOs) were also on the rise, such as the 12 flagship, time-limited, Urban Development Corporations. A small number of City Action Teams were also set up in 1985 with the remit to get different bodies working together. This phase was also marked by a tight geographical focus on initiatives during a period when the Conservative government was attempting to undermine the power of local authorities. In response to this, some Labour councils set up initiatives to address local problems, and there was some decentralization of services in these areas, under an alliance of Labour, trades unions and local communities. However, in the context of the erosion of local government powers by central government, the focus had switched to a defence of existing services.

A review of policy and the formation of Action for Cities (1988) marked the next, quite indistinct, fourth phase of community regeneration, which ran until 1990. During this period, the urban aid programme was re-organized, and 57 Priority Areas established, each having to submit an Inner Area Programme that identified local problems and strategies to address them. Several programmes were rolled together to try to improve co-ordination and, in some areas, rivalry between agencies developed.

The introduction of City Challenge in 1991 marked the beginning of the fifth phase of regeneration which saw an emphasis on inter-sector partnerships. It also saw growing recognition of the unambiguous need to encourage community participation which was a corollary of growing concerns about youth crime and family life. Bidding became more competitive and was led by local authorities. Key here was the Single Regeneration Budget (SRB), which began in 1994. Its resources were drawn from 20 programmes, but the overall budget was less than the sum of its previous parts and, despite the focus on need, priority was given to the best bids, rather than to the neediest areas. When Labour returned to power in 1997, it retained SRB, but introduced a sharper focus on need. However, out of office since 1979, a period during which the party's position on a number of social issues became less 'statist', Labour acknowledged the mixed economy of welfare where councils are enablers rather than providers, with a concomitant increase in involvement in provision facilitated by the 'not-for-profit sector'. Bitter controversy has raged here, with some critics arguing that Labour had (and without much difficulty) merely maintained the Conservative approach of market-managerialism to community regeneration which has superseded all other alternatives.

The current phase began in 1997 with New Deal for Communities (NDC) which had as its remit the task of reducing social exclusion. NDC, which is operational in 39 areas, draws together three strands of previous policy: local partnership for delivery; competition for funding; and citizen engagement in planning and implementation. NDC's five themes are indicative of what much contemporary community regeneration tries to achieve: getting people to work; getting place to work; building a future for young people; improving access to local public and private services; and making government work better. To achieve these aims, and ostensibly tied to the Third Way *communitarian* belief in community as the basis for moral and economic revival, 'capacity building' is seen as key (*see* 'Setting the Record Straight'). Capacity building focuses on equipping local people with skills which they would not otherwise have developed or obtained, with the explicit aim of helping them employ these skills in activities directed towards meeting their own individual needs and the needs of their community. This focus on people within community regeneration is a response to concerns that the poorest members of society are the least likely to adjust to social and business norms, and need to develop 'soft' skills to improve their chances of finding employment, or more secure or lucrative jobs in what is now a service economy. This 'up-skilling' of individuals is part of an attempt to break the vicious cycle of poverty which is 'uniquely destructive … unleashing a combination of forces that undermines what is in its path' (Pierson and Smith, 2001: 206).

In this current phase of community regeneration, there is an acceptance that cost and efficiency alone are too narrow a base to decide resource allocation, and there has been an explicit shift in policy towards need with the identification of 17 pathfinder areas in small geographical areas. There is also a greater emphasis on participation and an 'investment in people' in an attempt at joined-up thinking, with regeneration complimenting other initiatives such as Sure Start, which is a programme aimed at achieving better outcomes for children, parents and communities via increasing the availability of childcare, improving the health and emotional development of young children, and providing support for parents.

All this activity indicates that regeneration has become an increasingly high-profile area of government policy. The upshot is that the need for intervention to address urban deprivation is rarely an issue, but what is an issue is the *purposes* of such interventions, and their ability to bring about change. Miller (2001) claims that the majority of programmes and initiatives have had a limited impact, even when measured using the objectives of the partners involved. As Miller also points out, a good deal of regeneration initiatives have tended to be launched, not so much with the motivation to address need, but rather in the wake of unrest; and the upshot is that they are merely focused on 'managing local frustrations' (p. 141). Offering a more general critique, Ingamells (2007: 242) questions the assumption that regeneration is good *per se*, arguing that, over the long haul, the 'poorest residents experienced urban renewal dynamics as threatening rather than supporting their rights', and this has more often than not been accompanied with the feeling that regeneration is something which is done *to* communities, rather than *with* and *for* them.

What this suggests is that those in most need do not always derive the supposed benefits of regeneration; rather, they are often displaced by process as the regenerated space repopulated. Those involved in regeneration hope that new residents will bring with them new, much-needed skills, *social capital* and disposable income, and will assist the development of wider social networks, as well adding a sense of local vibrancy. However, evidence would seem to suggest that what often comes with new inhabitants are new problems or the intensification of existing ones. As Harvey (2008) points out, we are increasingly seeing the 'right of the city' switching from the right of everybody to change themselves and change the city to the right of individuals and private or quasi-private interests.

For example, gentrification often occurs when areas are taken over by those with higher incomes. This problem is often exacerbated by the new building of single-person housing such as apartments rather than family houses and existing properties converted into single-person housing. Another problem is that community cohesion is often undermined by a high turnover of new inhabitants drawn to regenerating areas, perhaps on short-term employment contracts, who are not able to put down roots. This can lead to antagonism between the existing population and those who have moved there more recently, but even more seriously to the displacement of that existing population.

This was clearly evidenced in the Marseille République regeneration project in France, which is discussed by Ruffin (2007), who outlines Guilluy and Noyé's step-by-step breakdown of a 'successful' gentrification process. The process gets underway with the arrival of the self-employed and pioneers such as artists and students who displace extant employees.

The status of the area increases with the development of new cultural facilities in the form of an ostensibly Bohemian culture which signals the arrival of trendy bars, cafés, art galleries and performance spaces. Very soon, developers, 'who are backed by finance, corporate capital and an increasingly entrepreneurially minded local state apparatus' (Harvery, 2008: 33), spot an emerging market and move in, which hastens the departure of the self-employed and signals the displacement of employed working-class people in manual jobs. As the number of developers and capitalists increases very quickly, the established working-class population collapses, and the pioneers are driven out by the non-renewal of leases and growing rents. Developers move in and instigate urban regeneration through the reconversion of property and the development of 'pedestrian precincts, gardens, cycle paths'. Working-class neighbourhoods become middle class and begin to exhibit the air of 'a lifestyle that encourages the arrival of ethnic cafes and restaurants', concert halls and galleries selling exotic art, all 'symbols of prestige that developers have learned to encourage in order to bestow upon certain areas the global brand that will attract those aspiring to membership of this global community' (Donzelot, quoted in Ruffin). This process of what Sharon Zukin calls 'pacification by cappuccino' (cited in Harvey, 2008) was summed up by Marseille resident, who argued that, supported by the local state apparatus who embraced gentrification for fear of appearing backward-looking or marginal, the Marseille République regeneration project ended up 'creating a European centre of culture for the middle classes. People like us were a blot on the landscape'.

Pierson and Smith (2001) argue that most successful efforts to revitalize deprived urban areas come from communities themselves, or are done with them, and it is this engagement that facilitates their legitimacy. However, evidence suggests that there are currently too many bureaucratic structures that hinder *community partnerships*, coupled with a lack of community capacity, which operate together to throw up barriers to genuine involvement. Much partnership is still cursory, with business and statutory agencies holding positions of power. The upshot is that there is little by the way of any contestation of 'norms' and community interests (*see* 'Community Action') that do not tally with the official, consensus-driven line. Another important, yet underplayed, stumbling block to participation by local communities in partnerships is that, whilst agencies may see themselves as having expertise, authority and legitimacy, to some communities, they may appear as the creators of local problems, rather than bodies equipped to address them.

Another source of criticism of current community regeneration has been the new managerialism which relies on market principles. Community regeneration has been developed under the auspices of the governmental management concepts of 'Value For Money' and 'Best Value', whilst, simultaneously, urban regeneration more broadly is driven by private sector development. Regeneration is marked by and reflective of a wider, commodification of space, a widening rift between public and privatized territories, with increasingly large amounts of space controlled by private companies, rather than local authorities. For all the talk that the market leads to more efficiency and flexibility in decision-making, Bradford and Robson (in Miller, 2001) note how small the funding for regeneration initiatives actually is, and how urban funding increases have been outstripped by mainstream budget cuts.

One of the key aims of community regeneration is the achievement of sustainability. Yet, as Arnold and Cole (1998) point out, typically, monitoring and evaluation of initiatives rarely looks at this, and many actual long-term benefits of regeneration often go undefined because of their implied nature. Where they are made explicit, as it was at one of Arnold and Cole's own case studies, where the aim was to 'leave behind a community equipped for the long-term with due regard to the sustainability of the various social and community infrastructure improvements made as part of its wider regeneration remit' (1998: 236), the focus is often on 'capacity building'. However, as Miller (2001) points out, the only phase of regeneration during which there was a genuine attempt to sustain capacity building was the second identified above, which saw the initiation of the Community Development Projects in 1969. The centralization of policy control by subsequent governments has sat uncomfortably with the *advocacy* of community empowerment through capacity building. In the current phase of regeneration, evidence of sustainability is thin, especially with regard to labour market initiatives, and attempts to achieve sustainability have not been helped by the externally driven aims and measures which can erode, rather than promote, community capacity by imposing 'solutions' on disparate and weary communities. The potential for sustainability is often further stymied by the short-term nature of much regeneration funding, which runs contra to advice that success is best achieved via long-term investment (DETR, 1997).

Reflecting on the efficacy of community regeneration, Robson et al. (in Miller, 2001) conclude that it is difficult even to decide what it has *aimed* to achieve, let alone whether it has been successful. Few inroads into the root causes and problems associated with urban deprivation have been made over the long run, and, indeed, there has arguably been continued urban disintegration and social malaise in some of the worst affected cities and towns in the United Kingdom. It is often argued that regeneration programmes often fail because they only focus their attention on dismantling these *pockets* of deprivation, without addressing their major structural causes. However, what the foregoing discussion suggests is that community regeneration needs to be returned to its proper function: as providing people with decent cities to live, work and leisure in, rather than for developers and capitalists to speculate on and middle-class cultural tourists to consume.

See also: *'Community Development'; 'Cosmopolitanism, Worldliness and the Cultural Intermediaries'; 'Political Community'; 'Social Capital'.*

Co-authored with Donna Woodhouse.

REFERENCES

Arnold, P. and Cole, I. (1998) 'Community Involvement and Sustainable Neighborhood Regeneration', in C. Cooper and M. Hawtin (eds) *Resident Involvement and Community Action. Theory to Practice.* Coventry: Chartered Institute of Housing.

Department of the Environment (1977) *Policy for the Inner Cities.* London: HMSO.

DETR (1997) *Regeneration – The Way Forward. A Discussion Paper.* London.

Harvey, D. (2008) 'The Right to the City', *New Left Review*, 53: September/October.

Henderson, P. and Armstong, I. (1993) 'Community Development and Community Care', in J. Bornat et al. (eds) *Community Care: A Reader.* London: Macmillan.

Ingamells, A. (2007) 'Community Development and Community Renewal: Tracing the Workings of Power', *Community Development Journal*, 42 (2): 237–250.

Miller, C. (2001) 'Community Regeneration and National Renewal in the United Kingdom', in J. Pierson and J. Smith (eds) *Rebuilding Community. Policy and Practice in Urban Regeneration.* Basingstoke: Palgrave.

Pierson, J. and Smith, J. (2001) 'Introduction', in J. Pierson and J. Smith (eds) *Rebuilding Community. Policy and Practice in Urban Regeneration.* Basingstoke: Palgrave.

Ruffin, F. (2007) 'The Politics of Urban Planning, Marseille: upgrades and degradation', *Le Monde Diplomatique*, February. Trans by D. Hounam.

community as policy and practice

The term 'youth work' is used to identify the process of creating settings conducive to engaging young people in informal education. The deviating term 'community youth work' can be distinguished in three ways: in terms of its methods of engagement; its explicit commitment to encouraging young people's participation in the youth work process; and through the ways in which it identifies social control and power as key to understanding the 'problem' of youth.

Section Outline: The starting point of this chapter is that the development of community youth work must be understood against the backdrop of the historical emergence of 'the teenager' and youth culture, and subsequently in relation to the place of young people in a society which has witnessed some profound social, cultural, economic and political changes that have led to the collapse of some homogeneous standards and structural patterns that were, once upon a time, taken for granted. It is argued thereafter that youth has suffered the brunt of 'respectable fears' about these changes and that community youth work approaches have emerged as a critical response to these conditions. After discussing three models of community youth work, the chapter closes with a discussion of how work with young people continues to operate in practice and what this implies for both young people themselves and society as a whole.

Most, though certainly not all, youth work in the modern liberal state is delivered by a publicly funded service – in the United Kingdom, this is known as the Youth Service – whose engagement with young people is distinctive from that of other statutory agency work because of the mainly voluntary nature of contact between it and young people. In the main, the kind of youth work carried out by publicly funded services has traditionally been concerned with personal and social development, growing out of mid-nineteenth-century concerns over the physical and moral welfare of young people. It was G. Stanley Hall, in his study of *Adolescence*, published in 1904, who invented the modern concept of problematic youth. In an effort to co-ordinate efforts to deal with this problem, the 1904 Committee on Physical Determination called for greater physical and mental education for 'adolescents', arguing that existing organizations provided amusement but little else, and only catered for small numbers. By World War II, such organizations were still mainly deliverers of leisure, not welfare.

The contemporary understanding of the problem of youth and responses to it developed in the light of the rise of the affluent society and relatively full employment in the 1950s and 1960s, which saw the growing cultural importance of the mass media, particularly film and popular music and their attendant subcultures – teddy boys, mods and rockers, skinheads and all the rest – which gave birth to the modern idea of 'the teenager'. 'Youth culture' was the term that was by now being used by sociologists to signify the subcultural features which surround young people as a distinctive social category.

The major social and economic development in the modern liberal state from the mid-1960s saw employment in services grow and employment in manufacturing decline. The upshot of this was that, compared with the aforementioned period of relative full employment, unemployment rates now increased dramatically, and long-term unemployment was by the 1970s, 1980s and 1990s a persistent problem. Unemployment was also on the whole a *selective* process: different *social groups* experienced different levels of unemployment. Young people were one of the social groups hit hardest, and it was in the shadow of this trend that certain sections of youth – especially men and those from the working-class and ethnic minority communities – came to be known as 'hard to reach'.

One of the upshots of this trend is that a social control imperative, with its ever-expanding matrix of surveillance, now looms large in the work of agencies and organizations working with young people. This is partly a response to moral panics around youth and concerns raised by, and reflected in, underclass theory, which, as MacDonald (1997: 181) points out, is 'rhetorical, ideological and, in the main, untainted by empirical facts', making young people scapegoats for complex problems and feeding the 'bourgeois appetite for moral panics', which bear 'respectable fears' and are marshalled by the powerful in the interest of historical moments (Pearson, 1983).

As Pearson shows, there has been a history of 'respectable fears' surrounding social breakdown and moral degeneration, most often directed at the working classes. Pearson's work is supported by Cohen (1972), who suggested that different societies go through stages of social change in which its fears are reflected in the emergence of folk devils. The 'folk devil' is a cultural archetype, the perpetual villain of the peace. To what extent particular social groups are considered as 'folk devils' is partly down to whether or not they have violated some law or tacitly understood social norm and partly on what social reaction this evokes.

According to Cohen, folk devils are seen as a threat to society and the values that come to symbolize that society. They are in essence seen as everything that is wrong with that society. That young people (and especially working-class youth) have historically tended to take the brunt of adult society's anxieties about its own predicament was not lost on Cohen, who also demonstrated the special significance of societal 'control culture' in this process and thus drew attention to its ideological role in actively constructing meanings, rather than merely 'reflecting' some supposedly shared reality. What Cohen's model suggests is that, to understand the management of fear, we must consider all the social actors involved, rather than ambiguously concentrating on the actions of 'folk devils'. In other words, we must examine the social audience and its reaction to folk devils since such labels are not automatically imposed on all rule breakers, and some escape labelling altogether. As Cohen points out, in the way that some groups are situated as folk devils, they are 'visible reminders' of what the rest of us should not be.

However, what this concentration on relatively contemporary events overlooks is that fear, or what Bauman (2007: 67) calls the problem of how to manage fear, is a recurring problem, which has been endemic to the modern liberal state since its inception. As he points out, political fears were born with 'the first bout of deregulation-cum-individualization', which accompanied the emergence of the modern liberal state, when the bonds of a pre-modern world run on the lines of community were broken (*see* 'A Theory of Community'). Bauman goes on to argue that today we live in an age when we have never been so secure, yet we have never felt so less in control of everything related to our security and safety. He also argues that our time in history is the age in which grand ideas have lost their authority, and where fear of an imagined enemy is all that politicians have to maintain their power. Implicit in Bauman's argument is that the idea that we are living in an age in which we have entered what he calls the 'second bout of deregulation-cum-individualization', when the modern liberal state, no longer certain of its authority, looks for *substitute* targets on which to unload the fears that uncertainty creates.

What Bauman's work suggests is that, if youth has long been a target for respectable fears, in an age when what is most fearsome is the sheer number of fears we encounter on a day-to-day basis, it is young people who are inevitably going to take much of the brunt. In response to this state of affairs, McDonald argues that it is high time that we developed a more 'balanced, empirically warranted and realistic representations of young people and their lives' (p. 183). What this suggests is that, as capitalism continues to deregulate our lives and the pattern of the world continues to change, so must our theories about how to understand the ways in which young people's lives are affected in the process.

Theories of community youth work have been defined in a variety of ways, and three distinctive approaches to the study of it may be identified (Banks, 1993). As its nomenclature suggests, *locality-based youth work* connotes a set of activities focused around a particular locale or area. There are a number of different approaches to locality-based youth work. Centre- and area-based work are both part of a broader move to decentralize services, with agencies feeling that these are responsive forms of delivery, which provide 'better value for money' than traditional youth work based in clubs. By the time of the publication of the 1982 Thompson Report, which followed a review of statutory and voluntary youth service provision resource deployment, many urban areas had adopted what came to be known as detached youth work approaches, partly as a response to the Albemarle Report (1960) and the Fairbairn-Milson Report (1969) which noted that some youths were not only 'unattached' but also 'unclubbable'. As Banks points out, in recent years, there has been a growing trend towards establishing specialist youth projects in the community through targeted work around homelessness, drug misuse and HIV and Aids. Targeted work is often born of the failure of other approaches to engage young people. It is also bound up with the move from generic *service* towards the targeting of problem populations, exemplified by a marked change within youth justice and social work (to which the Youth Service is intimately tied) which has introduced a number of schemes offering alternatives to custody.

Since the publication of Pearson and Cohen's important theoretical work, a substantial body of sociology and cultural studies research on youth culture has developed, primarily in the United Kingdom and North America. This research shows that prejudice and discrimination against young people (and the elderly) is deep rooted in the social, cultural, political and economic structures of society. Banks argues that the youth work approaches that have emerged as a critical response to these conditions can be summarized under the label *youth work with communities of interest*. These are interventions that work with young people as an interest group, or with the various 'sub' groups within the category of youth. In the United Kingdom, this approach developed in earnest in the light of figures published by the Commission for Racial Equality in 1980 which showed low take-up of youth work provision by Black Minority Ethnic (BME) youth. The Thompson Report (1982) recommended that youth work should reflect the values and attitudes of neighbourhoods, recommending separate provision for BME young people, if appropriate, suggesting that some local authorities have specialist workers, not just for BME youth, but also for girls and young women. However, as Youth Service aims are broadened, and as the age range of their client group expands, it may not be possible for the Youth Service, as currently constituted, to meet the demands of all its disparate constituencies.

The *community practice approach to youth work* is the third type of youth work identified by Banks. In her view, this approach is community youth work proper, in the sense that it is suggestive of the possibility of a way of working with young people which is much more than a feel-good label employed to give creditability to a variety of otherwise often mutually contradictory approaches to youth work. Banks questions whether much contemporary youth work is genuinely about working democratically with young people as valued community members, when the Youth Service's priorities are often not decided upon locally. The shift towards prioritizing work with particular groups, partly driven by reductions in funding and also the desire to target and control 'problem' populations, means that the idea of association, of young people working together, is now less powerful in youth work. Although nominally about encouraging positive change in young people in a group setting, empowerment, where it is achieved, tends to be atomized, at an individual, rather than collective, level. The line between youth work and social work has also become blurred, as the social control imperative takes prominence, and target setting and measurement sideline the *process* of working with young people, which is so vital to community-practice-style community youth work. Notwithstanding these problems, there is some hope that workers can find room for a community practice approach, by taking account of need and encouraging young people to work *together* towards incremental change. The shift from facility-based to outreach work, in the everyday spaces utilized by young people, may also be helpful in allowing practitioners to adopt the community youth work approach.

Taking a more empirically based approach to understanding recent trends in youth work, which on the one hand involves mapping the changes in the position of young people in society and on the other explores how community youth work operates in practice, MacDonald et al. (2001) identify two trends that have hitherto informed practice. The first of these is cultural studies, which prioritizes the analysis of how *lived culture* impacts on young people's lives and vice versa. A more recent trend is youth transitions, which focuses its attention more on the *structural constraints* that affect the lives of the young. However, the separation between the two has never been absolute, and the kind of transitions research with which these authors are involved can and should, they say, incorporate a concomitant analysis of youth culture. Transition studies carry many benefits. Not only do they tell us that transitions are extraordinarily complex and that young people do not view employment and education in the linear way that policy implies, but they also help us to understand how young people live their lives, not how policy writers perceive such lives. In this way, they call for the tracking of transitions over the long term and an examination of the complex relationship between personal agency and structural constraints. They also flag up the importance of locality in circumscribing the life chances of young people. In short, what transition studies suggest is this: not only must we understand how young people individually understand their lives, but also how they experience community. If we do not do both of these things, then youth work interventions are not likely to be effective.

Dean (1997) argues that both youth and the pejorative idea of underclass are symbolic constructions, and that, contrary to the ideological assumptions underpinning these, most of the young people she worked with had very ordinary ambitions. This especially runs contra to the underclass model, which portrays the socially excluded young as being individually, morally and culturally responsible for their lot and of having non-mainstream values. Although the stories of young people which are presented by authors such as Dean and MacDonald (2001) are unique to their specific studies, they reflect underlying common experiences which contradict the underclass theory, which over-emphasizes choice and underplays constraint. No one, claim MacDonald and Marsh (2001: 386), is wholly or permanently disconnected; rather, their lives are dominated by 'insecurity, instability and flux'. This is an important observation when we look at the issue of engaging young people.

Jeffs (1997) observes that the modern liberal state has never assembled a coherent youth policy. Rather, what we have seen over the long run is a myriad range of ad hoc inputs from agencies, both locally and nationally. In the United Kingdom, it is argued that government's aims for the Youth Service (DES, 2002) are now as grandiose as they are vague, and are driven by the new managerialism, a set of demands which extends to other agencies and organizations working with young people. Government expects those it funds to reflect key national *and* local priorities, and, to this end, says it is not appropriate to lay down a national curriculum for youth work. The Youth Service is required to promote active citizenship and encourage engagement with democratic and political processes, bringing together groups from different communities. DES has also instructed the Youth Service that work should begin where young people are at, but aim to move them beyond that point, providing interventions to promote personal and social development. The Youth Service must ensure user satisfaction, employing sufficient numbers of skilled staff, reflecting the diversity of the locality in which they operate. In order to counter the image of young people as problematic, the promotion of achievement is also expected. Importantly, the DES says that young people should play a part in setting the standards that the Youth Service aims to meet, and in evaluating these, sees involving young people in such endeavours as being the start of a transition from 'consumer to provider of youth services' (2002: 33). Such a move towards involving users in setting the priorities of service deliverers, and assessing their performance against targets, is also reflective of a broader trend to make agencies more accountable to their 'clients'.

Critics would argue that whilst there is this *official* agenda, as we have already seen, there is also an unwritten one which is about the effective social control and management of underclass youth. Funding for working with young people now favours short-term outputs, usually in high-stress urban areas, working with young males, meaning that community development modes of working are difficult to adopt. Good work is often patchy, geographically and conceptually, and experimentation is difficult. The focus of work with young people is seldom about encouraging participants to seek power; its aim rather is to limit young people to cajole and, if necessary, coerce them into fitting existing provision and bureaucracy. 'Participation' and 'empowerment' in youth work are even more tokenistic concepts than in much mainstream community development work.

Engaging young people as participants in community initiatives outside the domain of youth work is done infrequently, with adults invariably speaking on their behalf. Citizenship is equated with adulthood, rather than youth, and a lack of citizenship equates to a lack of participation, something which runs contra to United Nations Convention on Children's Rights (1989) which calls for protection, provision and participation. This lack of consultation means that the skills of young people are often ignored, compounding the view of young people as a problem constituency. Increasingly, adults find the presence of young people in public spaces threatening (West, 1998). Consequently, legislation, not always aimed specifically at young people, but which, in its application, controls young people's access to and behaviour in public spaces, such as the Anti Social Behaviour Act (2003) which, in addition to introducing Anti Social Behaviour Orders (ASBOs), allows the police to disperse groups of two or more people who are perceived as being intimidating or causing alarm or distresses, has been implemented and used by the police and local authorities, in an attempt to allay the fears of adults.

A stumbling block to boosting participation by young people in the kind of community approach identified by Banks is that it would inevitably involve adults, who may be keen to hold on to the little influence which they have over community work, which suggests that there would be the chance of them relinquishing some of their power. However, some local authorities in the United Kingdom, for example, have established youth councils and carry out consultation across administrative areas or in specific locales. Such initiatives can help young people to develop skills and acquire responsibility and a sense of ownership of initiatives, benefiting the areas in which they live, as well as bringing participants individual benefits.

Increasingly, youth work involves partnership working. Although aimed at promoting joined-up thinking and better utilization of resources, this is not without its problems. For instance, whilst sport is enthusiastically championed by government as a vehicle for the attainment of positive social objectives, and is often targeted at young people, Binks and Snape's (2005) examination of two youth sports projects highlight issues including interdepartmental rivalry, the setting of unrealistic objectives, problems with staff retention and the overall lack of ability to influence strategy.

In his classic work *Hiding in the Light*, Hebdige (1988) argues that youth is 'present only when its presence is a problem'. What the foregoing discussion has demonstrated is that much policy and hence mainstream youth work is about how to 'deal' with the youth 'problem' rather than how to include young people in community initiatives. As Rowlands points out, 'growing up in the context of pronounced inequality will bring in its wake poor health, poor mental health and poor social order', and the iniquitous treatment of young people, many of whom are already marginalized because of their economic status, is likely to contribute to, rather than address, issues of social order. Youth workers are often acutely conscious of the fact that they cannot address endemic structural problems to which Rowlands refers, but feel that they might be able to equip young people with the skills to deal with the complex personal and societal issues that confront them on a daily basis. Community youth work may be seen as a way of respectfully and pragmatically engaging with young people to address issues especially pertinent to them, as well as promoting the concept of young people as assets to their communities, rather than merely annoyances.

See also: *'Community Development'; 'Community Partnerships'; 'The "Dark Side" of Community'.*

Co-authored with Donna Woodhouse.

REFERENCES

Banks, S. (1993) 'Community Youth Work', in H. Butcher, A. Glen, P. Henderson and J. Smith (eds) *Community and Public Policy*. London: Pluto Press.

Bauman, Z. (2007) *Liquid Times: Living in an Age of Uncertainty*. Cambridge and Malden: Polity Press.

Binks, P. and Snape, B. (2005) 'The Role of Sport for Young People in Community Cohesion and Community Safety: Alienation, Policy and Provision', in A. Flintoff, J. Long and K. Hylton (eds) *Youth, Sport and Active Leisure. Theory, Policy and Participation*. Leisure Studies Association: University of Brighton.

Cohen, S. (1972) *Folk Devils and Moral Panics*. London: McGibbon and Kee.

Dean, H. (1997) 'Underclass or Undermined? Young People and Social Citizenship', in R. MacDonald (ed.) *Youth, the 'Underclass' and Social Exclusion*. London: Routledge.

Department of Education and Science (1982) *Experience and Participation. Review Group on the Youth Service in England ('The Thompson Report')*. London: HMSO.

Department for Education and Skills (2002) *Transforming Youth Work – Resourcing Excellent Youth Services*. London: Department for Education and Skills/Connexions.

Hebdige, D. (1998) *Hiding in the Light: On Images and Things*. London: Routledge.

Jeffs, T. (1997) 'Changing Their Ways. Youth Work and Underclass Theory', in R. MacDonald (ed.) *Youth, the 'Underclass' and Social Exclusion*. London: Routledge.

MacDonald, R. (1997) 'Youth, Social Exclusion and the Millennium', in R. MacDonald (ed.) *Youth, the 'Underclass' and Social Exclusion*. London: Routledge.

MacDonald, R. and Marsh, J. (2001) 'Disconnected Youth?', *Journal of Youth Studies*, 4: 373–391.

MacDonald, R., Mason, P., Shildrick, T., Webster, C. and Ridley, L. (2001) 'Snakes and Ladders: In Defence of Studies of Youth Transition', *Sociological Research Online*, 5 (4).

Ministry of Education (1960) *The Youth Service in England and Wales ('The Albemarle Report')*. London: HMSO.

Murray, C. (1990) *The Emerging British Underclass (Choice in Welfare)*. London: Institute of Economic Affairs. www.everychildmatters.gov.uk/

Pearson, G. (1983) *Hooligan: A History of Respectable Fears*. London: Macmillan.

Rowlands, J. *Childhood*. www.compassonline.org.uk

United Nations (1989) *Convention on the Rights of the Child, United Nations*. www.statistics.gov.uk/pdfdir/st0407.pdf.

West, A. (1998) 'What about the children? The involvement of younger residents', in C. Cooper and M. Hawtin (eds) *Resident Involvement and Community Action. Theory to Practice*. Coventry: Chartered Institute of Housing.

LEISURE AND ITS COMMUNITIES

Isaiah Berlin once said that some things change and some things do not, and that it is important that we distinguish which is which. There is no doubting the fact that the way in which community is understood has changed markedly in recent years. When the concept was initially theorized by leisure scholars, it largely mirrored orthodox sociological thought, which meant defining it first of all by breaking it down into the sum of its parts – namely, the ideas of geographical propinquity, communities of interest and forms of common affective union – and secondly by explaining that these constituent parts should only be understood with the proviso that community is also more than these. Yet, in defining the concept in leisure studies these days, it may not even be obvious what its constituent parts are anymore.

Section Outline: Notwithstanding this last point, 'community' is a term that is generally used in three ways in relation to leisure. The first refers to the large, diverse and conspicuous presence of communal leisure activities in everyday life. The second way it is used is in the sense of 'community leisure' which has found widespread currency in the leisure policy domain. The third comprises a more critical perspective, found in the work of Bishop and Hoggett (1986), who not only chart the breadth, depth and massive scope of communal, informal or voluntary leisure, but also provide a critique of attempts to subsume these myriad activities under the umbrella of a bureaucratic and centralized programme of 'state'-controlled leisure. This chapter looks at each of these three uses in turn.

community as policy and practice

195

Every society has its formal and informal leisure social formations and institutions which bring people together in their free time. To this extent, the notion of free time is central to most definitions of leisure. However, to say that leisure is simply free time, that is, an occasion, opportunity or period free from other obligations, when an individual is able to organize his or her own time in whatever ways he or she sees appropriate, tells us nothing about the content and quality of the leisure experienced. The idea also ignores the fact that time free to make deliberative choices about what to do with one's free time is always accompanied by the implication that the individual's ability to enjoy his or her free time has been, or is potentially, open to restraint or constraint. Such a definition, if it is useful for identifying in broad terms the quantity of time available for leisure, and how time is distributed among different social and cultural groups, also ignores, or at least marginalizes, how that free time has been created.

These caveats notwithstanding, it is in their free time that many individuals can be found engaging with what Stebbins (1999) calls serious leisure activities, such as amateurist and hobbyist pursuits and volunteerism, which often have the special capacity to support enduring careers of leisure which are marked by historical turning points and stages of achievement. Serious leisure also tends to be built on the kind of perseverance, which although at times might be experienced as particularly challenging for those involved, enables its participants to build special skills and knowledge; this, in turn, tends to engender self-confidence through achievement when they are successful. There are also other long-lasting benefits to be had through engaging with serious leisure that go beyond individual personal self-enhancement, such as material products and long-lasting personal relationships and friendships (compare these with the communal leisure activities discussed in the chapter 'Liminality, Communitas and Anti-Structure').

What Stebbins's work suggests is that leisure can be understood as a value-sphere, in Max Weber's meaning, which is one of those distinct realms of human activity that have their own 'inherent dignity' (Brubaker, 1984). The idea of leisure as a value-sphere suggests that not only is leisure governed by particular set of norms, rules, ethics and obligations that are inherent, but also that those who commit themselves to leisure often do so as a vocation. In other words, and to paraphrase what Zinzendorf (cited in Weber, 1930: 264, note 24) said about work, in making an existential commitment to leisure, people not only leisure in order to live, but live for the sake of their leisure, and if there is no more leisure to do, they suffer or go to sleep. The concept of value-spheres is useful because not only does it challenge the functionalist tendency to understand society as a totality, but it also understands that the modern world is not one in which 'everyone is related to a greater or lesser extent to the same ethical powers' (Heller, 1999: 37), and that men and women are capable of succeeding in establishing different ways of life in order to find meaning based on the shared values of their own communities of interest.

One particular, and obvious, criticism of the idea of leisure as a value sphere is that the guiding philosophy of the contemporary modern individualized and consumer society runs counter to the sort of dedication, moral principles and communal activities associated with such social arrangements. Indeed, much evidence would seem to suggest that the majority of men and women are more likely to be seen engaged in one-off leisure (individualized and consumerist) pastimes rather than vocational leisure, which tends to be communal and life-long.

In the light of the shift to a more consumer-driven society, community leisure has also been treated with suspicion by some critics, who argue that it is often used merely as 'a fashionable label with virtually no recognition that a particular set of practices and values is implied' (Haywood, 1994). Indeed, the community appendage is just as commonly used to describe leisure facilities, e.g., community leisure centres, community pools, etc., as it is used to describe particular ways of working with individuals and groups in local communities through leisure, e.g., community arts, community sport, etc. In the strongest use of the term, however, 'community leisure' is suggestive of an orientation to a particular model of public policy, whose underlying rationale is to use leisure to promote those types of collective association that put the accent on the promotion of community values such as solidarity, affiliation, coherence, participation and active citizenship. As such, it makes sense to give community leisure a general definition in relative terms, i.e., in terms of the relationship between the community practice model of public service delivery as it is developed through different kinds of leisure.

Community practice is a set of 'distinctive methods and practices concerned with promoting, fostering and implementing community policies' (Glen, 1993). This involves working from a community-based approach, where the users of services have some control over the resources required to provide those services (Donnison, 1989). This ideal-type model incorporates: top-down community services which involve providing leisure opportunities and activities to a user public;

bottom–up *community development* which encourages communities to define their own leisure needs and make provisions for those needs; *community action*; multi-agency coordination, which stresses co-participation between different providers and users of community services; and an action research approach which operates as a reflexive tool to enhance practice.

Bramham (1994) has identified how the community practice model has been developed through the arts, pointing out that community arts have a local focus; take popular local forms; have their basis in an artistic rationale, which is extrinsic rather than intrinsic (art is a process rather than an end in itself); and involve communal participation, which is integrated with everyday culture and takes place on the streets, in parks and community centres. The role of the 'professional' artist in the context of community arts is that of an *animateur* rather than an expert, whose adjunct responsibility is as a *cultural intermediary*, who encourages individuals and communities to become more aware of their own circumstances and importantly those of others in a society torn by conflicting interests, and in the process encourage them to develop their own creative potential, so that they can harness this for their own individual benefit and that of their local community. As Bramham points out, this cultural democratic approach to developing community leisure through the arts not only challenges the elitism that tends to pervade traditional engagement (suggesting in the process that there are no universal criteria of what constitutes proper art), but also opens the potential for neglected or hidden cultural and artistic forms while celebrating them in the process.

It is with these kinds of values in mind that Haywood (1994: 131) outlines a set of strategies for engaging hard-to-reach groups in community sport:

- The discouragement of leagues and tables and the encouragement of 'one off' encounters
- The selection of sports in which the rules emphasize co-operation and teamwork rather than individuality
- Deliberate stress on participation at the expense of performance, e.g., modifying rules in order to include as many people as possible
- Use of sports with low TV/media/professionalized profile
- In sports with a high media profile, such as football, the positive encouragement of fair play and respect for opponents, and an emphasis on attacking play and taking risks rather than safe defensive methods,

since the former highlights the essential process of playing, or the latter over states the importance of the end product, the result

• Encouragement of diversity of methods/rules within sports

Notwithstanding this recognition of the key role that community leisure has to play in the health and well-being of society by providing personal fulfilment to individuals and improving the quality of life in local communities, critics have argued that community interventions are often piecemeal and localized, conservative and unrepresentative, and often have limited impact on public policy, i.e., community leisure more often than not operates as another variation of market-managerialism and that, as a result, its stress on equality of access to leisure opportunities tends to support the status quo or hegemony. However, there is little doubt that, as an alternative approach to public leisure provision, community leisure has the *potential* to be radical, in the sense that communities formed around leisure interests can lead to the arrangement of alternative kinds of collective consciousness raising and/or forces for political change.

In developing a critique of bureaucratic and centralized programme of 'state'-controlled community leisure, Bishop and Hoggett (1986) chart the breadth, depth and massive scope of communal, informal or voluntary leisure. For Bishop and Hoggett, the so-called 'voluntary sector in leisure' is in fact comprised of myriad individuals, communities, groups and organizations. The idea of the existence of a 'voluntary sector of leisure' may be the essential element in the worldview of the leisure profession and the state formations surrounding it, but in their view leisure in the community is very much different to public sector and the more organized voluntary sector. Making reference to the wider voluntary sector already subsumed under the banner of 'state' provision of services through what they call 'state colonialism', Bishop and Hoggett (p. 128) stress that there is 'a key difference between communal leisure organizations and others such as trade unions or tenants' associations. The self-interest of the latter is based upon overt need, whereas in communal leisure we are speaking of that realm of human life beyond such need … Leisure, then begins beyond need. The self-interest underlying forms of communal leisure, is … not based upon neediness, but upon enthusiasm, pleasure and enjoyment. It may perhaps be more useful to talk about an enthusiast's desires than needs'.

Bishop and Hoggett also suggest that we should be very wary of assuming a purely instrumental concept for understanding why people organize around enthusiasms; people organize around leisure for any number of reasons to do with communality and mutual interest. Moreover, coming together in leisure may lack the perceived depth associated with long-standing social relations associated with neighbourhood or ethnic homogeneity, but under some circumstances leisure can bring people together in circumstances that yields transitory or ephemeral experiences of belonging that are felt as both deep and meaningful to those involved.

Following this theme, Wellman, Carrington and Hall (1988) demonstrate that the question of 'community' is no longer dependent on any notion of place (if it ever was) and that social networks and communities of interest spread beyond geographical boundaries. Indeed, their research evidence suggests that community today has been transformed and that we now see the co-existence of communities which represent, to different degrees, close-knit pre-industrial, or traditional, communities *and* communities which can be described as post-industrial. Community leisure, in other words, need not be confined to sociological interpretations that emphasize geographical propinquity or all-encompassing forms of social solidarity.

Other recent analyses have also challenged the notion that a sense of belonging, identification with a social group or place must necessarily involve deep, multiplex and enduring relationships. Dyck (2002), for example, argues that it is in suburban areas in particular where we have witnessed the decline of traditional communal relations, but, paradoxically, it is also here where people are more likely to generate social connectivity out of limited, voluntary and contingent, but deeply textured and meaningful leisure activities, in what are ostensibly heterogeneous, consumerist and individualized social settings.

See also: *'Setting the Record Straight'; 'Community Development'; 'Cosmopolitanism, Worldliness and the Cultural Intermediaries'; 'Liminality, Communitas and Anti-Structure'; 'Political Community'.*

REFERENCES

Bishop J. and Hoggett, P. (1986) *Organizing Around Enthusiasms: Mutual Aid in Leisure*. London: Comedia.

Bramham (1994) 'Community Arts', in L. Haywood (ed.) *Community Leisure and Recreation: Theory and Practice*. Oxford: Butterworth-Heinemann.

Brubaker, R. (1984) *The Limits of Rationality: An Essay on the Social and Moral Thought of Max Weber*. London: Allen and Unwin.

Donnison, D. (1989) 'Social Policy: The Community-Based Approach', in M. Bulmer, J. Lewis and D. Piachaud, *The Goals of Social Policy*. London: Unwin Hyman.

Dyck, N. (2002) ''Have you Been to Hayward Field': Children's Sport and the Construction of Community in Suburban Canada', in V. Amit (ed.) *Realizing Community*. London: Routledge.

Glen, A. (1993) 'Methods and Themes in Community Practice', in H. Butcher, A. Glen, P. Henderson and J. Smith (eds) *Community and Public Policy*. London: Pluto Press.

Haywood, L. (1994) 'Community Sport and Recreation', in L. Haywood (ed.) *Community Leisure and Recreation: Theory and Practice*. Oxford: Butterworth-Heinemann.

Heller, A. (1999) *A Theory of Modernity*. Oxford: Blackwell.

Stebbins, R. A. (1999) 'Serious Leisure', in T.L. Burton and E.L. Jackson (eds) *Leisure Studies: Prospects for the Twenty-First Century*. State College (Pen): Venture Publishing.

Weber, M. (1930) *The Protestant Ethic and the Spirit of Capitalism*. London: Unwin Hyman Ltd.

Wellman, B., Carrington, P. and Hall, A. (1988) 'Networks as Personal Communities', in B. Wellman and S. Berkowitz (eds) *Social Structures: A Network Approach*. Cambridge: Cambridge University Press.

POLITICAL COMMUNITY

Not to be confused with community politics (that decentred ingredient of civil society whose impetus lies in the mutual commitment and social solidarity of men and women who revel in their reciprocal independence from the state), 'political community' is the term used to describe the abstract, imagined (from without as well as within), ethical and self-determined totality of reciprocal interdependence, mutual commitment and social solidarity that underlies the state.

Section Outline: After outlining the central tenets of what constitutes a successful and moral political community, this chapter argues that the idea has recently been revivified in the politics of real-world affairs for two reasons: on the one hand, as a response to global concerns about mounting human rights abuses in particular nation-states, and on the other, the increased status given to community just at the same time that it was being argued by some commentators that politics were no longer ideological, and by others that communities in the orthodox sociological sense had become 'hard to find in real life'. Focusing its attention primarily on this second issue, the chapter subsequently argues that, contrary to the received wisdom, it is not the politics of communitarianism *that underlies this new politics, but rather neo-liberalism (see 'What is Community Today?'). The chapter closes by asking whether, in the light of these events, there is still a role for community in politics, other than its appropriation.*

In the view of Pelczynski (1984), it is in the ideal of political community where freedom reaches its fullest potential, because it is here where citizens can interact with other citizens and the state through free public debate, the exercise of the right to vote, representative politics and direct democracy. It is these kinds of social rights – rights which give men and women respect, recognition and dignity – which tie political community 'to the daily realities of its members and ... the solid ground of life experience; those rights certify, simultaneously, the veracity and realism of mutual trust *and* the trust in the shared institutional network that endorses and validates collective solidarity' (Bauman, 2008: 141).

To paraphrase Pelczynski, whose understanding lies in Hegel's idea that individual freedom develops only dialectically, the starting point of political community is the good of the ethical community itself, the common good or the public interest, which fully self-conscious and self-determined citizens promote for its own sake. In so doing, they actualize their own deepest freedom and realize their nature not simply as individuals but as universal, communal beings (1984: 32). What this suggests is that what Adam Ferguson, a leading philosopher of the Scottish Enlightenment, said of civil society in 1767 is also true of political community today: in any political community, the individual, while free to regard his or her happiness as a legitimate pursuit, should be willing to relinquish it if it interferes with the common good.

What this last reference makes manifestly clear is that political community has long been the focus of and subject to critical interpretation and interest. This observation notwithstanding, it is since the close of the short twentieth century (1914–1991), or what the historian Eric Hobsbawm otherwise calls the 'age of extremes', that the bringing together of politics and community has been revivified in the politics of real-world affairs. Indeed, no tail in politics today is longer, or broader, than political community; it has once again become the centre of consciousness in politics. There are two major reasons for this.

The first centres on the heightened attention given to human rights abuses within the borders of particular states, for example, Rwanda, Bosnia, Kosovo, Iraq, Burma, Zimbabwe, to name but a few, and the central issue of whether it is the responsibility of the world community as a whole or the right of the political communities that underlie those states to respond to these. Political theorists such as Michael Walzer (2007), for example, have argued that, notwithstanding what the rest of the world thinks about human rights abuses, it is always the prerogative of the political community in question to act, even in the case where an oppressive government regime is internally illegitimate (as in the case of Robert Mugabe's decision to ignore the results of the elections in Zimbabwe in 2008, for example). In the view of Walzer, it should be left to the people of the political community in question to decide what to do about human rights abuses that take place inside the borders of the state in which it resides, and they are likely to resent anyone who tries to appropriate this privilege (as in the aftermath of the US invasions of Afghanistan in 2001 and Iraq in 2003, for example).

The second reason why political community has once again become the centre of consciousness in politics is that its irresistible rise occurred just at the same time as when some commentators were arguing that politics were ostensibly no longer ideological (Giddens, 1998), and communities had become 'hard to find in real life' (Hobsbawm, 1995: 428) – in the orthodox sociological sense at least. What this suggested was that, paradoxically, the idea of political community came to the forefront of political life just at the very time that it seemed that it no longer necessarily represented a bringing together of politics and community, and that the two had become enjoined merely in a play of words, rather than on the basis of an ontological battle about the best way for humanity to live, the former seeking to appropriate and use the idea of the latter purely for its own political and ideological ends. Let us explore this argument in more depth by considering both Giddens's theoretical argument about the emergence of the 'third way' through the re-evaluation of leftist politics in the 1990s and the empirical reality of the political community that his ideas (these drew him into the inner circle of New Labour politics in the United Kingdom) have spawned.

The 'third way' is, according to Giddens, a political response to the altered societal conditions associated with the second stage of modernity. Giddens (1998) argues that, as a result of a combination of social, cultural, economic and political changes, such as de-industrialization, individualization, consumerism, information-technology-driven globalization and the emergence of 'life politics' at the expense of 'class politics' – all of which have undermined the viability of post-war social democratic politics and policies – modernity has been inexorably altered.

Taking into consideration the collapse of state socialism in the Soviet Union and the Eastern bloc, in addition to the above changes, according to Giddens, it no longer makes any sense to understand politics from either the perspective of the 'Right' or the 'Left'. Writing in 1998, he argued that this dichotomy needed to be replaced by a radical centre–left politics embodied with a 'utopian realist' outlook. If communism and capitalism had been central to the world order in the formative period of modernity, in the second stage of modernity, it was now the time for an alternative political ethic in its own right, defensible in its own terms and self-supporting – what Nikolas Rose (1999: 167) describes as a sort of 'natural, extra-political zone of human relations ... [that in its] ... 'natural-ness' is not merely an ontological claim but implies affirmation, a positive evaluation', which would provide the necessary impetus for renewing social democracy, especially by encouraging a more active civil society through community. In this view, the 'third way' can be seen as an attempt to install an alternative political, ethical and self-determined community centred in and governed by a state which is fit for the second modernity.

There is no doubt that the idea of this third space, which seeks to conjoin increased public participation with more individual responsibility, owes much to the moral canon of *communitarianism*. One of the key reasons for this is that politicians of both the Left and the Right feel unthreatened by communitarianism, because unlike that word of the same family resemblance, 'communism', it is a political ideology without socialism. As we shall see below, however, the 'third way' owes a great deal more to the ideology of neoliberalism and free market economics than communitarianism, not least because as a result of the failures of communism, there has emerged an almost fundamentalist belief in the market and the view that markets can be used to deal with everything. Indeed, everything in neoliberalism has to be judged by its market value and if it does not sell, it is not what is wanted, pure and simply. Community matters to neoliberals because it sells. As we shall see below, the appropriation of community was seen by 'third way' adherents as a smart political strategy, creating a new kind of hegemony that money could not buy – Community plc: gilt edged. This has been accompanied by the hugely successful creation of 'Brand Community', much copied in public policy circles.

Indeed, the idiom of community has become a symbol of a certain kind of neoliberal public policy interventions, at least those directed at the poorest denizens of society. The cast is a familiar one: 'community health', 'community policing, 'community housing' and so on. In living on a contemporary council estate, for example, you cannot be anything but intensely aware of the pressure of 'community' around you, the cacophony of need and want is hard to escape; and it feels like everybody is forced to feel the same experience of 'community' which is stultifying because it is to be imprisoned in the iron cage of other people's thoughts and judgements. However, what is most tellingly neoliberal is the phraseology of community policy discourse: 'social capitalism', 'capacity building', 'community empowerment', 'entrepreneurial values', 'efficiency', 'targets', 'evidence' (*see* 'Social Capital'). In short, community is about investing in social capital, welfare consumerism and self-actualized welfare, which is shorthand for more individual 'choice' and 'selectivity', with the hope of engendering marketwise community values in a modern setting through a new form of managerialism and, where possible, the decentralization of services. The way that community is used here is plain and simply as a family-friendly mechanism for mobilizing neoliberal values. This is community policy markedly at odds with that defined by Butcher et al. (1993), which associates it with the policy goals, outcomes and processes explicitly aimed at the realization of the community values such as solidarity, social justice and democracy by encouraging participation from all sections of the general public, in particular the socially disadvantaged and other marginalized groups.

For 'third way' adherents – Left or Right – the recipe is repetitive, additive, more community, impressing with its inexhaustible quality of power and plunder. The basic line is: more community – and more – still more community – still more. The major attraction of 'community' policies is, of course, that they promise the kinds of social intervention that are bottom–up, rather than top–down, and which in the process of delivery are more reflective of the interests of local communities (*see* 'Community Development'). Indeed, typical philosophies about political community put about high-minded politicians tend to offer the following kinds of 'benefits':

> Virtue regenerated – crime reduced – public safely enhanced – institutionalization banished – dependency transformed to activity – underclass included – democratic deficit overcome – idle set to work – political alienation reduced – responsive services assured – economy reinvigorated by seating it, as it were, within networks of trust and honour – the Gordian knot of the State versus individual not cut but untied, all by a simple idea of politics: community (Rose, 1999: 187).

However, as Bauman points out, public policy recast as community policy tends to rest on a promise of simplification which:

> brought to its logical limit … means a lot of sameness and a bare minimum of variety. The simplification on offer can only be attained by the separation of differences: by reducing the probability of their meeting and narrowing the extent of communication. This kind of communal unity rests on division, segregation and keeping of distance. These are the virtues figuring most prominently in the advertising leaflets of communitarian shelters (Bauman, 2001: 148).

As Jean Baudrillard (2005) might say, these shelters are most effective in depriving their clients of their 'right of revenge' and their capacity to take reprisals. To use an analogy from popular culture, 'all the rage' community initiatives work just like those 'all the rage' comedy television shows such as *Little Britain* and the 'comedy' work of BBC everyman Jonathan Ross, in the sense that by affecting a self-deprecating ironic tone in the delivery of their services, they effectively short-circuit our opportunities for criticizing them. As that most acerbic political commentator Peter Preston (2005) recently put it:

> Try community charge in poll-tax mode and it's a spoonful of sugar to help the medicine go down. Try care in the community and it's somebody over there calling on poor Mrs Bloggs once a week if she's lucky. Try America's community colleges and we mean comprehensives not city academies. Try community service orders, and the guy over there clearing rubbish could find himself in prison next time.

All of which suggests that community policy, as well as being limited to a game of second-best in which there is the tacit assumption that the market is the clear winner – community support officers as second-rate police officers employed to do policing on the cheap, or NHS dentists abandoning the health and hygiene side of their profession for the more lucrative but less public-oriented one of beautification – also tends to exacerbate the conditions it promises to rectify by intensifying the kinds of social and cultural separateness, human suffering, social disruption and the break up of local communities.

Both Bauman and Preston are perhaps guilty of over-egging their pudding by exaggerating the political influence of the communitarian project on UK public policy, which increasingly goes by the name of social capitalism and is the glossy packaged front end of the wannabe street-wise-community-cool that the government tries so desperately to trade under.

However, the idea of community is undoubtedly most attractive to the neoliberal adherents of the 'third way' because not merely does it speak the brand confident, popular and stylish, in a 'do-what-the-manual-tells-you' kind of way – stakeholding and capacity building, bridging capital and bonding capital, bottom-up and grass roots – but it also gives every appearance of having managed to embrace the ethos of community practice.

Having said that, community is most appealing to these politicians, first and foremost, because it offers public policy interventions 'managed' on neoliberal lines, but delivered with the kind of warmth and homeliness that the market and its public sector rival struggle to achieve (*see* 'What is Community Today?'). Yet, community is used at best as a sop to the limitations of market forces. In other words, it effectively occupies a space in the public sector that might otherwise have been filled with something much less desirable – either the 'pure' market itself or a public service. As that most astute observer of the current political scene Ross McKibbin (2006: 3) recently put it, the United Kingdom is governed by increasingly narrow political elite, who no matter what their formal political allegiances, 'are all the same kind of people who think the same way and know the same things' and who are committed to a 'model of market-managerialism [which] has largely destroyed alternatives, traditional and untraditional' – including the idea of any communitarian option proper.

As McKibbin goes on to point out, these politicians might not have conceded, contra Margaret Thatcher, that there is such a thing as '"society", a "we" as well as a "me"', but they nonetheless tacitly adopt the neo-liberalist mantra that ours is a 'highly privatized society increasingly shaped by "social entrepreneurs", charities, do-gooders, people with axes to grind, and our old friend "faith groups": in other words, a society based on the model of a market and restored social hierarchies'.

The upshot of this state of affairs is that the so-called political community often has nothing to do with community. Indeed, there is frequently not anything remotely 'community' about many so-called initiatives on offer other than what's in their labelling, namely, because they do not have the essential conditions or purpose that sustain a 'community'. Community merged with the market as public policy – endlessly appropriated, endlessly used to give credence to yet another strategy, another makeover – restricts real innovation and alternative thinking about a new route to social justice by keeping ideas bound in mental manacles that bind even tighter than the old dichotomy of the public sector versus the market.

This neoliberal marketized version of community is nothing less than the false face of political community. It has become the exemplar of a kind of postmodern aesthetic, embraced by policy makers for its discourse of pulling-togetherness as well as its social control function, and not least its overall family-friendly appeal. At both the popular and the political levels, community is little more than a feel-good label employed to give creditability to variety of otherwise often mutually contradictory social policy phenomena. Like Prospero, policy makers sprinkle problems with community fairy dust, and the spell is enchanting. However, we have seen, with the ideology of neoliberalism, not only politics, but also the market dominates. To reiterate, it merely appropriates community, and then pushes it aside, its values and goals substituted by market ones. We can conclude, somewhat paradoxically, that community values and goals do not provide any compelling basis for the dominant contemporary version of political community. What we have in this instance is a political community which is an aesthetical and neo-liberal ideologically determined community centred in and governed by a state.

In the light of this conclusion, it would be tempting to conclude that the immediate future of political community is bleak. It might also be tempting to conclude that there is no longer any role for community in politics, other than its appropriation. However, there is no compelling reason to suggest that this should necessarily always be the case from now on. As has been suggested by plenty of commentators, one of the major lessons of the short twentieth century was that the political fundamentalism of communism leads humanity nowhere but the graveyard. Yet, very few commentators to date have mustered a comparable critique of that alternative fundamentalism that has hitherto been the *idée fixee* of the twenty-first century, and which leads nowhere but to human suffering, social disruption and the break up of local communities: neoliberalism. Any new rendition of political community must not only include such a critique, but also those concerned with it – to paraphrase Dr Johnson – should also be just as interested in whether the two have been accommodated at all, as in whether they have been accommodated well.

See also: *'Setting the Record Straight'; 'Communitarianism'; 'Community Action'; 'Community Development'; 'Liquid Modern Communities'; 'Postmodern Community'; 'Social Capital'.*

FURTHER READING

Michael Walzer's (2007) *Thinking Politically: Essays in Political Theory* is the best introduction to contemporary debates about political community.

REFERENCES

Baudrillard, J. (2005) *The Intelligence of Evil or the Lucidity Pact*. Oxford: Berg.

Bauman, Z. (2001) *Community: Seeking Safety in an Insecure World*. Cambridge: Polity Press.

Bauman, Z. (2008) *Does Ethics Have a Chance in a World of Consumers?* Cambridge (Massachusetts) and London: Harvard University Press.

Butcher, H., Glen, A., Henderson, P. and Smith, J. (1993) (eds) *Community and Public Policy*. London: Pluto Press.

Giddens, A. (1998) *The Third Way: the Renewal of Social Democracy*. Cambridge: Polity Press.

Hobsbawm, E. (1995) *Age of Extremes: The Short Twentieth Century 1914–1991*. London: Abacus.

McKibbin, R. (2006) 'The Destruction of the Public Sphere', *London Review of Books*, 28 (1): January.

Pelczynski, Z. A. (1984) 'Political Community and Individual Freedom in Hegel's Philosophy of the State', in A. Z. Pelczynski (ed.) *The State and Civil Society*. Cambridge: Cambridge University Press.

Preston, P. (2005) 'There is No Such Thing as Community', *The Guardian*, 18th July.

Rose, N. (1999) *Powers of Freedom: Reframing Political Thought*. Cambridge: Cambridge University Press.

Walzer, M. (2007) *Thinking Politically: Essays in Political Theory*. Selected, Edited and with an Introduction by David Miller. Yale: Yale University Press.

SOCIAL CAPITAL

'Social capital' is a term that has recently come much into vogue in political circles to describe those social networks and relationships associated with civic virtue and social responsibility, which involve communities and other social groups establishing common values, trust and cooperative ways of being and working together for mutual benefit.

Section Outline: This chapter first locates the origins of contemporary interest in social capital in de Tocqueville's and Durkheim's respective deep anxieties about democracy and moral life. Thereafter, it outlines the conceptual basis of Robert Putnam's social capital thesis. The rest of the chapter is devoted to discussing the key ideological, theoretical and empirical problems with this thesis and what these imply for its efficacy as a force for defeating inequality, injustice and the humiliation of poverty.

The antecedents of the current interest in social capital can be traced to the political and social thought of Alexis de Tocqueville (1969) and the sociology of Emile Durkheim (1933; 1961), whose analyses of the problems associated with an emerging modernity have recently been revived by political scientists and sociologists to shed some light on some of our own. What this observation suggests is that, not only are social capitalists essentially proponents of a civic *communitarian* outlook that is functionalist in orientation, but also that this joint revival can been seen as attributable to an ideology that has on the one hand led to a wholesale rejection of the influence of Marxism in public policy and is on the other hand framed by a growing disillusionment with neo-liberalism, which has led to an uncontrolled and seemingly uncontrollable capitalism (*see* 'What is Community Today?'; 'Political Community').

If not unambiguously explicating either the communitarian or functionalist roots of his work, or its ideological import, the key proponent of social capitalism, the American political scientist Robert Putnam, acknowledges that 'social capital is closely related to what some have called "civic virtue"' (Putnam, 2000: 19), which is as Delanty (2003) points out underpinned by a 'Toquevillian discourse of the loss of community', whose abiding myth is both nurturing and consuming of those it holds captive. This is the myth perpetuated in other communitarian accounts, which imagine that the United States was once bound together by shared history (Lincoln's 'mystic chords of memory'), habits of the heart (the title of Robert Bellah et al.'s (1987) book and a phrase coined by de Toqueville), the 'proud craftsmen' of the Jacksonian era (Sandel, 1996), who shared a common ancestry (what is often referred to as consanguinity) and a collective pride in being American.

In his book *Bowling Alone*, where he observes that the bowling leagues of his youth with their legions of teams are no longer a dominant form of civic leisure participation in the United States and that people now tend to 'bowl alone', Putnam builds his own version of this 'Toquevillian discourse of the loss of community'. As he puts it:

> ... the last several decades have witnessed a striking diminution of regular contacts with friends and neighbours. We spend less time in conversation over meals, we exchange visits less often, we engage less often in leisure activities that encourage casual social interaction, we spend more time watching (admittedly some of it in the presence of others) and less time doing. We know our neighbours less well, and we see old friends less often. In short, it is not merely 'do good' civic activities that engage us less, but also informal connecting (Putnam, 2000: 115).

Obviously, people do not actually bowl alone, but in small, closed groups such that the activity does not involve interaction with people beyond the immediate social group. Insisting that this concern with the decline of social capital is not just a hankering for the nostalgia of the community of his youth, Putnam presents a wealth of research data contending that there is a positive relationship between social capital and education, economic prosperity, health and well-being, and the democratic process overall, and uses this to make the case that, through social capital, the problems of civil society are resolved more easily: sociability (like business transactions) is less costly; personal coping is facilitated; information flows are better; and increased mutual awareness between individuals, communities and organizations promotes tolerance in addition to challenging ignorance and distrust.

Social capital, then, is the conceptual basis of Putnam's thesis. He argues that it represents sets of actions, outcomes or social networks (relations and ties) that allow people and civic associations to operate more effectively when they act together. Social capital from Putnam's perspective, then, is simply functional. It can at the same time be a 'private good' and a 'public good', although its networks, relations and ties of reciprocity can also have either positive or negative functions for individuals and/or associations.

In their critical discussion of the ways that social capitalism has been incorporated into leisure policy discourse, Blackshaw and Long (2005) extend this basic definition to show that, in the work of Putnam, social capital tends to be accompanied by two kinds of reciprocity: bonding ties which signify interaction between 'like people' whose social networks are inward looking and exclusive; and bridging ties or inter-group links which are more outward looking and inclusive. At the same time, in Putnam's work, social capital has some further important characteristics: it is both a public and a private 'good' in that just as individuals benefit from their contribution to social capital, so do others; it is evidenced in many different kinds of social networks – family, neighbours, church groups, personal social circles, civic organizations, and e-groups. Some of these networks are repeated and intensive, some involve strong ties, while others involve weak ties; some are episodic and casual; some are formal, some informal; and its networks and reciprocity are largely positive for those inside particular communities and social groups, but its external effects are by no means always positive – some of the most robust communities and organizations are the same ones that have cultivated social networks that are exclusive and reproduce both inequality and/or what

Field (2003: 88) calls 'perverse goals'. Despite these negative or dysfunctional aspects, Putnam suggests that the real value of social capital lies in its positively functional capacity to transform itself 'from something realized by individuals to something possessed (or not possessed) by either individuals or groups of people' (DeFilippis, 2001: 785).

The above points notwithstanding, Putnam's thesis is far more than just functionalism. As has been suggested, it is an attempt to elaborate a civic communitarian philosophy in a way that offers some practical solutions for dealing with the decline in civil relations where a much more itinerant, anonymous life has taken shape, where people no longer know or care about their fellow citizens and find themselves oppressed or at least detached from the society of which they are a part. Yet, as compelling as these arguments are, it has been argued forcefully by some commentators that the picture which social capitalists paint of a civic society broken by neo-liberalism and the solutions they proffer piecing it back together do not stand up to critical scrutiny. In particular, social capitalism holds no panacea for dealing with that major public issue with which it is mostly associated: the poverty and the social exclusion that encumber communities where people eke out an existence with a pervasive sense of diminished possibilities.

Blackshaw and Long (2005) develop an especially sharp and comprehensive analysis of Putnam's understanding of social capital that brings our attention to three critical problems: the limitations of the research underpinning the thesis; the ideological implications of social capitalism; and the limitations of the theoretical basis of social capital. According to Blackshaw and Long, not only is Putnam's own research and the secondary research he tends to rely on hampered by a positivist orientation, but he also uses it in ways that are vague and misleading as well as evincing a tendency to ignore what the 'data' tells him about how social networks operate in the real world. For example, Putnam's asserts that changes in work patterns, principally women's increased involvement in full-time employment, has contributed 10 per cent to the fall in social capital. This idea is based on the observation that women are responsible for much social interaction and civic engagement at the community level through entertainment at home, volunteering or running community groups, and that with less disposable time available, these have suffered. However, this overlooks the massive injection of social interaction that is provided to women by involvement in the workplace.

Putnam also pays little or no attention to the feminist theoretical critique which argues that 'communities' often make claims on their members which are based on extant and often insidious hierarchies of patriarchal domination and subordination. As Blackshaw and Long point out, the problem is that Putnam is intent on bending the 'data' to fit his thesis that the single-biggest cause of the decline in social capital is the departure of his long civic generation, and he uses this taken-for-granted ideological assumption to form his research, rather than the other way round.

In the event, Blackshaw and Long argue that, in Putnam's work, ideology operates at two broad levels: as an ideology-as-culture, which is a body of civic communitarian political ideas, and as an ideology-in-process, whose symbolic action (symbolic exchange, symbolic power and symbolic violence) operates in tandem with the more explicitly material effects of the former. In terms of thinking about the symbolic nature of Putnam's own project – that is, the way in which it generates for Putnam and other like-minded communitarians their own social capital – Blackshaw and Long argue that the greater part of what Putnam offers is rhetorical rather than substantive, more an imaginary construction than a solution for the pains it claims to cure. They demonstrate that, through the idea of social capital, Putnam is navigating far from the use of language as a set of uninformed conventions, subsumed within the realm of an ideology of word and world realism, a discourse whose virtual effects verge on the real, but ironically, in terms of the real world, bears little relevance to the worlds of those people it purports to take care of. In other words, Putnam, in reputing his values before the fact, legislates the present and future by re-imagining the past and using it ideologically to maintain capitalistic (and hegemonic) ways of dealing with the defeat of inequality, injustice and the humiliation of poverty.

As a result, Blackshaw and Long argue, Putnam overlooks Bourdieu's theoretically important point that what he calls 'the profits of membership' of civic associations and social networks are not available to everybody. As they indicate, drawing on the work of Ball (2003), the point of all 'capitals' – not just social capital – is that they are resources to be exploited, and it is their exclusivity that gives them their value. In a nutshell, people are able to realize social capital through their social networks precisely because they are able to exclude others. This ostensible failing of Putnam's thesis is normally presented as a bonus, in that some aspects of social capital are seen not as positional goods in a zero sum game; those contributing to trust, support and security might be seen to be strengthened if shared; moreover, in using it, social capital is seen to grow. However, Putnam ignores the fact that the 'profits' of community life are not things that you can so easily cost, measure or bank on.

Blackshaw and Long (2005) conclude that social capital has two decisive (and divisive) features: on the one hand, it is a tangible resource made by advantage of social networks, and on the other, like all forms of capital, it has a symbolic dimension, which contrives to hide networks of power woven into the fibres of familiarity. In the event, they suggest, following Bourdieu (1993), that in understanding social capital we must take into account the extent, quality and quantity of social actors' networks *and* their ability to mobilize these, which is always governed by the mutual understanding that any given field is an arena of struggle. In other words, and as Bourdieu would have said, it is the battle for distinction that gives social capital its ostensible qualities.

See also: *'Communitarianism'; 'Community Action'; 'Locality, Place and Neighbourhood'; 'Nostalgia'; 'The "Dark Side" of Community'; 'Political Community'; 'Social Network Analysis'.*

REFERENCES

Ball, S. J. (2003) 'It's Not What You Know: Education and Social Capital', *Sociology Review*, November.

Bellah, R., Madsen, R., Sullivan, W., Swidler, A. and Tipton, S. (1987) *Habits of the Heart*. Berkeley: University of California Press.

Blackshaw, T. and Long, J. (2005) 'What's the Big Idea? A Critical Exploration of the Concept of Social Capital and Its Incorporation into Leisure Policy Discourse', *Leisure Studies*, 24 (3): 239–258.

Bourdieu, P. (1993, trans. 1999) *The Weight of the World: Social Suffering in Contemporary Society*. Cambridge: Polity Press.

DeFilippis, J. (2001) 'The Myth of Social Capital in Community Development', *Housing Policy Debate*, 12 (4): 781–806.

Delanty, G. (2003) *Community*. London: Routledge.

Durkheim, E. (1933) *The Division of Labour in Society*. Glencoe, IL: Free Press.

Durkheim, E. (1961) *Moral Education: A Study in the Thoery and Appicaltion of the Sociology of Education*. Glencoe, IL: Free Press.

Field, J. (2003) *Social Capital*. London: Routledge.

Putnam, R. D. (2000) *Bowling Alone: The Collapse and Revival of American Community*. New York: Simon & Schuster (Touchstone).

Sandel, M. (1996) *Democracy's Discontent*. Cambridge: Cambridge University Press.

Toqueville, A. de (1969) *Democracy in America*. New York: Doubleday.

key concepts in community studies

index

References to notes are indicated by 'n'.

index

key concepts in community studies

The Qualitative Research Kit

Edited by Uwe Flick

Read sample chapters online now!

Doing Ethnographic and Observational Research — Michael Angrosino — The SAGE Qualitative Research Kit

Using Visual Data in Qualitative Research — Marcus Banks — The SAGE Qualitative Research Kit

Doing Focus Groups — Rosaline Barbour — The SAGE Qualitative Research Kit

Designing Qualitative Research — Uwe Flick — The SAGE Qualitative Research Kit

Managing Quality in Qualitative Research — Uwe Flick — The SAGE Qualitative Research Kit

Analyzing Qualitative Data — Graham Gibbs — The SAGE Qualitative Research Kit

Doing Interviews — Steinar Kvale — The SAGE Qualitative Research Kit

Doing Conversation, Discourse and Document Analysis — Tim Rapley — The SAGE Qualitative Research Kit

www.sagepub.co.uk

⑤SAGE

Supporting researchers for more than forty years

Research methods have always been at the core of SAGE's publishing. Sara Miller McCune founded SAGE in 1965 and soon after, she published SAGE's first methods book, Public Policy Evaluation. A few years later, she launched the Quantitative Applications in the Social Sciences series – affectionately known as the "little green books".

Always at the forefront of developing and supporting new approaches in methods, SAGE published early groundbreaking texts and journals in the fields of qualitative methods and evaluation.

Today, more than forty years and two million little green books later, SAGE continues to push the boundaries with a growing list of more than 1,200 research methods books, journals, and reference works across the social, behavioral, and health sciences.

From qualitative, quantitative, mixed methods to evaluation, SAGE is the essential resource for academics and practitioners looking for the latest methods by leading scholars.

www.sagepublications.com